MORAL ACTION, GOD, AND HISTORY

IN

THE THOUGHT OF IMMANUEL KANT

MORAL ACTION, GOD, AND HISTORY

IN

THE THOUGHT OF IMMANUEL KANT

by

CARL A. RASCHKE

Published by

AMERICAN ACADEMY OF RELIGION

and

SCHOLARS PRESS

DISSERTATION SERIES, NUMBER 5

1975

Distributed by

SCHOLARS PRESS
University of Montana
Missoula, Montana 59801

MORAL ACTION, GOD, AND HISTORY

IN

THE THOUGHT OF IMMANUEL KANT

Library of Congress Cataloging in Publication Data

Raschke, Carl A
  Moral action, God, and history in the thought of
Immanuel Kant.

  (Dissertation series - American Academy of Religion ; no. 5)
  Bibliography: p.
  1. Kant, Immanuel, 1724-1804--Ethics. 2. God.
3. History--Philosophy. 4. Progress. I. Title.
II. Series: American Academy of Religion. Dissertation series - American Academy of Religion ;
no. 5.
B2799.E8R34   193   75-11787
ISBN 0-89130-003-1

Copyright © 1975

by

AMERICAN ACADEMY OF RELIGION

Printed in the United States of America

Printing Department
University of Montana
Missoula, Montana 59801

To my mother

and

to my wife, Lori

TABLE OF CONTENTS

	Page
Chapter I. The Problem of Moral Agency in Kant . . .	1
A. Reason and Moral Action	1
1. Kant's "Moral Anthropology"	1
2. Moral Action and Motivation	6
3. The Notion of Practical Reason	11
4. Action and Willing	15
B. The Pure Will and Laws of Morality	18
1. Rules and Laws of Action	18
2. Subjective and Objective Principles . . .	24
3. The Moral Law	26
C. Kant's "Formalism"	35
D. Intentionality	48
1. The Faculty of Desire	48
2. Inclination and Interest	51
3. Moral Feeling	55
4. Human Purpose	59
E. Moral Agents in a Moral Universe	68
1. Ultimate and Final Purposes	68
2. Happiness	74
3. The Highest Good	77
Chapter II. God as Moral Agent	85
A. God as a Postulate of Practical Reason	85
1. Willing and Hoping	85
2. Believing	89
3. Postulation	95
B. The Grammar of Divine Agency	104
1. God as World Cause	104
2. God as Supreme Will	108
3. God as Moral Purposer	111
C. Postulation and Agency	116
1. The Language of Analogy	116
2. The Language of Limitation	125
3. The Language of Intention	131
Chapter III. Autonomy and Theonomy	143
A. The Autonomy of the Moral Agent	143
1. Self-legislation	143
2. Man as an End-in-Himself	148
3. The Kingdom of Ends	150

		Page
B.	Theonomy	154
	1. God as Person	154
	2. Divine Grace	162
C.	The Inter-relation of Autonomy and Divine Action	170
	1. The Failure of Theodicy	170
	2. The Dilemma of Theism	176

Chapter IV. Historical Action and the Idea of Progress 181

A.	The Foundation of the Idea of Historical Progress in Kant	181
	1. The Paradox of Perfectibility	181
	2. The Social Context of Moral Progress	185
B.	The Concept of Historical Progress	191
	1. Nature, Teleology, and Morality	191
	2. The Providential View of Nature	199
	3. The Socialization of the Race	206

Conclusion 223

Bibliography 229

EXPLANATION OF SYMBOLS

Date of
Original Publication

1798	Anthr. = <u>Anthropologie</u> in <u>pragmatischer</u> <u>Absicht</u>.
1763	Beweis. = <u>Der einzig mögliche Beweisgrund</u> zu <u>einer Demonstration Gottes</u>.
1790	CJ = <u>Critique of Judgement</u>. Translated by J. H. Bernard. New York: Hafner Publishing Company, 1966.
1788	CP_rR = <u>Critique of Practical Reason</u>. Translated by Lewis W. Beck. New York: Bobbs-Merrill, The Liberal Arts Press, 1956.
1803	E = "Education." Translated by Annette Churton. Ann Arbor: The University of Michigan Press, 1960.
1786	Gebrach. = <u>Über den Gebrauch teleologischer Principien in der Philosophie</u>.
1785	GMM = <u>Groundwork of the Metaphysic of Morals</u>. Translated by H. J. Paton. New York: Harper & Row, Torchbooks, 1964.
1781	K_rV = <u>Kritik der reinen Vernunft</u>. (B) signifies second edition.
1775-82*	LE = <u>Lectures on Ethics</u>. Translated by Louis Infield, London: Methuen & Company, 1930.
1800	Log. = <u>Introduction to Logic</u>. Translated by Thomas K. Abbott. New York: Philosophical Library, 1963.
1797	MEJ (MM, Intro.) = Introduction to the <u>Metaphysics of Morals</u> in <u>The Metaphysical Elements of Justice</u>. Translated by John Ladd. New York: Bobbs-Merrill, Library of Liberal Arts, 1965.
1797	MPV = <u>Metaphysical Principles of Virtue</u>. Translated by James Ellington. New York: Bobbs-Merrill, Library of Liberal Arts, 1964.

*Given as lectures

Date of
Original Publication

1797	Nach. = Nachlass.
1764	Nat. Theol. = Untersuchung über die Deutlichkeit der Grundsätze der natürlichen Theologie und der Moral.
1796	Neuer. = Von einem neuerdings erhobenen vornehmen Ton in der Philosophie.
1784	("Idea") = "Idea for a Universal History from a Cosmopolitan Point of View"
1795	("Perpetual Peace") = "Perpetual Peace"
1798	("Question") = "An Old Question Raised Again: Is the Human Race Constantly Progressing?"
1784	("Enlightenment") = "What is Enlightenment?"
	OP = Opus Postumum.
1786	Orient. = Was heisst: sich im Denken orientieren?
1783	Prol. = Prolegomena to Any Future Metaphysics. English translation. New York: Bobbs-Merrill, The Liberal Arts Press, 1950.
1792	RWL = Religion within the Limits of Reason Alone. Translated by Theodore Greene and Hoyt Hudson. New York: Harper & Row, Torchbooks, 1960.
	Schriften = Kants Gesammelte Schriften, Prussian Academy Edition. Berlin and Leipzig: Walder de Grupter & Company.
1798	SF = Der Streit der Fakultäten.
1791	Theod. = On the Failure of all Theodicies. Translated by Michel Despland. Unpublished typescript, Harvard University.
1793	Theor. Prax. = Über den Gemeinspruch: das mag in der Theorie richtig sein, taugt aber nicht für die Praxis.

Date of
Original Publication

1796 <u>Verkünd</u>. - <u>Verkündigung</u> <u>des</u> <u>nagen</u> <u>Abschlusses</u>
<u>eines</u> <u>Traktats</u> <u>zum</u> <u>weigen</u> <u>Frieden</u>
<u>in</u> <u>der</u> <u>Philosophie</u>.

<u>Vorles</u>. = <u>Eine</u> <u>Vorlesung</u> <u>Kants</u> <u>über</u> <u>Ethik</u>.
Berlin: Pan Verlag Rolf Heise, 1924.

All German texts except <u>Eine</u> <u>Vorlesung</u> <u>Kants</u>
<u>der</u> <u>Ethik</u> are contained in the <u>Schriften</u>.
Where no English translation is represented
in the symbol, the translation of the text
is my own.

PREFACE

I have deliberately placed the phrase "moral action" before the term "God" in the title of this dissertation, contrary perhaps to literary convention, in order to accent the logical sequence of the argument I unfold. Kant's concept of God cannot be made intelligible without prior analysis of what it means, it terms of the critical philosophy, to be a moral agent. For Kant, the very necessity of postulating the idea of God comes from consideration of certain problems that confront man in his quest for moral perfection and for a coherent universe of meaning in which his actions take their place. For that reason, I have launched a lengthy and probing survey in the first chapter concerning Kant's ideas about moral agent in general. I treat extensively such interrelated issues as actions versus specifically moral action, the nature of the will, phenomenal and noumenal causality, desires and inclinations, intentionality, the need for a moral universe, etc. Each phase of my analysis is designed to build upon the preceding one. Only when the intricate questions concerning moral action as a whole have come into focus can the question of God as agent be raised.

On raising the question of God as moral agent, I attempt to interpret the idea of God with critical attention to its essential meaning vis-a-vis Kant's specific criteria for morality. I try to distill a meaning from Kant's concept of divine "action" that cannot be readily extracted from the literal wording of the texts. I then undertake to show that in certain of his writings, which in earlier discussions I have not treated with any real care (in particular, the writings on history), Kant seems to move toward a resolution of the God-problem in a different way than the one for which he is usually given credit.

Although I want to argue, in some sense, that I am taking a "developmental" approach to Kant's thought, I do not submit that such a development is chronological, or even evident to Kant himself. The development takes place according to a kind of "inner logic" within Kant's whole critical philosophy, a logic manifesting itself through subtle twists and turns of his formulation of an issue, shifts in his use (or disuse) of key language forms, apparent inconsistencies in his own argument, etc.

That Kant was not outspokenly aware of this general movement does not undermine the standpoint I have taken. As Kant himself wrote in the second *Critique*, "consistency is the highest obligation of a philosopher and yet the most rarely found." That Kant did not consistently adhere to one stance throughout his life does not tarnish his greatness; it only exposes him as engaged in a life-long search for the internal truth of his own insights. In other words, it reveals him as human.

CHAPTER I.   The Problem of Moral Agency in Kant

A.   Reason and Moral Action

1.   Kant's "Moral Anthropology"

Kant defines man as a species, not only by his ability to reason, but also by the fact that he acts morally. To act morally means in some sense to originate events in the world which cannot be accounted for other than as human effects. To "act" per se is not man's solitary privilege. The usages put by our language to the term "act" concern a variety of things, animate and inanimate alike, that are not specifically human. We say without metaphor or trope that, for instance, a rabid dog seems to "act funny." A meteorologist reporting on the movements of a hurricane through the Atlantic notes that the storm is not "acting as predicted." Chemists talk all the time about chemical "agents" that "act" and "re-act" in certain ways when they come in contact with each other. Only man, however, acts in a fashion that is appropriately "moral." He alone, therefore, merits the title of "moral agent."

What is that peculiar property of human action that goes by the name "morality"? Kant's effort to answer such a question crowds a major portion of his work during the "critical" period. His attempt to delineate the nature of morality joins with a concerted analysis of the essence of man himself. Hence, Kant's account of moral agency is equivalent to a moral anthropology. All philosophical elaboration of moral concepts, Kant insists, must derive from a careful investigation of "ordinary human reason" (die gemeine Menschenvernunft).[1] Like his mentor in ethical theory, Jean-Jacques Rousseau, Kant took it for granted that the man on the street had as much moral acumen as the professional philosopher, and therefore he believed ethical propositions could only stand on their own if they conformed to the way the

---

[1] GMM, p. 71.   Schriften, IV, 403.

common man reasoned about the moral life. Kant had this particular type of "anthropological" analysis in mind when he set about to develop a "metaphysics of morals" (Metaphysic der Sitten).[1]

But this moral anthropology, Kant holds, does not assimilate to a plain description of the manner in which men, in the main, do in fact reason and act. Indeed, Kant advances the seemingly peremptory claim that it is doubtful whether any genuine morality can be discerned in the world at all.[2] Furthermore, Kant constantly enjoins us against making our judgments about morality on the basis of "experience" (Erfahrung) of things as they actually happen. This reservation highlights an apparent paradox in Kant's conception of human morality: although the metaphysics of morals does somehow replicate man's native form of reasoning, it is questionable whether we can speak affirmatively of any authentic moral experience. As we shall see, the paradox is more apparent than real. That man is capable of reasoning about the moral life does not imply, Kant tells us, that he is equally capable of acting morally. The discrepancy between reasoning and acting points to a kind of transcendence which moral concepts have over the empirical course of events. The true foundation of morality, according to Kant, "must be

---

[1] According to Kant, "a moral principle is really nothing but a dimly conceived metaphysics, which is inherent in every man's rational constitution--as the teacher will easily find out who tries to catechize his pupil in the Socratic method concerning the imperative of duty and its application to the moral judgement of action." MPV, p. 32. Schriften, VI, 376. Moral anthropology takes as its point of departure this "dimly conceived metaphysics" (dunkel gedachte Metaphysik) in the structure of human reasoning. "Since moral laws have to hold for every rational being as such, we ought rather to derive our principles from the general concept of a rational being as such, and on this basis to expound the whole of ethics -- which requires anthropology for its application to man -- at first independently of a pure philosophy, that is, entirely as metaphysics." GMM, p. 79. Schriften, IV, 412.

[2] GMM, p. 75. Schriften, IV, 407.

looked for, not in the nature of man nor in the circumstances of the world in which he is placed, but solely a priori in the concepts of pure reason."[1] The a priori means that moral ideas do not derive from how men in fact behave, but from the way in which they reason they ought to behave.[2] The "oughtness" of moral claims represents the heart of morality in Kant's view of the world. The supremacy of the "ought" in moral claims has been taken by those who have followed Kant as the colophon of the study of ethics -- that is, the examination of moral phenomena.[3] For that reason, what we have called Kant's "moral anthorpology" demands an inversion of the empirical subject matter which, as the etymology of the term "moral" suggests, might readily pass for the concern of any "science of morality." Mores, whence we derive the expression "moral," mainly signify the numerous modes of man's relations with others that come readily to hand, that can be observed, described, and adduced as inductive concepts. A "science of morality" would concern itself only with the empirical operations that account for such relations. Yet "morality," in its proper sense, according to Kant, has little to do with empirical relations. The meaning of its concepts does not lie in the fact that they simply are discoverable in the nature of things, but in what ought to be. So morality is not what it appears to be at all.

Behavior, regarded as "moral" only in virtue of its conventionality, loses its ultimate claim to morality, for Kant,

---

[1] GMM, p. 57. Schriften, IV, 389.

[2] "Reason by itself and independently of all appearances commands what ought to happen; that consequently actions of which the world has hitherto given no example -- actions whose practicability might well be doubted by those who rest everything on experience -- are nevertheless commanded unrelentingly by reason..." GMM, p. 75. Schriften, IV, 408.

3Henry Sidgwick distinguishes ethics from the descriptive or "positive sciences" insofar as it has for its object "to determine what ought to be, and not to ascertain what merely is, has been, or will be." The Methods of Ethics (London: Macmillan and Company, 1901), p. 1.

precisely because it is conventional.¹ Genuine morality is
a *priori*: it makes demands concerning how men *should* act
"prior to" all experience of the forms in which they *do* interact with one another. But what is the character of these
moral demands if they cannot be observed as conventional or
regular acts? How does Kant believe we can speak of moral
agency at all, if we cannot acquire adequate evidence that
there are such things as moral acts taking place in the world
around us?

Again, Kant says that to act morally and to reason morally
are not the same. Reason constructs an idea of the good, what
ought to be (*das Sollen*). This idea transcends our acquired
ideas of human behavior cognizable as "empirical motives
which understanding raises to general concepts by the mere
comparison of experiences."² The idea is not measurable by
visible acts *per se*.³ As a "fact of reason" (*Faktum der Vernunft*) it exists in its own right.⁴ The bifurcation between

---

¹Kant distinguishes between "morality" as *mores* and morality as a nonempirical claim in a passage from the *Metaphysics of Morals*. "Instruction in the laws of morality is not drawn from observation of oneself and the animality within him, nor from the perception of the court of the world -- how things happen and how men in fact do act (although the German word *Sitten*, like the Latin word *mores*, designates only a manner and way of life). But reason commands how one ought to act, even though no instance of such action might be found; moreover, reason pays no attention to the advantages which can accrue from such action, which admittedly only experience could teach." MEJ (MM, Intro.), p. 15 *Schriften*, VI, 216.

²GMM, p. 59. *Schriften*, IV, 391.

³"...when moral value is in question, we are concerned, not with the actions which we see, but with their inner principle (*auf jene innere Principien*) which we cannot see." GMM, p. 75. *Schriften*, IV, 407.

⁴CP_rR, p. 31. *Schriften*, V, 31. For an important exposition of what may be dubbed the "transcendental" or "formal" view of morality in Kant, see W. T. Jones, *Morality and Freedom in the Philosophy of Immanuel Kant* (London: Humphrey Milford, 1940), esp. chs. IV and V, which will be discussed later in this chapter. The "formal" interpretation of Kant holds that moral ideas must be judged solely according to their rational self-consistency without any reference to their possible realization in concrete life.

the independent value of the rational ought and the relative value of the concrete acts, therefore, makes for a dichotomy in Kant deserving precise interpretation.

On the face of it, this dichotomy suggests the age-old distinction between the intention and the act. To intend something does not necessarily mean it will be accomplished. This is illustrated in Saint Paul's famous plaint, "For I do not do the good I want, but the evil I do not want is what I do."[1] The moral idea eludes being realized in our actual deportment. Hence, it becomes impossible to infer morality straightaway from what men do, for men are congenitally powerless to carry out their intentions. The problem of moral agency, therefore, does not turn exclusively on the fact that morality cannot be adduced from descriptions of the phenomenal order. Because men do not, as a rule, act morally does not make moral actions eo ipso impossible. Kant does not contest whether there are, in fact, moral acts. Their existence he, with certain qualifications, assumes.[2] The rent between reason and experience, between the ought and the is, shows us only that we must go after the problem of moral agency, not by examining the character of human action as it appears to us, but by ferreting out the motive of action.[3] The problem of

---

[1] Romans 8:19 (Revised Standard Version).

[2] Kant, in fact, waffles on the question whether there exist, or ever have existed, genuine moral acts in the world. While he admits it may be impossible for genuine virtue to occur, he concedes that it may be possible as well. Kant's guarded optimism concerning the possibility of morality stems from his conviction that pure ideas (especially moral ideas) are at least convertible into their phenomenal manifestations. "An idea," he writes elsewhere, "is nothing else than the conception of a perfection which has not yet been experienced." $E_{,}$, p. 8. Schriften, IX, 444. The possibility of such experience is Kant's concern. But even Kant's provisional skepticism about the facticity of moral actions disappears with certain pragmatic considerations. "Out of love for humanity," Kant admits, "I am willing to allow that most of our actions may accord with duty." GMM, p. 75. Schriften, IV, 407.

[3] Kant states unequivocally that ethics, or the study of moral agency, "is not merely a philosophy of the good act, but

moral agency hinges first of all on the problem of how men
reason about the moral life, how they intend to follow through
their reasoning in action. The complicated relationship of
moral reasoning to moral action fixes the standpoint for looking into the question of moral agency.[1]

2. Moral Action and Motivation

In his Lectures on Ethics, composed during the second half
of the 1770's while the beginnings of the critical philosophy
was in gestation, Kant maps out in perhaps its most lucid form
his conceptual framework for treating moral agency. "Morality" (Moralität), Kant declares, has "either an empirical or
an intellectual basis (entweder auf empirischen oder intellektuellen Gründen beruhe), and must be derived either from
empirical or intellectual principles. Empirical grounds are
derived from the senses, so far as the senses find satisfaction in them. Intellectual grounds are those in which all
morality is derived from the conformity of our actions to the
laws of reason (aus der Übereinstimmung unserer Handlungen mit

---

of the good disposition" (der guten Gesinnung). LE, p. 72.
Vorles., 90. This approach to the problem of agency is the most
fruitful way of interpreting Kant. Kant, of course, does use
the term "action" in a double sense: 1) visible concrete behavior for which the person is accountable; 2) the intention
manifested in such an act. All action, however, for Kant, is
ultimately significant only in the first sense. Cf. J. Kemp,
Reason, Action, and Morality (New York: The Humanities Press,
1964), p. 172.

[1] Kant's moral anthropology, which investigates the a
priori in human action, cannot be disengaged completely from
a merely descriptive anthropology of human behavior. "Practical philosophy (that is, the science of how man ought to behave) and anthropology (that is, the science of man's behavior)
are closely connected, and the former cannot subsist without
the latter: for we cannot tell whether the subject to which
our consideration applies is capable of what is demanded of him
unless we have knowledge of that subject. It is true that we
cannot pursue the study of practical philosophy without
anthropology, that is, without the knowledge of the subject.
But our philosophy is then merely speculative (nur spekulativ),
and an Idea (Idee). We, therefore, have to make at least some
study of man." LE, pp. 2-3. Vorles., 2-3.

den Gesetzen der Vernunft). Accordingly, systema morale est vel empiricum vel intellectuale."[1] Here is a concise statement of the inherent dichotomy that Kant discerns in man's moral life. All moral action arises out of some inner compulsion: ground (Grund), principle (Grundsatz), motive (Bewegungsgrund), incentive (Triebfeder), or determing ground (Bestimmungsgrund). These compulsions spring from one of two general sources: the rational and the sensible. Sensible compulsion Kant terms "pathological" (pathologisch). It is compulsion "by stimulus" which man shares with animals.[2] In modern parlance, we call this sort of compulsion "instinctual" or "reflexive." Rational compulsion, on the other hand, applies only to man; it counters compulsion by stimuli. Unlike a dog, for example, who at the sight and smell of food is overpowered by the instinct to eat, man, under similar circumstances, "can restrain himself."[3] Man can restrain himself, because his reason takes control of his appetite or instinct. In fact, reason compels man to act in a way not befitting the dog, and hence it must be viewed as a different kind of motivation. In the Lectures, Kant enrolls this kind of motivation under the broad rubric of "intellectual." Intellectual or rational compulsion differentiates man from the brutes. The problem of morality strikes man, because he is torn between sensible and rational compulsions, between his (definitively) human and animal natures.[4]

---

[1] LE, pp. 11-12. Vorles., 14.

[2] "Animals are determined per stimulus. Thus when a dog is hungry and there is food, he must eat." LE, p. 28. Vorles., 34.

[3] Ibid.

[4] This dual set of compulsions -- the rational and the sensible -- is what Kant really has in mind with his doctrine that man exists as a citizen (Bürger) of "two worlds." "Now man actually finds in himself a power which distinguishes him from all other things -- and even from himself so far as he is affected by objects" or stimuli. "This power is reason." GMM, p. 119. Schriften, IV, 452. Reason, Kant says, "manifests its highest function in distinguishing the sensible and intelligible worlds from one another..." Ibid., p. 120 (Ibid.). Instead of

But morality is not simply identified as a clash of motivations. Morality, Kant insists, while presenting itself as a task or challenge in consequence of this strife of opposites, exists as an immediate state of action only when the rational principle gains the upper hand in compelling what we do. For "the principles of morality must be intellectual. The moral judgement never occurs at all in virtue of the sensuous or empirical principles, for the ethical is never an object of the senses (Gegenstand der Sinne), but purely of the understanding (bloss des Verstandes)."[1] The "understanding," in this early formulation of Kant, serves as the genuine yardstick of the moral life; it generates the rational principles that compel action.[2] The more actions are rationally motivated, the more they deserve to be deemed moral.

---

interpreting Kant's sensible/intelligible (phenomenal/noumenal) distinction metaphysically, as is often done, we may perhaps regard it as simply a division of motives. Man's citizenship in the two realms is thus a metaphor for the clash of compulsions, or conflict between the power of reason and the power of instincts. For further analysis of the distinction, see below.

[1] LE, pp. 13-14. Vorles., 17.

[2] In the Groundwork of the Metaphysics of Morals (1785) and the Critique of Practical Reason (1788) as well as in Kant's subsequent writings, "reason" in the sense of "pure reason" as it is denominated in the critical philosophy replaces "understanding" (Verstand) as the organ of moral judgements. This development owes mainly to the special role which Kant assigns the understanding in the "Transcendental Analytic" of the first Critique: the role of entertaining a priori concepts that have meaning only when schematized in relation to sense-intuition. Given this specification of roles, reason then becomes the mind's purely constructive activity which, unfettered by sensible criteria or data, independently provides the "intellectually" pure concepts of morality. The constructive, or originative, function of reason, in contrast to the synthetic work of the understanding, is spelled out by Kant. "As pure spontaneity reason is elevated even above understanding in the following respect. Understanding -- although it too is spontaneous activity (Selbstthätigkeit) and is not, like sense, confined to ideas which arise only when we are affected by things (and therefore are passive) -- understanding cannot produce by its own activity any concepts than whose sole service is to bring sensuous ideas under rules

But what do we mean by rational motivation? Rational motivation means merely that there is a certain ratio, a proportionality or consistency (in a word, a regularity) in one's plan of action. A "plan of action" is an intelligent choice as to how one proceeds prior to the action itself. The "regularity" of actions motivated by reason signifies that the actions take place according to a rule. "In all our actions that which is called moral is regular. It conforms to a rule."[1] The understanding furnishes rules. In cognitive operations the mind employs these rules for the synthesis of sense-data into empirical concepts.[2] Kant labels such rules of cognition "categories" (Kategorien) or a priori "forms of judgment" (Formen des Urteils). The category of causality, for instance, ensures that "if we experience that something happens, so do we at the same time presume that something precedes it, whereupon it follows as a rule."[3] Rules of cognition enable us to organize the welter of sense impressions into a pattern that is intelligible by dint of its repeatability and consistency. Without the rule of causality, Kant says, we could not infer that an impression of an object at $time_1$ and $position_1$ has a clear relation to an impression of the same object at $time_2$

---

and so to unite them in one consciousness: without this sensibility it would think nothing at all (gar nichts denken). Reason, on the other hand, in what are called "Ideas" -- shows a spontaneity so pure that it goes far beyond anything sensibility can offer..." GMM, 119-20. Schriften, IV, 452. This view of reason, according to Paton, breaks from the traditional conceptions which treat understanding as one branch of "reason as a whole," or "thinking in general." H. J. Paton, The Categorical Imperative (London: Hutchinson and Company, 1965), p. 96. In the Lectures Kant seems to uphold the traditional view of reason and understanding.

[1] LE, p. 42. Vorles., 51.

[2] K_rV (B): Schriften, III, 167ff. The second edition of the Kritik der reinen Vernunft is hereon always cited.

[3] K_rV (B): Schriften, III, 171.

and position$_2$. Kant uses the example of a ship moving down a stream. The rule of causality allows us to link together the two sensations of the ship in situation A and situation B, and to draw the same valid connection over and over again under like circumstances.[1] Otherwise, the two sensations would not have any meaningful affinity with each other.

The fact that all persons affected by the same impressions draw the same connections lends these rules of cognition a definite "universal" character. The rules are universal, because all rational beings experience the world uniformly. Moreover, there are also universal rules for moral experience. These the understanding likewise furnishes. "Understanding is the faculty of the rule of our actions, and actions which are in harmony with the universal rule are in harmony with the understanding, and thus their impulsive grounds are in the understanding."[2] The understanding, then, imposes a universal form and regularity on the way in which we act, as well as on the way we know. "Moral goodness...is the submission of our will to rules whereby all our voluntary actions are brought into a harmony which is universally valid."[3] Whether we are knowing or acting through rules, our experience is shaped by the peculiar human capacity for understanding or reason. In knowing, reason constructs a world homogeneously conceived by all men. In acting reason seeks a world in which all men will behave consistently vis-a-vis their fellows. That world is possible, according to Kant, since all men share the gift of rationality. For animals, who are not rational, the world cannot be conceived on a universal model. Affected only by sensations, they do not possess the regulative power of reason or understanding. Their world, along with the world of madmen, does not compose a world in any coherent sense: it

---

[1] K_rV (B): Schriften, III, 169f.
[2] LE, p. 44. Vorles., 53.
[3] LE, p. 17. Vorles., 21.

consists only in a private chaos of disconnected givens, what William James called a "blooming, buzzing confusion." Similarly, animals do not act according to universal rules. Their motions are purely mechanical reflexes of sense.[1] Their bondage to sense impulsion precludes them from action consistent with all other animal acts. A dog's horizon of moral experience is not a universe of other animals. A dog will pilfer a piece of meat from another dog merely from the stimulus of hunger without any respect for his congener. Dogs can never act morally in the reflective and rule-directed manner that human beings do.

3. The Notion of Practical Reason

In the Groundwork Kant furbishes the meaning of rational motivation slightly. Here the simple parity between the terms "reason" and "understanding," evidenced in the Lectures, drops away. As a result, reason is now enshrined as the main faculty of the supersensible. Reason alone provides the transcendent norms for moral judgement and, by extension, the incentives for moral action.[2] The essentials of the new view in the Groundwork reside largely in the distinction previously forged in the first Critique between reason in the wider sense ("the whole higher faculty of knowledge" [das ganze obere Erkenntnisvermögen]) and reason in the narrower sense ("the highest power of knowing" [die oberste Erkenntniskraft]), that is, as "pure reason" (reine Vernunft).[3] Unlike the

---

[1] Kant's conception of animal behavior as irrational, sensible, and mechanistic parallels the idealist views of his predecessors that originate with Descartes. Descartes, we remember, thought of animals simply as automata or "machines" impelled by sensation without any influence of reason or "thought." Cf. Descartes' Letter to Henry More (1649) excerpted in Henry Torrey, The Philosophy of Descartes (New York: Henry Holt and Company, 1892), pp. 284ff.

[2] LE, p. 44. Vorles., 53.

[3] LE, p. 17. Vorles., 21.

understanding which supplies the mind with categories whose sole use is to regulate sense impressions, pure reason develops and entertains a system of ideas (Ideen). These ideas

> ...are still further removed from objective reality than the categories; for no phenomenon can ever present them to the human mind in concreto. They contain a certain perfection, attainable by no emperical cognition; and they give to reason a systematic unity, to which the unity of experience attempts to approximate, but can never completely attain.[1]

Through the employment of ideas pure reason regulates not sense data, but the very process of thinking in general. The ideas, heretofore, constitute rules for reflection irrespective of what is cognized and judged relevant in sensory input.[2] With the ideas thought is able to reach a total consistency or rational "perfection" (Vollkommenheit) that would be impossible were empirical concepts the criteria of truth and falsity.

Empirical concepts themselves draw their relevance or significance from the ideas of reason which contain a "schema" (Schema) of a world that does not necessarily correspond to that cognized in the understanding. All human knowledge, Kant asserts, "begins with sense, then proceeds to the understanding and finally to reason, beyond which the human mind can discover nothing for elaborating the stuff of intuition and subjection it to the supreme unity of thought."[3] Pure reason attempts to regulate all conceptions, just as the understanding regulates the material of sensation, and to unify them in

---

[1] $K_r V$ (B): Schriften, III, 383. An idea transcends sense-experience because it has for its aim comprehension (Begreifen), just as the concepts of understanding (Verstandesbegriffe)... serves for the understanding (of perception)." $K_r V$ (B): Schriften, III, 244.

[2] "The understanding may be a faculty of the unity of appearances mediated by rules; the reason is the faculty of the unity of rules of understanding under principles. Reason thus never applies to experience nor to any object..." $K_r V$ (B): Schriften, III, 239.

[3] $K_r V$ (B): Schriften, III, 237.

a highest synthesis. The idea of God as First Cause, for example, while not a "cognizable object," is "merely a regulative principle of the reason which demands that we consider all connections between phenomena as though they derived from an all-sufficient necessary cause, in order to ground therein the rule of a systematic and necessary unity according to general laws in the explanation (of phenomena)."[1]

Ideas of this kind function chiefly as "hypotheses" (Hypothesen). Their role is to provide a heuristic unity to our modes of knowledge of the world. While in themselves they do not contain a "theory" about the way the world is, they do nevertheless have their primary use in a "theoretical" vein. They serve as aids for the understanding in its effort to open up a farthest horizon of meaning that helps clarify more elementary theoretical insights. But the ideas of reason have another important service to perform besides the theoretical. The ideas have a practical function where "human reason exhibits real causality (wahrhafte Causalität), and where the ideas become effective causes (of actions and their objects), namely in ethics, but also in respect to nature itself..."[2] Reason displays its own special praxis: a means of bringing about concrete effects in the universe as moral acts. Pure reason, according to Kant, gives rise to morality by dint of the vigor of the "oughtness" contained in a practical idea. This idea of "oughtness," or what Kant calls an "imperative" (Imperativ), necessitates an order of events quite distinct from the ordinary course of things.[3] The "oughtness" of the imperative cannot be represented by the understanding, which merely tries to make some sense out of

---

[1] $K_r V$ (B): Schriften, III, 413.

[2] $K_r V$ (B): Schriften, III, 248.

[3] "That...reason has causality, or at least that we can represent it as such, is clear from the imperatives, which in a practical way we ascribe as rules to the executive powers (den ausübenden Kräfte). The ought expresses a kind of necessity and connection with principles which otherwise are not found in all of nature." $K_r V$ (B): Schriften, III, 371.

the given objects of sensation through the synthesis of cognition.[1] "This *ought* expresses a possible action (mögliche Handlung), the ground of which is nothing other than a pure concept..."[2] Such a pure concept is realized by changing the empirical succession of events to fit the pattern it prescribes.

The pure concept does not have its source in our observation of the sequence of actual events. The pure concept is essentially *sui generis*. Pure reason, which produces the concept, struggles to realize an ideal order in the universe.[3] The causality of pure reason through concepts is tantamount to the peculiar rule-directed behavior we have designated as moral agency. Like every cause, reason "presupposes a rule according to which certain appearances follow as effects, and each rule demands a uniformity of effects, which grounds the concept of a cause (as a power)."[4] Pure reason in its practical exercise expresses itself in terms of moral actions, or as an *ought* with phenomenal manifestations.[5] It bodies forth

---

[1] "The understanding can know only what exists, or has been, or will be. It is impossible that something [in nature] should be other than it is, in fact, through all relations of time..." Ibid.

[2] Ibid.

[3] "...reason does not give those grounds which are given empirically and does not follow the order of things as they appear, but makes for itself with complete spontaneity its own order according to ideas, to which it adjusts (passt hinein) empirical conditions..." K_rV (B): Schriften, III, 372.

[4] Ibid.

[5] The distinction Kant makes between theoretical and practical reason is only semantic. One must be able, Kant says, to "show the unity of practical and theoretical reason in a common principle, since in the end there can be only one and the same reason, which must be differentiated solely in its application." GMM, p. 59. Schriften, IV, 391. The same point is made in a common sense way in W. H. Walsh, Kant's Moral Theology (London: Oxford University Press, 1963), p. 268.

the _ought_ as a rule of action that does not simply duplicate
the conventional patterns of action perceived in nature.[1]
In short, pure practical reason functions as a cause of moral
action so far as it furnishes rules of such action. The
capacity for these rules is unique to rational beings. Not
the blowing of the wind, the running of the time, the migratory flights of birds, but only human action can have reason
as its cause. For man alone can rationally conceive what
ought to be, what never has gone before. Only man has the
talent for transforming the conditions under which he lives
by projecting an ideal state of existence and laboring to
actualize it. Only man is able to put his ideas "into
practice."[2] But this capacity exists precisely because man
possesses a _will_.

4. Action and Willing

"Reason," for Kant, "is the constant condition (_beharrliche Bedingung_) of all acts of will..."[3] Moreover, reason is

---

[1] In the practical use of reason "we find a wholly different rule and order than the order of nature (_Naturordnung_)."
K_rV (B): _Schriften_, III, 373.

[2] The disjunction in Kant's thought between _ought_ and _is_ resulting from the moral claims of reason represents a markedly revolutionary shift in philosophical reflection about man's place in nature. According to L. W. Beck, "Kant's ethics, historically, represents a transition between two great conceptions of the relation of man to the world. Against the eighteenth-century position that man is a part of nature and ought to be subservient to her laws, Kant reacted by inverting the order and making nature what she is because of how she appears to us. Then he transcended even this Copernican venture by daring to weigh nature in the scales or reason and to declare what she is wanting and does not contain the destiny of man. The practical -- what man ought to be and how he ought to transform his existence -- in this conception takes precedence over what nature is and what she demands of man as part of her order." _A Commentary on Kant's Critique of Practical Reason_ (Chicago: The University of Chicago Press, 1960), p. 125.

[3] K_rV (B): _Schriften_, III, 374.

as we have seen, "a faculty...originating by itself a series of events,"[1] that is, creating a new pattern of action that is distinctively moral. All willing, therefore, is that process whereby rational rules of action are translated into visible effects that can be compared with their ideal form or origin.[2] Hence, "the will is nothing but practical reason."[3] The human will is the operation of reason in the natural or sensible realm. Through his will man can change what goes on around him to conform to his ideas. If a man "wills" to do a good turn for a stranger, this means that he has acted according to an idea that conduces him in a manner conspicuously unlike the way he might act under ordinary circumstances. People ordinarily give short shrift to the needs of strangers. Such disregard is habitual, not willed in the sense of being conscious of a discrete idea of how one should act toward the stranger.[4] Human willing is behaving with reason as one's motivation. In this regard, the notion of will

---

[1] Ibid.

[2] "Thus every man has an empirical character to his will which is nothing but a certain causality of his reason, so far as [his reason] manifests in its effects the presence of a rule, according to which man can examine the rational grounds (Vernunftgründe) and its actions in its different forms and degrees, and to judge the subjective principles of willing." K_rV (B): Schriften, III, 372.

[3] GMM, p. 80. Schriften, IV, 412.

[4] Of course, habits are often formed as the unthinking repetition of what were originally conscious choices. In short, the teleological character of the original act (the exercise of ideas of reason in informing a decision), many times repeated, becomes habitual and, in a certain sense, "instinctive." However, Kant would distinguish a "habit" of a rational or good will from the habits of a pathological or mere animal will. Habitual disregard of another person's welfare, Kant would probably say, is a product of a selfish or irrational impulse that never had an original telic character, unlike a man, for instance, who makes a habit of doing good turns for his fellows from day to day. The latter man has made a reasoned and deliberate choice in favor of the moral law, and his "good habit" of altruism is merely the repetition of that initial choice.

encapsulates Kant's theory of moral action.

More specifically, Kant is concerned with what he calls "pure will" (reiner Wille), a will motivated by concepts of pure reason. The pure will is distinguished from "willing as such" (das Wollen überhaupt)[1] which comprises sensible as well as rational motivation. It is instructive to note that Kant makes use of two separate terms to indicate human will: Willkür and Wille. By Willkür Kant means primarily the general power of "choice" or the capacity of an "action to produce its object."[2] Thus the Willkür can be either sensuously affected or rationally motivated; it is "willing in general" as signified in the Latin term arbitrium.[3] Wille, on the other hand, "is the faculty of desire whose internal ground of determination and, consequently, even those likings are found in the reason of the subject..."[4] Unlike the power of mere choice, Wille has not so much to do with the effectiveness of an action as with "the ground determining the Willkür to action."[5] Such

---

[1] GMM, p. 58. Schriften, IV, 390.

[2] MEJ (MM, Intro.), p. 12. Schriften, VI, 213.

[3] "A will (Willkür) is purely animal (arbitrium brutum) when it is determined by sensuous impulses and instincts...in a pathological manner. A will, which can be determined independent of sensuous impulses, consequently by motives presented by reason alone, is called a free will (arbitrium liberum)." K_rV (B): Schriften, III, 521.

[4] MEJ (MM, Intro.), p. 12. Schriften, VI, 213.

[5] MEJ (MM, Intro.), p. 13. Schriften, VI, 214. The distinction between Wille and Willkür may be thought of on an analogy with the legislative and executive branches of government. The Wille legislates rules of action through reason; the Willkür merely executes them or carries them out through choice. Like the two branches of government, legislation and choice are necessary functions of the unified process of will. It is also possible to translate Willkür as "agency" instead of "choice" and Wille as "moral agency" instead of, say, "practical reason." While the agency/moral agency distinction perhaps is more precise and distinct than the traditional choice/practical reason distinction, the former pair has been retained to remain consistent with the various conventional translations cited in this dissertation.

a ground we have in reason. In willing reason in varying degrees determines how we elect to do one thing or another.[1] Human choice, as distinct from the stimulus to action in animals, does never completely consist in sensible impulses; it only comes to be "affected by them."[2] The sensible impulses ceaselessly vie with the rational or moral grounds of action. The aim of reason is to regulate such strife by producing a pure will: a will not guided pre-eminently by the sensible. In the exercise of a pure will lies genuine morality.

Still, it remains to be seen exactly how the pure will in Kant's estimation can originate in human activity sparked by conflicting compulsions. The problem of the pure will preoccupies the Groundwork, Kant's tightly argued overture to his moral philosophy. In our analysis of the pure will we must examine three sub-topics that are necessary to understanding the problem as a whole. These are 1) the relation between rules and laws of action 2) the distinction between subjective and objective principles of conduct 3) the general concept of what Kant calls the "moral law." These sub-topics will be investigated in close detail in the following section.

B. The Pure Will and Laws of Morality

1. Rules and Laws of Action

In the Groundwork Kant construes the notion of the will in terms of its agreement with certain "laws" (Gesetzen):

> Everything in nature works in accordance with laws. Only a rational being has the power to act in accordance with his ideas of laws -- that is, in accordance with principles -- and only so has he a will.[3]

---

[1] "Will is a kind of causality belonging to living beings so far as they are rational." GMM, 114. Schriften, IV, 416.

[2] MEJ (MM, Intro.), p. 13. Schriften, VI, 214.

[3] GMM, p. 80. Schriften, IV, 412.

Kant's use of the term "law" here stands as something of an innovation. Prior to the Groundwork, Kant is inclined, on the main, to speak of moral agency merely as following "rules" instead. Is Kant only substituting a new figure of speech for an old, or does he make a substantive division between rules and laws?

The concept of a rule, as we have shown, implies a consistent method of the mind for ordering or regulating different modes of experience. As Kemp notes, the chief property of a rule is that it must apply to several occasions of experience and not obtain only for a single person or situation.[1] When one contends, for instance, that "as a rule" people pay their income tax before the deadline, he means simply that it is generally the case that they will do so. He does not mean that every person will pay his income tax on time, for there are always delinquents and chiselers. Instead he means that he has sufficient grasp of the way people behave toward the Internal Revenue Service, and thus he can ascertain a definite pattern of behavior concerning payment of taxes. A rule is a plan for making a uniform series of judgements or completing operations. Such is the case when we speak of a rule for balancing coefficients in algebra. An algebraic rule is not a fool-proof prescription for balancing coefficients and exponents, yet it is general enough to arrange properly different sets of numerical data. A rule, sufficiently general, can also be called "universal," so far as it applies in all instances. Universality is implied when we say "as a rule night follows day," or "as a rule people grow old and die." But such phrases grate slightly on our ears, since the expression "as a rule" does not usually occur in syntaxts of the form "in every single conceivable occasion." When we use the expression,

---

[1] Kemp, op. cit., p. 113. For example, "the words, 'Don't smoke in here,' addressed to a particular individual in a particular occasion, do not state or express a rule, whereas the same words exhibited on any notice may perhaps do so." Ibid.

we frequently point to some contingency, to the fact that the rule has exceptions. If a mother says, "As a rule my Sally minds her manners in public," she does not mean that her daughter never commits a pecadillo or two.

Kant, indeed, makes reference in the first *Critique* to "universal rules" both of cognition and action. Yet not all rules are universal. Thus the expression "universal rule" needs a more precise lection. Kant finds such a rendering of "universal rule" in the term "law." Laws, for Kant, signify "objective rules" (<u>objektive Regeln</u>). By "objective" Kant simply means universal applicability. Judgements of cognition or perception (<u>Wahrnehmung</u>) are objective, because they are universal (<u>allgemeingultig</u>).[1] One of Kant's purposes in composing the "Analytic" to the <u>Critique of Pure Reason</u> (1781) is to demonstrate that the "laws of nature" (<u>Naturgesetze</u>) which Newton claimed to have discovered, in truth, constitute objective rules of scientific knowledge in virtue of their status as universal rules of perception seated in the structure of the human understanding. All men, Kant insists, experience nature consonant with these rules. If universal rules, or laws of the understanding, are possible, then is not such the case with laws of practical reason? There exist laws of practical reason, for Kant, so far as these laws are objective and universal: valid for all men. A second feature of laws, theoretical or practical, is their "necessity" (<u>Notwendigkeit</u>). If something is universal, it is <u>eo ipso</u> necessary, as it cannot have exceptions; it <u>cannot be any other way than it is</u>. That a law of nature is necessary means it cannot be qualified or annulled under any conditions. That a practical law is necessary means one <u>ought not</u> to act in any other way than he

---

[1] "...when a judgement agrees with an object, all judgements concerning the same object must likewise agree among themselves, and thus the objective validity of the judgement of experience signifies nothing else than its necessary universal validity." <u>Prol.</u>, p. 46. <u>Schriften</u>, IV, 298.

is so compelled irregardless of the actual conditions or extenuating circumstances at the moment of decision. The compulsive effect of a practical law upon the human will Kant denominates an "imperative" (Imperativ).[1]

Imperatives, or commanded practical laws, arise because men do not live up to the demands made upon them by reason. If they did live up to them, right action would not have to be demanded; it would be a fact. Unlike laws of perception (theoretical laws) which are strictly descriptive of the way natural events invariably happen, practical laws are prescriptive, inasmuch as they mark out not what is, but what ought to be the case. Laws of perception are inviolable. Practical laws, however, are infringed as often as a man does not choose them as the principle of his conduct.[2] Practical laws have their universality and necessity in that they oblige all men in all circumstances. But to oblige someone does not entail compliance. The apocryphal Kantian epigram, Du sollst denn du kannst ("You ought since you can") emphasizes that a man always has the capacity to carry out the ought by virtue of his rational will.[3] But the "can," as a contingent term, also signifies that one has a similar capacity to ignore the promptings of his reason. The necessitation of practical laws, therefore, does not allude to an actual world in which men do

---

[1] "The conception of an objective principle so far as this principle is necessitating for a will is called a command (of reason), and the formula of this command is called an Imperative." GMM, p. 81. Schriften, IV, 413.

[2] Cf. Brendan Liddell, Kant on the Foundation of Morality (Bloomington: Indiana University Press, 1970), p. 105.

[3] "...this, 'I ought,' is properly an 'I will' which holds necessarily for every rational being -- provided that reason in him is practical without hindrance (ohne Hindernisse)." GMM, p. 117. Schriften, IV, 449. This is one of Kant's statements which have the force of the famous epigram connecting Wollen and Sollen, although the exact expression, "Thou canst because thou shouldst," nowhere exists in Kant's writings. Cf. Beck, op. cit., p. 200n.

perform what they should but to an ideal world where all men act rationally. The contradiction between the real and ideal gives rise to a situation in which the demands of the latter must be addressed to the former as an imperative. The imperative stipulates what the will need accomplish instead of giving an empirical account of how things occur. Thus the objective necessity of a practical law, for Kant, rests on its ability to make an incontrovertible demand on the will. This demand has the force of what Kant calls "obligation" (Verbindlichkeit).

Kant defines obligation as a "constraint" (Nötigung) to action, albeit a constraint which is "only that of reason and its objective law."[1] It is "only that of reason" because it cannot necessitate action in the manner an empirical cause necessitates its effect, viz., by drawing an inalterable rule of connection between two actual events. A moral action can never appear an ineluctable effect of moral reasoning in the sense that two events observed in nature are connected, because of the contingency of volition in all man's decision-making. The formula for obligation always reads in terms of "ought," never "is."[2] Yet the necessity of this ought contains within itself the possibility of becoming an is, since it is an axiom of logic that necessity entails possibility. This possibility is represented in the "I can," and thus yields the old saw in

---

[1] CP_rR, p. 32. Schriften, V, 32.

[2] "One ought to do this or that and leave the other; such is the formula according to which each obligation gets expressed." Nat. Theol.: Schriften, II, 298. The split between ought and is, between man's ideal (rational) and real (sensible) constitutions, as we have seen, not only underlies the concept of obligation, it also serves as the "condition for the possibility of the moral life." In this sense, constraint, for Kant, is ingredient in all morality. A being with no sensible motives would not require constraint or obligation, and hence would not confront the task of living morally. Cf. Allen Wood, Kant's Moral Religion (Ithaca: Cornell University Press, 1970), p. 4.

ethics that "ought implies can," which contemporary moralists often view as Kant's bequest.[1]

The proposition that one can do what he ought means that one can adopt the implied imperative as a rule for his will. On the other hand, a rule of willing, merely because it is a rule, does not in itself constrain to action as an objective law. Obligation compels more strongly than a mere rule. A rule gives us the "how" of action, not its "must." I can say that "it is a good rule to take brisk daily walks if I wish to stay healthy," but such a rule does not oblige me to take brisk walks. No demand is made on me. There is no intrinsic obligation in such a rule, because it does not universally (and thus not necessarily) hold for all persons under all circumstances. People with severe heart conditions or paralysis of the limbs, for example, should not take such walks. Obligation requires that a rule have the status of universal law. The ought of obligation means that "everyone ought to do such and such." Jesus' saying, "You ought to love your neighbor," means something far different than the conditional statement, "You ought to love your neighbor if he happens to look like you, is Jewish, has plenty of money, etc. Laws of practical reason, specified as obligations, for Kant, never have conditions, qualifications, or exceptions.[2] Their unconditioned character renders them objective. Conditional rules of willing, however, are merely subjective. They compel only insofar as they hold for particular persons in particular situations. The distinction between subjective and objective rules of willing, therefore, serves as a point of departure for closer

---

[1] Cf. Stuart Hampshire, Thought and Action (New York: The Viking Press, 1959). Hampshire's book represents an important and thorough effort to discount the Kantian position that men have clear ideas of their obligation and that moral agency consists in merely fulfilling or failing to carry out imperatives.

[2] Cf. John Hospers, Human Conduct (New York: Harcourt, Brace & World, 1961), pp. 276ff.

examination of Kant's analysis of moral volition in its "pure" sense.

2. Subjective and Objective Principles

Every human action, according to Kant, is motivated or compelled in some way. This signifies that all willing proceeds from some "practical" principle (Grundsatz) or basic rule of action.[1] In some measure reason, by equipping the will with rules to follow, gives impetus to action. So far as the rule of action is wholly rational and not infected with sensation, it becomes universal and objective. An objective principle, or "practical law," consistutes a rule "valid for the will of every rational being." A principle, however, remains "subjective" when "the condition is regarded by the subject as valid only for his own will."[2] Subjective principles, in general, Kant identifies as "maxims" (Maximen).[3] Maxims, indeed, account for all human actions. Every man, because he is an individual subject of action, has his own particular maxims in choosing a court to take. Every action, in other words, involves a choice which can only be one's own. The choice invariably depends on a rule which determines what he himself elects to do. Even if a subjective rule, or

---

[1] "Practical principles are propositions which contain a general determination of the will (allgemeine Bestimmung des Willens), having under it several practical rules." CP_rR, p. 17. Schriften, V. 19.

[2] Ibid.

[3] "Subjective grounds of actions" (subjective Gründe der Handlungen) or "subjective principles" (subjective Grundsätze) are terms maxims." K_rV (B): Schriften, III, 527. "A maxim is the subjective principle of volition: an objective principle (that is, one which would also serve subjectively as a practical principle for all rational beings if reason had full control (volle Gewalt) over the faculty of desire) is a practical law." GMM, p. 69n. Schriften, IV, 400n.

maxim, ultimately gains objective worth, it has, from the point of view of the acting individual, a distinctively singular meaning. Although, for example, my choice of giving money to charity can perhaps be construed as a possible choice for all men, the choice itself, first and foremost, is valid for me as an agent. Therefore, all choices have a prior subjective validity.[1] Thus, the problem of moral willing is not posed because men act according to subjective rules, but because it is not always the case that their maxims comport with objective principles, or practical laws. The moral imperative requires that subjective and objective principles of action somehow agree with each other.[2]

The contradiction between objective and subjective principles emerges when a man simply adopts a maxim without any thought to its possible universality. The maxim then becomes a rule of action for that man only. Subjective choices, taken generically, are only universal in the peculiar sense that every individual, in order to act, must choose in one way or another. Yet subjective choices in themselves do not universally oblige; they have no moral necessity. A simple choice signifies only an arbitrium, an "arbitrary" principle of acting that causes one to act in one way just as well as the other. Just because I choose to have lunch at the refectory today does not mean I ought to do so. I could just as well dine at some lunch stand. My choice to dine wherever I do is prima facie valid for me only as an individual. However, any choice need not be arbitrary. One may choose something he feels must be chosen because all men, including himself, should so so in that situation. In that case, the choice loses its sub-

---

[1] "The rule which the agent adopts on subjective grounds as his principle is called his maxim; hence the maxim of agents may be very different with regard to the same laws." MEJ (MM, Intro.), p. 26. Schriften, VI, 225.

[2] An "imperative contains only the necessity that our maxim should conform to this law, while the law...contains no condition to limit it, there remains nothing over to which the maxim has to conform except the universality of a law as such..." GMM, p. 88. Schriften, IV, 420-1.

jectivity. If one chooses only for himself, he isolates himself. He does not choose according to a law of choice that unqualifiedly applies to all rational beings. Certainly it is possible to formulate an empirical law that every man does in fact choose for himself (an egotist or a cynic might well argue that such is the way everybody chooses); but an empirical law is not, for Kant, an objective law of morality. For if every man did indeed choose for himself alone, he would not ipso facto be choosing in a fashion that would have validity for anyone other than himself. If a man chooses to embezzle a large sum of cash from his employer to increase his own income, he cannot claim to act from an objective principle; since, if all his fellow workers also embezzled to the extent he did, there would be no money left to steal. Similarly, if all men made a habit of lying (to recall Kant's example) for personal advantage, such advantages ultimately would be unattainable, as no one would trust anyone else sufficiently to be duped any longer. A contradiction inexorably interposes, Kant notes, between the adoption of purely subjective principles and objective demands of the moral reason. The contradiction centers on the fact that subjective principles by themselves cannot be universalized into objective laws of action in terms of obligation. The subordination of subjective choices to the objective law of reason is the sufficient condition for a pure will. The pure will as Wille, therefore, transcends mere choice (Willkür) inasmuch as it is guided by an objective principle, or the "moral law" (Sittengesetz).

3. The Moral Law

The moral law, for Kant, denotes the authentic rule of moral agency. The moral law can only be deduced a priori and demands unqualified obedience, i.e., it obligates us.[1] It is

---

[1]"Pure reason is practical of itself alone, and it gives (to man) a universal law, which we call the moral law." CP_rR,

the law of pure willing. When one wills the moral law, no sensuous or subjective factor can count as the governing principle. The ideal *oughtness* of the law cancels all contingent motives and renders it universal.[1] To will the moral law is to prescribe a definite maxim for all men in any context of action without exception or qualification. Kant's term for the unqualified character of the moral law is the adjective "categorical" (Kategorisch). The obligatory form of the moral law Kant dubs the "categorical imperative."

By introducing the concept of the categorical imperative into his discussion of morality, Kant modulates slightly his notion of "oughtness" as contained in an imperative. At the outset of the *Groundwork* he describes imperatives simply as demands upon a refractory will[2] which are valid "for every rational being as such."[3] One gets the impression, therefore, that "oughtness" alone defines the moral law. With the intro-

---

p. 32. Schriften, V, 32. "Everyone must admit that a law has to carry with it absolute necessity if it is to be valid morally -- valid, that is, as a ground of obligation; that the command, 'Thou shalt not lie' could not hold merely for men, other rational beings having no obligation to abide by it -- and similarly with all other genuine moral laws; that here consequently the ground of obligation must be looked for, not in the nature of man nor in the circumstances of the world in which he is placed, but solely *a priori* in the concepts of pure reason..." GMM, p. 57. Schriften, IV, 388.

[1]"Since I have robbed the will of every inducement that might arise for it as a consequence of obeying any particular law, nothing is left but the conformity of actions to universal law as such, and this alone must serve the will as its principle. That is to say, I ought never to act except in such a way that I can also will that my maxim should become a universal law." GMM, p. 70. Schriften, IV, 402.

[2]"All imperatives are expressed by an 'ought' (Sollen). By this they mark the relation of an objective law of reason to a will which is not necessarily determined by this law in virtue of its subjective constitution (the relation of necessitation)." GMM, p. 81. Schriften, IV, 413.

[3]Ibid.

duction of the idea of a categorical imperative, however, Kant adds the <u>proviso</u> that "oughtness" really can have two senses, only one of which is specifically <u>moral</u>. There may be a condition attached to the "ought" statement, in which case the imperative is not categorical at all, but "hypothetical." Hypothetical imperatives "declare a possible action to be practically necessary as a means to the attainment of something else than one wills (or that one may will)." A categorical imperative, on the other hand, "would be one which represented an action as objectively necessary in itself apart from its relation to a further end."[1] Kant makes this belated distinction between hypothetical and categorical imperatives, perhaps because he recognizes the fundamental ambiguity in the grammar of "oughtness." The unconditional sense of "ought" is implied in most imperative sentences that simply command us to do such and such, that in a sense simply speak for themselves. The Mosaic commandment, "Thou shalt not commit adultery," has the ring of an unconditional imperative. No condition is attached, because it is not permissible to conceive a counter-instance in which the injunction against adultery might not obtain. On the other hand, it is possible to qualify the commandment to read, "You ought not to commit adultery, <u>if</u> you want to preserve your marriage." Such an injunction is only valid because one, for instance, is afraid of a broken marriage and not because it is wrong to have an extra-marital affair in itself. The "ought" is qualified by an "if" clause. By the same token, the rule of refraining from adultery is limited by the particular purpose one has in mind (i.e., good relations with one's wife). The conditional sense of "ought" occurs

---

[1] <u>GMM</u>, p. 82. <u>Schriften</u>, IV, 414. Similarly, "the categorical (unconditional) imperative is one that does not command mediately, though the representation of an end that can be attained by an action, but immediately through the mere representation of this action itself (<u>blosse Vorstellung dieser Handlung selbst</u>)...which the categorical imperative think as objectively necessary and makes necessary." <u>MEJ</u> (<u>MM</u>, <u>Intro</u>.), p. 23. <u>Schriften</u>, VI, 222.

throughout everyday speech. For example, it is commonplace to say something like, "You ought to shop at the market today if you want to take advantage of their weekend special on vegetables," or "You ought to finish your doctoral dissertation if you want to land a good job." This sense of "ought," like the unconditional, is syntactically correct.

The conditional, or hypothetical, imperative alone does not pretend to objectivity, since the basis of its validity (the "if" clause) does not have to apply to all men. Not all men worry about the prospect of divorce. A man who hates his wife and does not expect social ostracism for illicit intercourse is a case in point. All conditional imperatives, therefore, are "problematic." On the other hand, there do exist kinds of conditions which are objective in the sense that they do have meaning for all men. Kant takes as a fact of nature, for instance, that all men desire happiness, and thus achieving happiness can be posited as a condition for a certain type of "objective" imperative. The idea that all men naturally seek happiness Kant takes over from Aristotle, who was the first to formulate a version of this imperative: if you want to be happy, you must attain to the contemplative life.[1] Such an imperative, conditioned by a universal end of life like happiness, Kant calls "assertoric;" it <u>asserts</u> what must be the general case (i.e., that all men desire well-being) if the imperative is valid. Kant's acknowledgement of assertoric imperatives (especially the imperative of happiness) prompts him to reconstruct the notion of the moral <u>ought</u> as a universal demand of reason.

Assertoric imperatives, according to Kant, are merely "pragmatic." Only categorical imperatives are truly "moral."[2] An imperative built on the desire for happiness, though it does express a universal rule of man's will in some sense, does not

---

[1] Aristotle, <u>Nichomachean Ethics</u>, 1177^a-1179^b.

[2] <u>GMM</u>, p. 85, <u>Schriften</u>, IV, 416.

whatsoever typify the moral law. That is because "all the elements which belong to the concept of happiness are without exception empirical -- that is, they must be borrowed from experience."[1] These elements, Kant argues, are so myriad and diffuse that "although every man wants happiness, he can never say definitely and in unison with himself (mit sich selbst einstimmig) what it really is that he wants."[2] Although each man desires happiness, he nonetheless has to rely on his own subjective hunches, piecemeal observations, and hasty inferences in order to ascertain exactly what might promote his own well-being. He cannot say for certain how every man, himself notwithstanding, might necessarily will to live happily. Hence, the maxim to seek happiness as an end carries no moral necessity; it can only be a counsel of "prudence" (Klugheit). It cannot be universalized into a practical law. One must reserve this honor for the categorical imperative.[3]

The categorical imperative summarizes the moral law. "There is...only a single categorical imperative and it is this: 'Act only on the maxim through which you can at the same time will that it should become a universal law.'"[4] To will a maxim to become a universal law means, above all, that such a maxim not be tainted with any subjective desire or intention. A maxim directed toward a particular end, or what

---

[1] Ibid. Schriften, IV, 418.

[2] Ibid. Schriften, IV, 418. "Is it riches that he wants? How much anxiety, envy, and pestering might he not bring in this way on his own head! Is it knowledge and insight? This might perhaps merely give him an eye so sharp that it would make evils at present hidden from him and yet unavoidable seem all the more frightful..." Ibid.

[3] "...the categorical imperative alone purports to be a practical law, while all the rest may be called principles of the will but not laws; for an action necessary merely in order to achieve an arbitrary purpose can be considered as in itself contingent, and we can always escape from the precept if we abandon the purpose..." GMM, p. 87. Schriften, IV, 420.

[4] GMM, p. 88. Schriften, IV, 421.

Kant calls a "matter" (Materie),[1] cannot be universalized. A universalizable maxim must have a non-specific "form (Form), or general plan of action, in which consists its universality.[2] Thus, the moral law, Kant says, is universal so far as it is "formal." A formal law is a rule of action abstracted and generalized from all particular instances of its validity.[3] A formal law prescribes how one ought to act in a particular case, but only so far as that case represents an instance of a broader pattern of conduct.

The term "form," like "idea," betokens Kant's Platonic heritage. The form is something transcending, yet conferring reality on, material entities. The form is universal and immutable, the material thing particular and transitory. The form provides the shape for the empirical content which is known. With respect to moral agency, the form determines the concrete pattern of specific actions. But the form can only determine action insofar as it lays down a rule governing many particular actions. If universal, the form must govern every action. The form is a paradigm for structuring through man's will the totality of his behavior. A law, which is a general conception comprising acting as well as knowing, must be sufficiently formal, or inclusive of particulars, to have the far-ranging and consistent application it connotes.

On the other hand, the formality of the law does not imply that rules of action must always be computed at an ideal or abstract level, like some Euclidean theorem, and certified in

---

[1] Cf. GMM, p. 104. Schriften, IV, 436.

[2] GMM, p. 103. Ibid. "If a rational being can think of its maxims as practical universal laws, he can do so only by considering them as principles which contain the determining ground (Bestimmungsgrund) of the will because of their form and not because of their matter." CP_rR, p. 26. Schriften, V, 27.

[3] "For the law in respect to the form of the will is that which alone remains if I have left out of the question the matter of the will (the purpose...)." Theor. Prax.: Schriften, VIII, 281.

themselves without any further eye to how the law might work
out in practice. Such a caricature of Kant's position, un-
fortunately, has appealed to enough generations of his inter-
preters to inspire the charge of what has come to be known as
his "formalism." Kant's formalism, however, is a misnomer.[1]
The moral law legislates not merely as a reasoned intention,
but as the basis for concrete action, although the worth of
the law, as we have seen, is adjudged exclusively according
to its conception. That the moral law is a rule not only of
a formal or ideal order, but of the natural world itself,
understood now as lived morality, becomes evident in Kant's
corollary to the first formulation of the categorical imperative, "Act as if the maxim of your action were to become through
your will a universal law of nature."[2]

The formula of the law of nature points up an important
refinement of the principle that morality lies mainly in the
universalizability of a maxim. In a sense, the difference
between the formula of the law of nature and the formula of
universal law as such, as Paton notes, is quite sharp.[3] For
the idea of a universal law of nature requires more extensive
moral criteria than simply logical consistency, or absence of
contradiction, in the expansion of maxims into general rules.
It requires that, in formulating maxims, we must account for
how they, as rules, would generate a total system of effects.
A system of effects, regulated by universal rules of laws, is
"nature," for Kant, in its broadest sense.[4] A universal law

---

[1] In his essay on "Theory and Practice" Kant explicitly re-
buts the insinuation that he has only an abstract "theory of
action": "Only in a theory founded on the concept of duty does
the concern about the empty ideality of this concept completely
fall away; for it would not be a duty to aim to achieve (auszu-
gehen) a definite effect of our will, if the effect were not
possible in experience..." Theor. Prax.: Schriften, VIII, 276-7.

[2] GMM, p. 89. Schriften, IV, 421.

[3] Paton, op. cit., p. 146.

[4] "...the universality of the law governing the production
of effects, constitutes what is properly called nature in its

of nature signifies, from the theoretical stand point of the
natural observer, the general categorical scheme which determines how one is used to understanding the mode in which
things happen. From the practical vantage point, however,
such a law tells how things would happen if men behaved ideally.
It differs from the primary formula of the imperative so far
as to show that the moral agent must, in composing his maxim,
take into account the consequences of his actions, especially
their bearing on the actions of all other beings, sentient and
insentient alike.

The rule of thumb behind the formula of universal law in
the general sense is that a given maxim of conduct cannot contradict itself when extrapolated formally. Such examples of
contradictory maxims we discussed earlier.[1] Into the formula
of the law of nature enters the dictum that there can be no
contradiction in reality as well. Kant illustrates how one
employs the formula of the law of nature with several examples,
such as a man contemplating suicide. His death wish, however,
springs mainly from the motive of self-love, inasmuch as he can
no longer shoulder the burden of pains and misfortune. "The
only question to ask," Kant asserts, "is whether this principle
of self-love can become a universal law of nature."[2] In light
of the function of human responses and feelings, Kant, concludes, the urge to suicide ultimately contradicts itself;
since "a system of nature by whose law the very same feeling
[the feelings of self-love] whose function is to stimulate the
furtherance of life (zur Beförderung des Lebens anzutreiben)
should actually destroy life would contradict itself and consequently could not subsist as a system of nature."[3] Suicide

---

[1] See above, p. 27f.
[2] GMM, p. 89. Schriften, IV, 421.
[3] Ibid. Schriften, IV, 422.

may be possible, or not fully self-contradictory in abstracto (that is, if one brackets the meaning of suicide as a desperate reaction to our own physical suffering); it can be seen simply as another instance of the act of killing. Yet when we reflect on the prospect of taking our own life in view of its concrete Sitz im Leben, which takes into account the meaning of human life as a whole, the contradiction leaps to the eye. The formula of the law of nature emphasizes that moral willing has no real significance apart from its participation in a world of effects which it produces. Kant's notion of morality, as Kemp has rightly observed, does not simply involve "making rational inferences from rational first principles," but the exercise of keen judgement "as to the particular circumstances of each case."[1]

Consequently, the whole issue of moral agency hangs on the question of how universal rules of willing can strike an empirical sequence of events. In a word, how does thought become action? The critics who father "formalism" on Kant deny that he really has a theory of action. Taking their nod from Kant's assigning priority to the study of inner motivation in morality, these critics want to deny that the critical philosophy makes any appreciable link between man's reasoning about the moral life and his creation of that life in action. For analytic purposes, the problems of reasoning and action can be treated separately; but it is arguable whether one can discuss the one intelligently without the other.

Before examining the key features of Kant's thought which disabuses the critics of their complaints, we must review in brief the formalist charge. For this end we shall turn to two interpretations of Kantian ethics, those of Max Scheler and W. T. Jones.

---

[1]Kamp, op. cit., p. 71. The same point is made by Paul Schilpp, Kant's Pre-Critical Ethics (Evanston: Northwestern University Press, 1968), p. 183.

C. Kant's "Formalism"

1. The charge of formalism in Kant, while recurrent, usually sounds from those critics who have never closely read the critical philosophy. Noteworthy among these critics is the twentieth century German phenomenologist Max Scheler. In his book *Der Formalismus in der Ethik und die Materiale Wertethik*,[1] Scheler twits Kant for overvaluing the intellectual principle of ethical decision-making as the a priori.[2] The upshot of glorifying the a priori, Scheler claims, is that the moral act becomes wholly dependent of any "law of action" (Aktgesetz).[3] Reason is shut off from sensibility, while the "will appears ...as a mere instrument of logic" with no spontaneity for creating actual events in the phenomenal order.[4] In the same breath, the "transcendental meaning of the a priori" turns into a purely "subjective meaning."[5] The concepts of necessity and universality have relevance only as formal, or thoroughly ideal, properties of reason which in no way affect the real processes by which we will and act. Scheler denies Kant has the right to speak of "objective necessitation," because Kant has an idea of the will as something which can produce no objective or extra-mental effects. Necessitation, for Kant (according to Scheler), is proper only to the rational deductions of the reasoning subject. The empirical act itself does not in any way derive from the deliberations of the subject, since the two events of reasoning and behaving are radically disjoined; one does not influence the other.[6]

---

[1] Max Scheler, *Der Formalismus in der Ethik und die Materiale Wertethik* in *Gessammelte Werke*, Bd. 2 (Bern: A. Francke, 1954).

[2] "Still, another not less profound error proves to be the identification of the 'a priori' with thought, 'apriorism' with rationalism, as Kant, especially to the detriment of ethics, poses it." Ibid., pp. 83-4.

[3] Ibid. p. 84.

[4] Ibid.

[5] Ibid., p. 94.

[6] Ibid., p. 96. Cf. also p. 98n.1.

Kant's formalism, according to Scheler, is a stark dualism between moral reflection and moral deeds, between intention and consequence. Kant definitely uses language, of course, that would suggest such a basic polarity in moral experience, as we have seen. But question arises whether Kant's dichotomizing human conduct does not merely serve as a functional distinction between two sides of the same unified process. The distinction between man as *homo noumenon* ("man insofar as he is a moral being") and *homo phenomenon* ("insofar as he is a physical being" who plays an active role in the observable universe of events) is really a heuristic device for explaining the peculiar manner in which human reason transforms the regular operations of nature.[1] Kant develops this heuristic distinction through his view that the rational (noumenal) and empirical components of moral action are nothing more than two "standpoints" (*Standpunkte*) for looking at human agency. "Regarded as the causality of a thing in itself...[the acting self] is *intelligible* in its action; regarded as the causality of an appearance in the world of sense, it is *sensible* in its effects."[2]

---

[1] It is not to be denied, of course, that Kant's account of the noumenal/phenomenal distinction lends itself to a metaphysical interpretation rather than to the "heuristic" rendering which we are advancing here. Kant tends to make absolute distinctions between the two realms which suggest an irreconcilable dualism -- e.g., his claim that the causality of moral freedom "is not subordinated (*steht unter*) to another cause, which determines it according to time" (K_rV (B): *Schriften*, III, 363); or that reason is "determining, but not determinable" (K_rV (B): *Schriften*, III, 376). Kant provides some strong evidence for the heuristic interpretation in his "solution" to the third antinomy with the "two-standpoints" theory; but it is questionable whether this solution really overcomes the metaphysical language in Kant's own descriptions of freedom.

[2] K_rV (B): *Schriften*, III, 366. Cf. also *GMM*, p. 118. *Schriften*, IV, 450: "We can enquire whether we do not take one standpoint when...we conceive ourselves as cause acting *a priori*, and another standpoint when we contemplate ourselves with reference to our own actions as effects which we see before our eyes."

The basis of the "two standpoints" distinction lies in Kant's recognition that, while man through his transcendental powers of reason can prescribe "laws of such effects and actions as accord with the principles of an intelligible world," he nevertheless can only render them laws concretely (that is, laws which actually determine something) in imposing them on himself in his everyday comings and goings.[1] As *homo noumenon* man devises and attempts to implement rules of action "altogether different from the order of nature."[2] The "altogether different" character of these rules rides on the radical distinction between the *ought* of reason and the *is* of experience.

The discrepancy between noumenal and sensible activity, between ideation and facticity, does not mean that the mind through will cannot produce something outside the mind. Scheler's error springs from the tacit Cartesianism that informs so much of phenomenological analysis. Cartesianism holds that mind and corporeal reality are disassociated substances, and that the activity of the two can be correlated, if at all, only in an indirect or accidental fashion.[3] The process of reasoning, therefore, practical as well as theoretical, belongs exclusively to the individual subject of thinking (the *res cogitans*) which detaches itself from all physical objects, including its own body. Scheler's charge of "intellectualism" and "subjectivism," therefore, owes to his reading of Cartesianism into the Kantian texts. Such a rendition of Kant is patently mistaken. The formalist criticism, based on the premise that there is a Cartesian mind/matter dualism in Kant's thinking, misconstrues the real meaning of the moral *a priori*. Whereas it is true that Kant's demand for the "formal" coherence

---

[1] GMM, p. 125. Schriften, IV, 457.

[2] K_rV (B): Schriften, III, 372.

[3] Descartes, in fact, believed the only connection between thought and action occurred because of the activity of the "pineal gland" -- a rather strange notion later challenged by his successors, notably Gassendi.

alone of moral rules (which cannot be tested by the exigencies of life) indeed suggests a rigid essentialism of some kind, it is also the case that Kant wants to preserve an interrelation between rational values and the empirical data of the moral life.[1] Moral behavior, like all empirical events, can only be known as a system of appearances (Scheinen). This is because something, in truth, appears: the rational will.[2] The will itself, as it puts into effect moral rules, is the link between the world conceived by reason and the world experienced through the senses. It is what E. Ballard has called the "moral pineal gland" in Kant's philosophy.[3]

If the will did not connect rational essence with human existence, the concept of reason as praxis would ring hollow. Intentions alone cannot count as willing.[4] Intentions demand execution. Otherwise, they would not be intentions but mere whimsy. Pure willing is the generation of a visible pattern

---

[1] The logical expression of Kant's apriorism is found in his statement: "The essence of things does not vary with their external relations..." GMM, p. 107. Schriften, IV, 439. Scheler misinterprets such a statement as an avowal of Cartesian essentialism. He seizes upon Kant's discussion of a priori constructs as "facts of reason" and wrongly concludes that "Kant in no way is able to show us how the 'fact' on which an a priori ethics must rest -- if it is not to be an empty construct -- differs from the facts of observation and induction, and how it differs in its being established from any manner of establishing something; if we are rightly to demonstrate it as a principle." Scheler, op. cit., p. 67.

[2] Kant notes that appearances considered as human action are merely "the empirical character of reason" which produces through rules of willing phenomena following "as effects from its cause." K_rV (B): Schriften, III, 372. While reason as the origin of willing cannot be cognized through sense-intuition like appearances, "it nevertheless has a real application exhibited in concreto in intentions or maxims; that is, its practical reality can be pointed out." CP_rR, p. 58. Schriften, V, 56.

[3] E. G. Ballard, "The Kantian Solution to the Problem of Man," Tulane Studies in Philosophy III (1954), 35.

[4] Cf. Sir David Ross, Kant's Ethical Theory (Oxford: The Clarendon Press, 1954), p. 12: "It is important to note,"

of events. The moral law, once incorporated as a maxim of the will, is designed to be effective as a univeral law of nature.[1] As a result, the so-called "transcendental" use of practical reason "is changed into an immanent use, whereby reason becomes, in the field of experience, an efficient cause through ideas."[2] Immanent reason realized by the execution of rules of action is a seminal concept in Kant which tends to slip past the critics of his "formalism." Scheler's cavils concentrate only on Kant's construction of the *a priori* while ignoring his whole theory of willing.

A more respectable, albeit perhaps no less jaundiced, exposition of the formalist thesis about Kant comes from W. T. Jones, whose book on the subject remains something of a *piece de resistance* in Kant scholarship.[3] Before trying to get beyond the formalist impasse, let us look briefly at this work. Jones' interpretation of Kant succeeds for the most part where Scheler failed, because it subtly avoids the Cartesian fallacy by attacking the whole question of action in terms of motivation. Since motivation is the only issue, the reason/reality problem does not arise. The nub of Jones' thesis is this: what Kant means by practical reason is that man recognizes the value of

---

Ross says, "what Kant means by will. Good will without good action is common and properly judged to be ineffective and worthless; 'the road to hell is paved with good intentions.' Kant is careful to point out that this is not what he means by good will. He means 'not a mere wish, but the sommuning of all means in our power.'"

[1] Hence "the moral law is, in fact, a law of causality of sensuous nature." CP_rR, p. 49. *Schriften*, V, 47. There are however, certain intimations in the text of an unbridgeable dualism which would tend to contradict Kant's own claims about reason's causal impact on nature. Cf. above, p. 37, n. 2.

[2] *Ibid*. *Schriften*, V, 48. Cf. also: "For...reason can suffice to the determination of the will at least, and has objective reality, if willing only is in question. And this use of reason the critical philosopher terms immanent."

[3] Jones, *op. cit.*

reason in his own person as an end in itself and affirms this value accordingly. Moral motivation, for Jones, is grounded in "respect for reason," for that in man which defines his humanity.[1] Jones' interpretation banks largely on his understanding of the moral law which he thinks is grounded not in the first but in the third formulation: the command to treat all rational beings as ends in themselves.[2] Practical reason, Jones argues, is simply reason as a faculty recognizing itself and dignifying itself as a value. Willing, therefore, is only the act of safeguarding the intrinsic worth of reason by esteeming rational beings in our own person and other persons.[3] Jones is saying that practical reason implies action only in the performative sense. An illustration is the performative use of language. When I make a promise, for example, I perform an act merely by uttering the promise, not by guaranteeing anything real. Similarly, when I reason about moral values and commit myself to them, I am thereby *acting* morally, even though I may not have acted in any visible fashion.

This appraisal of what Kant means by "pure will" shows up the view that reason need not be concerned with an intention in order to have accomplished a moral act. The idea of a causality of reason thus goes by the board. This is precisely the stance at which Jones arrives. Jones wants to deny that reason can have any impact on the empirical order. He implies that reason only aims to secure itself as an end, as a self-contained valuation in the guise of a categorical imperative.[4] The value reason has "is not an event and not empirically conditioned."[5] Naturally, Jones finds himself confronted with a

---

[1] Op. cit., p. 111.

[2] For my discussion of the concept of an end-in-itself, see below, ch. ii.

[3] Op. cit., p. 80ff.

[4] Op. cit., p. 114.

[5] Op. cit., p. 115.

number of passages, particularly in the section of the first
Critique on the antinomy of freedom and necessity, which baldly
describe the causal spontaneity of reason, and which Jones endeavors
to explain away. Jones tries to dismiss these passages
as having a strangely "critical" instead of literal meaning.[1]
Happily this critical meaning seems to square with Jones' own
previous interpretation. The causality of reason, Jones says,
"refers simply to the existence of a certain kind of state of
affairs which has supreme worth because it is a morally good
act of will in which personality is realized. It does not
refer to the way in which this state of affairs is produced."[2]

Jones has an idiosyncratic understanding of "morally good
act of will." The will, he implies, signifies nothing more
than some kind of avowal of intention concerning rational principles.
It were as though one could will entirely pro forma,
that is, will by positing the ideal without acting. Jones
assimilates the concept of willing to "wanting" in its strict
sense, that is, an expression of a mere desideratum. To will
something is different from doing it. Jones tells us that such
actless willing characterizes Kant's view of how practical
reason works.[3] But if Kant did not see the concrete act as an
indispensable feature of a coherent theory of moral agency, he
would not need to talk about reason as having causality in the
first place. He would not have to qualify the formula of the
universalizability of one's maxim with the formula of the law
of nature.

The formalist interpretation of Jones is more sophisticated
than Scheler's, inasmuch as it acknowledges the counter-evidence
in the Kantian texts against formalism. But it misses the
target widely in pleading that in these instances Kant does not
really mean what he says. The formalist interpretation is nurtured
by Kant's bending of language in the first two Critiques.

---

[1] Cf. K_rV (B): Schriften, III, 372, 375f., 376f.

[2] Op. cit., p. 120.

[3] Op. cit., p. 116.

The problem stems from his pressing us to accept the proposition that the will, undetermined by the rules of natural causation (and in the negative sense, thus, has a certain "freedom"), can nonetheless produce effects determined by such rules.[1] The apparent paradox of a non-determined agent acting in a fashion that is yet determined fosters the supposition that Kant simply bisected human action into two levels of significance -- reason and action -- without assuming their overall unity. Admittedly, if we try to clarify Kant's theory of moral agency solely in the context of the issue of determinism versus indeterminism, the formalist solution becomes very tempting. If, though, we suspend the whole determinism issue (and stop worrying about whether natural events, which are always determined, can ever be caused by something undetermined), we can meet formalism straight on. Let us assume instead that Kant, with his noumenal/phenomenal "paradox," is groping toward a theory of moral agency not amenable to the deterministic categories of nature drawn from the science of Newtonian mechanics. With his notion of rational willing, Kant seems to be proffering the idea that human action cannot be explained in the same fashion as we explain the action of billiard balls on a table, or a falling meteorite. Kant's "paradox" of nature

---

[1] Kant entitles the particular section of the first Critique in which he makes this claim the "Explanation of the Cosmological Idea of Freedom in Agreement with the Universal Laws of Natural Necessity." Reason, Kant says, "is determining (bestimmend) but not determinable (bestimmbar)." K_rV (B): Schriften, III, 376. For "it does not impair [our observations of nature] in the least, even granted that it should be merely fictitious (erdichtet), for one to assume that among natural causes (Naturursachen) those which have a power (Vermögen) that is only intelligible, insofar as they are never determined to action by empirical conditions, but derive from pure grounds of the understanding (Verstandes); so that actions as appearances of these causes are conformable (gemäss) with all laws of empirical causality." K_rV (B): Schriften, III, 370. The whole question of the determinability of an action which in its inception is completely undetermined has sparked much controversy in philosophical circles since Kant first tendered this solution.

and freedom serves as a didactic construct to point out that the model of determinism does not account for the whole of human experience. We cannot go so far as to say Kant himself understood his own use of the noumenal/phenomenal distinction exactly in this way; but his explanation of the distinction as representing two "points of view" toward human agency gives hint that he really has in mind a heuristic construction for making intelligible conflicting items of experience.

Kant's contention that "reason has a causality in relation to phenomena"[1] is less a privileged insight than common sense. Modern behaviorist theory aside,[2] this contention describes how we actually experience our own acts. Our own volition strikes us as unique and self-caused, because we are inclined to attribute it to nothing save ourselves. If, for instance, I fall ill with some hereditary illness, I do not attribute this act to myself; rather, I view it as something irremediably caused by a prior happenstance (such as bad genes) that suffices to explain it. The same is true if I roll out of bed while sleeping. In judging myself not responsible for leaving my bed, I assume certain irrational factors (sub-conscious physio-motor impulses) caused such an event. I do not consider myself responsible, because these factors are not a part of my

---

[1] K_rV (B): Schriften, III, 374.

[2] Modern behaviorism represents a clear instance of the dogma that the "methods of the natural sciences" must be "applied ...in the field of behavior." Cf. B. F. Skinner, Science and Human Behavior (New York: The Macmillan Company, 1953), p. 297. The model of human agency which behaviorism presents is solely that of man as machine, or a consistent system of reflex actions that can be measured and manipulated by the proper stimulus/response techniques. Ibid., p. 45ff. Behaviorism tries to preserve the mechanistic conception of Newtonian physics in its explanation of organic life. It is an article of faith among behaviorists that any "free causality" that might be ascribed to human beings, that is, a "spontaneity," merely "is negative evidence" only that a given scientific theory is weak in its explanation. Ibid., p. 48. This, of course, was Kant's point; although he denied that empirical science in its mechanistic form could ever account for all man's acts.

deliberative, waking life in which I have some sense of volition. On the other hand, let us take as an example a decision to divorce one's wife. Rarely would I refuse to attribute such a decision to myself, especially if I had deliberated long hours about it. If I did not account the decision to myself, I would probably not get the divorce I wanted, as the courts usually will not grant a legal estrangement unless both involved parties can be said to opt intelligently for such a course of action. Naturally, I could explain my desire for the divorce as having been "forced upon" me by my wife's extreme cruelty, but still I know that my ultimate choice to file for separation was my own insofar as it was "I" who wanted the divorce. If I were a mere automaton, there would be no real first person endowed with consciousness and reason to attribute the act of filing for divorce to myself. Rather, the act would be seen by another observer as merely the necessary consequences of a preceding series of events.

The power of reason to produce effects, or "noumenal causality," differs from the concept of causation in the ordinary sense.[1] Rather, it refers to the fact, which every man experiences, of attributing certain kinds of acts to his own person and, by extension, to other persons. Kant so much as vouches for what, in respect to noumenal causality, may be called a theory of attribution or "imputation" in a passage in the first Critique. The passage is long, but it should be quoted in full:

> In order to illustrate the regulative principle of reason by an example of its empirical use...let us take a voluntary (willkürliche) action, for instance, a malicious lie, through which a man has brought definite confusion into society, and which one judges...according to its motives (Bewegursachen) from which it springs, and the consequences of the act im-

---

[1] "...when we say e.g. that a man ran because he was afraid of a snake, or wanted to escape from it, we are not describing inner (mental) events which are causally antecedent to other (bodily) events..." Theodore Mischel, "Kant and the Possibility of a Science of Psychology," The Monist 51 (1967): 620.

puted (zugerechnet) to the agent. One's first aim is to trace the empirical character of the offence back to its source, which one seeks in bad education, an evil society, a shameless and unfeeling natural malignity (Bösartigkeit), frivolity, or recklessness (Unbesonnenheit): without letting slip from one's attention the original cause that óccasioned the act. In all this one proceeds, as in general one does in investigating the sequence of determining causes, to given natural effects. If one believes the action to be determined at once by these conditions, he does not reproach in any less way the offender (Täter) on account of his unhappy disposition nor on account of circumstances influencing him, not even on his previous mode of life (Lebenswandel), for one presumes that one can set aside these factors ...and the sequence of former conditions may be seen as never having happened, and the action regarded as unconditioned in respect to former circumstances, as though the agent commenced (anhebe) by himself entirely a sequence of effects. One's reproach to the offender is founded on a law of reason, by which we regard reason as a cause that could and should have determined otherwise the relations between men irrespective of all so-called empirical conditions. To be sure, one sees the causality of reason not merely as an accompanying event (Concurrenz) but as complete in itself, if the sensible impulses did not favor but opposed the action. The act is estimated in its intelligible character; the offender incurs at the moment of his falsehood his guilt. Thus as reason entirely free, despite the empirical circumstances of the act, it is entirely imputable for what it does.[1]

Kant is saying, in effect, that we reproach the criminal for his misdeed simply in virtue of our imputing rational choice to him. We make such an imputation, because we have a firm and transparent idea that what he did he ought not to have done.

---

[1] $K_r V$ (B): Schriften, III, 375-6.

Had we no such idea, we would probably not hold the criminal responsible, just as we do not blame a rain-swollen river for overflowing its banks and flooding a city. In the case of the river we know that, granted a certain confluence of circumstances, like unusually heavy rains in the area, nothing but a flood could have taken place. But this sense of inevitability does not arise with human action. We praise or blame human action, because we impute to it an independent causality.

Kant refers to our imputation of free causality to an agent as a "regulative idea" (*regulative Idee*). By a regulative idea Kant means a notion that, while it has application in the ordering of sense experience, cannot be confirmed through sense observation and induction: by scientific method or experimentation so far as the category of causality holds.[1] Common sense, or what Kant calls "ordinary reason," tells us that we ourselves are the source of our actions, even though science may look askance at such a sentiment.[2] The principle of imputation serves to attach a concrete meaning to human

---

[1] Cf. R. G. Collingwood, *The Idea of Nature* (New York: Oxford University Press, 1960), p. 118f. Collingwood claims that Kant's view that moral action cannot be cognized or explained by empirical principles owes to his belief that the human mind, although a part of nature, cannot be understood by the methods of science for exploring the natural realm. Newton was only competent as a physicist, not as a psychologist. The mind can only be studied by taking account of the phenomenon of the will. Practical reason, as a function of mind, does not simply "appear" in nature like most events because mind is the constitutive force that gives form to nature as a whole.

[2] Similar common-sense views of the explanation of rational behavior can be found within contemporary philosophical literature. I cite some significant articles on the subject, taken from Norman Care and Charles Landesman (eds.), *Readings in the Theory of Action* (RTA) (Bloomington: Indiana University Press, 1968) and Alan White (ed.), *The Philosophy of Action* (PA) (London: Oxford University Press, 1968). These are Donald Davidson, "Actions, Reasons, and Causes," PA, pp. 79-94; Joel Feinberg, "Action and Responsibility," PA, pp. 95-119; Theodore Mischel, "Psychology and Explanations of Human Behavior," RTA, pp. 214-37. The common-sense view usually hinges on the distinction between "reasons" and "causes" as principles of explanation for action. A "reason" for an action is something

action, especially when the perspective of action is our own
and not that of a disinterested spectator. Thus we can ascribe a causality to willing without becoming imbroiled in any
metaphysical squabble about the determination of actions.[1]
Kant, as is well known, eschewed metaphysics of this ilk.
Instead he opted for "critical" or what we might dub "tuitional"
solutions. Such tuitional solutions instruct us in the complexity, and perhaps impenetrability by ordinary language, of
certain problems. One of these problems, for Kant, is the
whole nature of man's will. By juxtaposing, as if in paradox,
"noumenal" and "phenomenal" causes, Kant brings to our attention
the fact that neither account, though each is relevant for
certain purposes, adequately portrays "the whole man in his
environment."[2] The formalist thesis, which tries to leap the
contradiction between human action viewed from "inside" as
personal decision and action observed from "outside" as a

---

the agent subjectively attributes as an explanation of his behavior which satisfies himself, if no one else. A reason is
that by which I "rationalize" a particular action of mine
(Davidson, p. 79) without concern as to whether my account
offers an adequate public explanation. Thus I may give as a
reason for my refusing to view an obscene motion picture my
"dislike for nudity," even though a psychiatrist, for example,
may assign a different explanation (such as negative attitudes
toward sex instilled in me by my parents) for my refusal. Such
a reason is <u>ascriptive</u>; that is, I <u>ascribe</u> it as the <u>explanans</u>
of my own action. A "cause," on the other hand, is <u>descriptive</u>.
Unlike a reason, which consists of an internal rationalization
of my own prejudices, that would satisfy any number of neutral
observers in the situation. In respect to the example given
above, the psychiatrist's explanation would count as a "causal"
account of my actions.

[1]For a couple of good summaries of what I have called the
theory of "imputation" or "attribution," as regards Kant's
understanding of noumenal causation, see Hans Kelsen,
"Causality and Imputation," Ethics 61 (1951): 1-11 and A.R.C.
Duncan, <u>Practical Reason and Morality</u> (New York: Nelson
and Company, 1957).

[2]Cf. Edward Ballard, "The Kantian Solution to the Problem
of Man," <u>Tulane Studies in Philosophy</u> III (1954): 34. Also,
G. J. Warnock, "Kant," in D. J. O'Connor (ed.), <u>A History of
Western Philosophy</u> (New York: The Free Press, 1964), p. 309.

determined system of events by extruding reason from the world, only pictures man as a schizoid creature. Hence, the familiar lament about Kant's "dualism."

We have posed the theory of imputation as one way of softening, or at least bracketing, this dualism. But this theory, particularly as implied in the first Critique, does not comprise Kant's final method of working out the dilemma. The noumenal/phenomenal distinction betrays Kant's intrinsic lack of all-sufficient categories for describing moral agency. Thus he must depict man as living in "two worlds." Subsequent to the first and second Critiques Kant begins to shed the two-world dichotomy and to develop a "one-world" or organic concept of human agency. The rudiments of that one-world concept comes under the general heading of what from now on we shall call "intentionality."

D. Intentionality

1. The Faculty of Desire

Intentionality is man's power as a natural being to project ends or purposes, and to seek to accomplish them with the means available to him. Man's capacity for projection resides in his reason. Through reason, Kant contends, man can set before himself objects to be acquired or achieved, whether they be objects of the senses or ideal objects of morality. The use of reason to attain ends Kant terms "life" (Leben) or the "faculty of desire" (Begehrungsvermögen). Desire, for Kant, is the faculty of a rational being for "causing, through its ideas, the reality of the objects of these ideas."[1] In one form, desire is simply the will or practical reason itself.[2]

---

[1] CP_rR, p. 9n. Schriften, V, 3. Cf. also MEJ (MM, Intro.), p. 10. Schriften, VI, 14.

[2] "The faculty of desire whose internal ground of determination and, consequently, even those likings are found in the reason of the subject, is called the Will." MEJ (MM, Intro.), p. 12. Schriften, VI, 213. Also CJ, p. 13ff. Schriften, V, 177ff.

Desire represents man's ability to transcend his given nature
by projecting in consciousness his idea of an "ought" that he
attempts to materialize through action. Man, therefore,
desires what in the current situation he lacks: a good which
does not reflect his experience of himself in the universe.
Appropriately, he posits this good as an aim yet unfulfilled.

In the second Critique Kant refers to the aims of these
rational desires as "objects (Gegenstände) of pure practical
knowledge," Kant says, "as such signifies...only the relation
of the will to the action whereby its opposite is brought into
being. To decide whether or not something is an object of the
pure practical reason is only to discern the possibility or im-
possibility of willing the action by which a certain object
would be made real, provided we had the ability to bring it
about..."[1] Such objects possess a "reality" quite distinct
from the reality of the objects of empirical cognition. Not
from sense perception, but from the constructive work of pure
reason itself do these objects derive.[2] "Practical reason is
concerned not with objects in order to know them but with its
own capacity to make them real (according to the knowledge of
them), i.e., it has to do with a will which is a causal agent
so far as reason contains its determining ground."[3]

Practical reason does not <u>receive</u> objects to be delimited
by the understanding; it actually creates these objects <u>de novo</u>
apart from sense perception. The "truth" of such objects is
not experimental, but conational. The proof of these objects
lies in the inborn nisus of reason to realize a world in its
own image. Kant says the objects of pure practical reason do
not constitute empirical concepts so much as moral values.

---

[1] CP_rR, p. 59. Schriften, V, 57.

[2] "This objective reality, however, is only of practical
application, since it has not the slightest effect in enlarging
theoretical knowledge of these objects as insight into their
nature by pure reason." CP_rR, p. 58. Schriften, V, 56.

[3] CP_rR, p. 92. Schriften, V, 89.

moral values possess an intrinsic worth not amenable to descriptive evidence. Per contra one must judge values by a priori standards. Moral values fall under the rubrics of "good" and "evil." One does not deem them valid or invalid as facilely as one might rate a scientific hypothesis, i.e., by induction. One either desires or shrinks from them in the way one might respond, for instance, to hearing a Chopin piano concerto. Still, the criteria for judging moral values has nothing to do with real or anticipated sensory pleasure. I say I like Chopin, because his music sounds delightful to the ear, but it is improper for me to make a similar claim regarding the categorical imperative. The touchstone of moral values is not simply that they arouse desire, but that they agree with reason undiverted by sensible attachments.[1] Moral values are irreducible to mere preferences.

The faculty of desire has as its supreme objects certain transcendental values constructed by pure reason.[2] Yet desire projects things also which are a product of man's sensible constitution. In that sense, desire describes the intentionality of the "whole man." Man desires many sensible objects: sleep, palatable food, sexual release, a congenial environment.

---

[1] "The sole objects of a practical reason are thus those of the good and the evil (vom Guten and Bösen). By the former, one understands a necessary object of the faculty of desire, and by the latter, a necessary object of aversion (Verabscheuungsvermögens), both according to a principle of reason." CP_rR, p. 60. Schriften, V, 58. Cf. also A.E. Teale, Kantian Ethics (London: Oxford University Press, 1951), p. 99.

[2] It should be noted here that Kant is no "apriorist" who posits a pantheon of moral values that float mysteriously above the natural order, like Plato's forms. Such a Platonic exiology was the error of Neo-Kantianism. Kant's notion of the "good" must be understood in terms of the nature of the will without assuming any independent value-entities. For my special discussion of Kant's notion of the "good will" as concerned only with the action itself, see below. Kant's own use of Platonic idealism is found in a brief passage in the first Critique. Cf. "On Ideas as a Whole" (Von den Ideen überhaupt), K_rV (B): Schriften, III, 245-50.

These things he cannot totally forbear, even if his will be disciplined by reason. He cannot forbear, because he has an animal as well as a rational nature. Beset by desires in countless guises with varying intensities, he has cravings, wishes, appetites, as well as sheer fantasies. Some desires, like those of sustenance and sex, are relatively easy to accommodate. Others seem impossible dreams. The ambivalence and imprecision of what man desires gives rise to what Kant points to as the "anthropologico-teleological problem."[1] This is the problem of man as an intentional being. That man desires such a vast spectrum of different objects is due to the conflict within him as a genus between reason and unreason.

The crucial matter is why man can desire the reasonable in preference to the simply bestial. Neither a priori nor empirical considerations can settle this matter alone. Instead, we must examine man as a special organism who completes within himself the natural order. We also require a more plastic conception of nature than what suffices for Newtonian physics. We need a picture of man and nature as forming an integral totality. The significance of this totality we shall explore shortly. But first we must consider the two chief modes in which desire, for Kant, expresses itself. In this respect, we must grasp what Kant means by the terms "inclination" and "interest."

2. Inclination and Interest

The "dependence" of the faculty of desire "on sensations," according to Kant, "is called an inclination (Neigung)."[2] Inclination is a "habitually sensible appetite" (Begierde).[3] In practice, inclinations are nothing more than particular feelings of pleasure and pain projected toward an object of desire.[4]

---

[1] CJ, p. 14n. Schriften, V, 173n.
[2] GMM, p. 81n. Schriften, IV, 413n.
[3] Anthr.: Schriften, VII, 251.
[4] GMM, p. 94. Schriften, IV, 427.

In consequence, the exercise of inclinations as a motive of will "constitute self-regard (solipsismus)" which can be broken down into "self-love (philautia)" and "self-satisfaction (arrogantia)."[1] Inclination expressed as self-satisfaction, Kant maintains, occurs when man's will has succumbed to his sensible impulses. Self-satisfaction, or "self-conceit," represents a state in which the moral law has been excluded as a principle of action. Self-satisfaction is the use of inclinations for immoral ends. Self-love (Selbstliebe), or "selfishness" (Eigenliebe), on the other hand, is only the universal condition of man that precedes all willing. Self-love bespeaks the "lower faculty of desire" which informs material maxims or subjective rules of conduct.[2] Unlike self-satisfaction, therefore, inclinations organized as self-love are not immediately immoral. "Natural inclinations, considered in themselves, are good, that is, not a matter of reproach (unverwerflich), and it is only futile to want to extirpate them;" rather they should be "tamed" (bezahmt) and disciplined.[3] Inclinations are the natural affective source of all willing viewed subjectively. Instead of destroying the immediate inclinations of self-love, practical reason simply checks them; it incorporates them as maxims subordinate to the universal law of reason.[4]

Kant's point is that man's phenomenal nature with all its sensible desires and feelings does not intrinsically oppose morality. Rather, this nature provides the material of action

---

[1] CP_rR, p. 75f. Schriften, V, 72f.

[2] CP_rR, p. 21. Schriften, V, 22f.

[3] RWL, p. 51. Schriften, VI, 58.

[4] "Pure practical reason merely checks (thut Abbruch) selfishness, for selfishness, as natural and active in us even prior to the moral law, is restricted by the moral law to agreement with the law; when this is done, selfishness is called rational self-love (vernünftige Selbstliebe). CP_rR, p. 76. Schriften, V, 73.

to which practical reason lends a durable and irresistible form. Moral motivation can include sensible feeling as well as the principle of self-love, because reason has the power to take control of all other principles in the will.[1] Immorality, or self-conceit, occurs when self-love becomes the supreme principle.[2] Kant is commonly misinterpreted as refusing to grant morality to any action that involves inclination or sensible desire.[3] Such a misinterpretation bolsters the formalist thesis. Man's sensible fiber is woven into the process of moral action as much as his reason. The sine qua non is whether his sense nature does not dominate in his deliberations.

Inclinations regularly co-operate with reason in decision-making. Kant employs the term "interest" (Interesse) to designate the mode in which sensible feelings collaborate with practical reason. The concept of interest underscores the fact that man, for Kant, does not act wholly from either rational or irrational compulsions, but learns to balance and harmonize the competing forces within him. Nietzsche called this tendency of man to give form to his dark and sensible energies the "Appollonian" element in his personality. Kant is saying, therefore, than man does not act simply rationally or irrationally, but in both ways at once. Interest may favor

---

[1] "Now everything in self-love belongs to inclination, and all inclination rests on feelings; therefore, whatever checks all inclinations in self-love necessary has, but that act, an influence on feeling. Thus we conceive how it is possible to understand a priori that the moral law can exercise an effect on feeling, since it blocks (ausschliesst) the inclinations and the propensity (Hang) to make them the supreme practical condition...from all participation in supreme legislation." CP_rR, p. 77. Schriften, V, 74.

[2] "This propensity to make the subjective determing grounds of one's choice into an objective determining ground of the will in general can be called self-love; when it makes itself legislative and an unconditional practical principle, it can be called self-conceit (Eigendünkel)." Ibid.

[3] Paton, op. cit., p. 48.

satisfaction of the sensible drive, or it may be directed toward fulfilling the demands of pure reason. But interest always involves the use of reason for some end.[1] Whether interest be primarily rational or sensible, it invariably leads to the sensible satisfaction of a desire.[2] In short, interest gives to a rational being an expectation of pleasure (Angenchm). If the rule of willing is sense-oriented, the interest becomes an "interest of inclination."[3] The interest is "pathological," inasmuch as it aims purely for the satisfaction of the inclination mindless of the law of practical reason. It employs rational considerations "only at the service of inclination -- that is to say, where reason merely supplies a practical rule for meeting the need of inclination."[4]

On the other hand, if the rule of willing is objective or moral, the interest becomes an "interest of reason." An interest of reason allows no sensible pleasure into the concept of an object desired. A rational principle, not the principle of pleasure, enters into the rule of desiring.[5] Pleasure, therefore, "would...be not the cause, but the effect of a pure interest of reason."[6] An interest of reason, or more properly

---

[1] "The dependence of a contingently determinable will on principles of reason is called an *interest*." GMM, p. 81n. Schriften, IV, 413n.

[2] "The satisfaction which we combine with the representation (Vorstellung) of the existence of an object is called 'interest.' Such satisfaction always has reference to the faculty of desire, either as its determining ground or as necessarily connected with its determining ground." CJ, p. 38. Schriften, V, 204.

[3] MEJ (MM, Intro.), p. 12. Schriften, VI, 212.

[4] GMM, p. 81n. Schriften, IV, 413n.

[5] "...only of a rational being do we say that he takes as an interest in something: non-rational creatures merely feel sensuous impulses. Reason takes an immediate interest in an action only when the universal validity of the maxims of the action is a ground sufficient to determine the will. Such an interest alone is pure." GMM, p. 128. Schriften, IV, 459n.

[6] MEJ (MM, Intro.), p. 12. Schriften, VI, 213.

a "moral interest," is what Kant terms a "pure non-sensuous interest of the practical reason alone."[1] This interest is "non-sensuous," only because it does not primarily aim to gratify an inclination. Yet sensible pleasure may certainly be part of the satisfaction we feel when we obey the moral law.

The passages defining interest tend to fly in the fact of the conventional wisdom that Kant was a dour old moralist who forbade men pleasure, even when acting virtuously. Pleasure, according to Kant, is a welcome appurtenance to morality. However, one must not let pleasure reign supreme in determining how one ought to behave. All interests incorporate an anticipation of pleasure. The difference between rational and sensible interests has to do with the fact that, for the former, such an anticipation cannot serve as motivation.

All willing and acting, Kant suggests, depends on our pursuit of some interest. There is no such thing as "disinterested" action. Disinterested action is impossible, since every act eventuates from a will spurred on by a desideratum one has in mind. If I say, I want to do such and such "for its own sake," I am at least doing what I do for the sake of something. The action itself is still desired, and hopefully I will obtain pleasure of some kind in doing it. The desideratum itself always arouses feelings of pleasure or aversion. When I think about how I want to buy a ticket to hear the Boston symphony, for instance, I am assuming that I will reap enjoyment from it. Feeling or sensation, then, is not banished from Kant's conception of the moral life. The positive sensations that go with moral action Kant denotes by the special term "moral feeling" (Moralisches Gefühl).

3. Moral Feeling

Practical reason, as we have seen, has the power not only to give a universal form to action, but to induce a feeling of

---

[1] CP$_r$R. p. 82. Schriften, V, 79.

pleasure associated with the act. Thus practical reason, instead of subverting man's sensible life, disciplines and directs it.[1] Practical reason regulates the affective aspects of willing (inclinations, emotions, sensible desires) by unifying them all as a higher form of sense awareness which Kant calls "moral feeling."[2] Moral feeling arises, like all feeling, out of man's senses. Nonetheless, it is distinguished by the fact that it is possible only when pure practical reason has been exercised in a moral situation.[3] Moral feeling thus appears in man as a sensible testimony that he has been faithful, or desires to be faithful, to his idea of morality. It is a feeling of pleasure associated with the idea of the moral ought. Or, as Kant says, it is "the susceptibility to pleasure or displeasure merely from the consciousness of the agreement or disagreement of our action with the law of duty (Pflichtsgesetz),[4] and "can only follow the representation of the law."[5]

Of course, Kant takes pains to set moral feeling apart from "moral sense" -- the notion developed by his contemporary Francis Hutcheson that all men have an innate perceptivity about what is right and wrong. "Moral feeling," Kant demurs, "(like pleasure or displeasure in general) is something merely

---

[1] "If we are to will action for which reason by itself prescribes an 'ought' to a rational, yet sensuously affected, being, it is a feeling of pleasure or satisfaction in the fulfillment of duty, and consequently that it should possess a kind of causality by which it can determine sensibility in accordance with rational principles." GMM, p. 128. Schriften, IV, 460.

[2] Kant uses the term "reverence" (Achtung) sometimes as a synonym for "moral feeling." Achtung can also be translated "respect."

[3] "...sensuous feeling, which is the basis of all our inclinations, is the condition of the particular feeling we call respect (Achtung), but the cause that determines this feeling lies in pure practical reason." CP_rR, p. 78. Schriften, V. p. 75.

[4] MPV, p. 58. Schriften, VI, 399.

[5] Ibid.

subjective, which yields no knowledge."[1] Moral feeling, still, is a universal ingredient in human experience. "No man is devoid of moral feeling; for if he were totally unsusceptible to this sensation, he would be morally dead."[2] Indeed, "his humanity would be dissolved (as if by chemical laws) into mere animality, and would be irretrievably mixed with the mass of other natural beings (mit der Masse anderer Naturwesen)."[3]

The concept of moral feeling in Kant's writings, like the concept of interest, tends to lay the foundation for a model of human agency which in many ways offsets the formalist thesis. The formalist thesis, we recall, turns immediately on the Cartesian disjunction between transcedental reflection and the activity of the corporeal agent in the world of sense-experience. The notions of interest and moral feeling, however, suggest that, au contraire, there is distinct cooperation (though not perhaps absolute unity of action) between practical reason and the sensible side of man in all moral conduct. Were the formalist thesis tenable, man could behave morally without consistently experiencing any corresponding change in his bodily or sensible condition. Nor would man find himself compelled to use his powers of moral scrutiny as a response to certain alterations in his sense make-up. In denial of the latter possibility, we have seen that, for Kant, man possesses

---

[1] Ibid. Schriften, VI, 400. We must remember, however, that Kant himself in the pre-critical writings on morals intimated at times that man can know the "ought" as a datum of feeling. Kant calls this feeling "moral sympathy" (moralische Sympathie) which he otherwise defines as "the feeling of the beauty and dignity (Würde) of human nature." Beobach.: Schriften, II, 217. Kant's discovery of moral feeling as the lens that refracts the universal element in moral experience derives from Rousseau. Cf. Ernst Cassirer, Rousseau, Kant, Goethe (Princeton: Princeton University Press, 1945), p. 6ff. Kant later, however, substituted the notion of "practical reason" for moral feeling, the latter of which he left an appendage to the moral act.

[2] MPV, pp. 58-9. Schriften, VI, 400.

[3] Ibid.

certain interests (specially "interests of inclination") consisting in the employment of the rational faculties to gratify a sensible need. In this case, reason responds to the urgings of sense and is programmed to complete the aim of these urgings. Man strives to fulfill an intention which, though not precisely moral, nevertheless depends on the interpenetration of rational and sensible activity. In regard to moral feeling, the subordination of reason to sense desire is reversed; yet the marriage of the two orders of motivation is preserved. When man acts morally, or when he merely contemplates the ideal majesty of the moral law itself, he necessarily experiences a feeling originating in the senses which cannot be extirpated as some recrement of consciousness alien to the moral life. Moral experience only comes full circle, Kant seems to say, once the rational and sensible elements are combined in their due proportions. If the formalist thesis were correct, the very idea of "moral" feeling would appear a contradictio in adiecto, since feeling properly belongs, for Kant, to the phenomenal realm and morality to the noumenal.

Thus we begin to see dimly how Kant's anthropology implies the view, about which we spoke earlier, of man and nature as a totality. In the foregoing discussion we have occupied ourselves with certain concepts which unfold what might be called Kant's "psychology" of action, as opposed to his metaphysics of morals. The standpoint of psychology, in this case, contains empirical considerations which must be harmonized with the transcendental position of metaphysics. Our approach is more phenomenological than ontological. Our analysis here has gone so far as to try to bring out the inter-connection between the activities of man's "higher" and "lower" natures. Thus we have begun to descry the contours of a monistic anthropology which is somewhat distinct from Kant's strictly "moral" anthropology. Such a monistic conception of man -- if that is what Kant really had in mind -- must, like the "two standpoints" interpretation of the noumenal/phenomenal distinction, remain purely heuristic. Kant never develops a positive metaphysics of man as a sensible/rational unity. Nevertheless, this monistic anthropology is more intellectually satisfying than the dualistic or "two worlds" metaphysic which may be read into Kant. This anthropology sharpens the true picture of human agency, even though Kant himself may never have been fully prepared to endorse such a picture. The picture looks as follows. Man acts, Kant seems to be saying, only because he is the creature in nature with intentions. It is the intricate relationship between his intentionality and his animality which composes man as a totality.

In the Critique of Judgement Kant orchestrates the idea of man as an intentional being, as a complexus of physical and rational forces working in concert toward the attainment of some purpose. The concept of man as having purposes, therefore, specifies him in his unique totality. What Kant means exactly by human purposes we shall take up next.

4. Human Purpose

Initially, Kant defines a "purpose" or "end" (Zweck) as "the concept of an object, so far as it contains the ground of the actuality (Wirklichkeit) of this object."[1] What does Kant mean by the "ground" (Grund) of a thing's actuality? Later in the third Critique Kant dilates this remark in noting that "the purpose is the object of a concept, insofar as the concept is regarded as the cause of the object (the real ground of its possibility)."[2] But how can a concept be a cause? We have seen that, for Kant, concepts or ideas have causal power when they occur as rules of man's will. The will, again, signifies man's ability to accomplish certain objectives or purposes ideated as desires.[3] To will something, in the sense that one

---

[1] CJ, p. 17. Schriften, V, 180.

[2] CJ, p. 55. Italics mine. Schriften, V, 220.

[3] "The faculty of desire, so far as it is determinable to act only through concepts, i.e. in conformity with the representation of a purpose, would be will." Ibid.

"intends" it, means to "have in mind" a state of affairs which one wants to come to pass. The word "purpose," itself, etymologically speaking, suggests an idea affecting the human volition, insofar as the idea is to be made concrete at a future moment. To purpose something is to propose it, i.e., to "set forth" something which one would like actualized. It is to place among an assortment of possibilities a desired condition that one knows can become real by dint of his own capacity, and that of others like himself, to make it so. For example, when one "proposes" marriage, he has in mind a real prospect of joining in wedlock with a certain woman. All that is required for the proposal to become fact is the man's willingness, together with the woman's consent -- not to mention, of course, their both following through the prescribed routine of obtaining a marriage license, blood test, and performing the marriage ceremony.

For Kant, all willing has some purpose. In general, the purpose or end sets down a subjective rule which guides the action.[1] Purposes as such, therefore, can only be ascribed to creatures with wills. For only a will, or practical reason itself, has its own causality which can produce effects or objects represented beforehand as projects or proposals to be accomplished. Such a causality diverges sharply from the mechanical causality of Newtonian science.[2] The two types of

---

[1] "Now what serves the will as a subjective ground of its self-determination is a [purpose](Sweck)..." GMM, p. 95. Schriften, IV, 427.

[2] "in order to see that a thing is only possible as a purpose, that is to be forced to seek the causality of its origin, not in the mechanism of nature, but in a cause whose faculty of action is determined through concepts, it is requisite that its form be not possible according to merely natural laws, i.e. laws which can be cognized (erkannt) by us through the understanding alone when applied to objects of sense, but that even the empirical knowledge (Erkenntnis) of it as regards its cause and effect presupposes concepts of reason...For reason, which must cognize the necessity of every form of a natural product in order to comprehend even the conditions of its genesis (Erzeugung), cannot assume such (natural) necessity in that

causality -- that of nature and of practical reason -- Kant analyzes in perhaps his most straightforward language in the introduction to the third *Critique*. Both kinds of causality, Kant observes, constitute rules for ordering experience objectively by furnishing "laws." Law-giving, or "legislation through natural concepts is carried on by means of the understanding and is theoretical. Legislation through the concept of freedom is carried on by the reason and is merely practical."[1] The two modes of legislation apply "to the same territory of experience, without prejudice to each other."[2] On the other hand, this division of legislation between understanding and practical reason conjures up a dualistic interpretation with which Kant seems uncomfortable. For the world of nature and the world of morality (if indeed they are really obverse aspects of the same world) must somehow be tied together.

In the third Critique Kant does undertake to tie the two worlds together. Kant considers this effort imperative, because of the very presumption in the idea of noumenal causality that practical reason "is meant to actualize in the world of sense the purpose proposed by its laws."[3] At first blush, the presumed efficacy of practical reason seems implausible, unless morality and nature do somehow coalesce into a single concept. Consequently,

> ...nature must be so thought that the conformity to the law of its form harmonizes with the possibility of the purposes effected in it according to laws of freedom. There must, therefore, be a ground of the *unity* of the supersensible, which lies at the basis of nature, with that

---

particular given form. The causality of its origin is then referred to the faculty of acting in accordance with purpose (a will), and the object which can only thus be represented as possible is represented as a purpose." CJ, p. 216. Schriften, V, 369-70.

[1] CJ, pp. 10-11. Schriften, V, 174.

[2] Ibid., p. 11. Schriften, V, 175.

[3] Ibid., p. 12. Schriften, V, 176.

> which the concept of freedom practically contains; and the concept of this ground, although it does not attain either theoretically or practically to a knowledge of the same, and hence has no peculiar realm, nevertheless makes possible the transition from the mode of thought according to the principles of the one to that according to the principles of the other.[1]

The ground of unity between nature and the transcendental sphere of morals Kant finds in his notion of man as a "natural purpose" (Naturzweck).

For Kant, "a thing exists as a natural purpose if it is... both cause and effect of itself."[2] This type of causality, which we shall call "self-causality," bears nothing in common with the notion of causation as the principle of necessary connection between two events observed in nature. No natural or empirical cause can be causa sui, since on the mechanistic model every cause must have an effect subsequent to it in time. If something were both cause and effect of itself, its causality would be independent of temporal succession (We could not say event ^{A} at $time_1$ caused event ^{B} at $time_2$, but only that ^{A}, t_x caused ^{A}, t_x, which would mean there was no differentiation between two time/object moments), and that, from the Newtonian standpoint, would appear impossible. The self-causality of a natural purpose, according to Kant, cannot be adduced simply by applying the rule of necessary connection to successive phenomena. Rather, self-causality pertains solely to the activity of an "organized and self-organizing being" in which "every part not only exists by means of other parts, but is thought as existing for the sake of the others and the whole -- that is, as an (organic) instrument."[3] A self-organizing being, which alone can be called a natural purpose, has the peculiar property of causing itself, since "an idea is to be the ground of the possibility of the natural product."

---

[1] Ibid.

[2] CJ, p. 217. Schriften, V. 270.

[3] CJ. p. 220. Schriften, V, 373.

In short, it is a conception of the effect which serves as the causal rule of action.

In mere mechanical causation (or what we shall term "linear" causation), the effect follows only adventitiously from the cause. No intrinsic relationship obtains between an event and its antecedent condition. But in a natural purpose, the relationship between event and prior condition is intrinsic, because the idea of the effect (or objective to be attained) specifies just what must take place beforehand for the effect to be achieved. The connection between cause and effect is made prior to the effect in the idea of what ought to be the case, rather than simply in hindsight or post hoc. The rule of drawing a connection after the effect has occurred, as is the case with linear causality, applies only to that which actually happens, not what is merely possible in thought.

Kant calls the complete philosophical schematism of nature, which includes self-caused action a teleology. He considers the teleological vantage point indispensible for grasping the character of the activity of organic or living beings. Every organic being, Kant says, has an indwelling purpose or "internal possibility" that cannot be explained away by invoking the "mechanical principles of nature."[1] We can, for instance, explain how a plant continues to reproduce itself by developing into the same form or genus only by supposing that there exists some "idea" delimiting the course of its growth. Linear causality excludes the possibility that there might be a conceptual determinant of the growth-event that is not merely the various extrinsic circumstances at any moment prior to the maturation of the organic being. Thus, we cannot sufficiently account for why a certain kind of plant repeatedly attains its generic form simply by pointing to such contingent facts as rich soil, ample rainfall, sunlight, etc. The enigma of organic life, Kant indicates, cannot be cleared

---

[1] CJ, p. 223. Schriften, V, 377.

up by the available scientific method of explanation. Thus we have Kant's celebrated remark that it is "absurd for men...to hope that another Newton will arise in the future who shall make comprehensible by us the production of a blade of grass according to natural laws which no design has ordered."[1]

Natural products cannot be cognized through the categories of the understanding. Such a mechanistic rendering of living forms is superficial at best. Natural products cannot be secured as empirical concepts by what Kant, at least in the third Critique, labels the "determinant judgement" (bestimmende Urteilskraft). Instead, natural products are deemed "purposive" by the special faculty called the "reflective judgement" (reflektierende Urteilskraft). The reflective judgement accounts for natural products according to different rules or laws than that provided by the understanding.[2] The reflective

---

[1] CJ, p. 248. Schriften, V, 400.

[2] Kant's notion of the "reflective judgement" is a highly interesting, albeit problematic, one. It supplies an important clue to how he attempts to combine the concepts of noumenal and natural causality in a unified principle. "Judgement in general," Kant states, "is the faculty of thinking the particular as contained under the universal." CJ, p. 15. Schriften, V, 179. Cf. also K_rV (B): Schriften, III, 131. "If the universal (the rule, the principle, the law) be given, the judgement which subsumes the particular under it...is determinant. "But if only the particular be given for which the universal has to be found, the judgement is merely reflective." Ibid. Kant considers the use of the reflective judgement necessary because "the forms of nature are so manifold, and there are so many modifications of the universal transcendental natural concepts (Naturbegriffe) left undetermined by the laws given, a priori, by the pure understanding -- because these only concern the possibility of nature in general (as the object of sense) -- that there must be laws for these [forms] also." CJ, p. 16. Schriften, V, 179. The reflective judgement, then, seeks laws for understanding certain phenomena which are not ready-to-hand, like the law of succession according to a scheme of cause and effect. It must find a law, such as the internal purpose of a thing (what Kant calls a "particular" versus a "general" law) in order to comprehend nature in its totality. Thus the reflective judgement trades in teleological concepts, which subsume "nature under a causality" that does not meet with the criteria necessarily of the scientific judgements, but is "only thinkable through reason

judgement discerns purposes in nature not as things in themselves; natural purposes have no independent ontological status, but are merely regulative ideas for reflecting on Nature as a complex whole that is not limited to the nature of Newtonian science nor the "super-nature" of moral reason.[1] Such regulative ideas are constructed on analogy with the purposes the human agent sets before himself in his own life. The fact that all purposiveness (Zweckmässigkeit) in nature reflects the purposive character of human activity reveals something about the

---

(durch Vernunft Denkbar)." CJ, p. 243. Schriften, V, 396. On the other hand, such teleological judgements establish "objective" (objektiv) purposes, because they supply a meaning to natural phenomena, albeit not a strictly scientific one. Their objectivity refers to the fact that they ascribe a lawlike order to the world. In this sense, the reflective judgement is capable of representing certain types of events, such as human action, as an integral part of nature, though not Newtonian nature. The "laws" of these events -- i.e., their "purposes" -- thus give an account of these events in a fashion that is neither "practical" nor "theoretical," but heuristic so far as they show us how phenomena and noumena can be viewed as events within a larger framework of meaning than the merely scientific world view, or the transcendental perspective of morality, provides. We may call this larger framework of meaning "Nature" with a capital "N." However, we cannot go so far as to call this perspective on the totality of events a real metaphysics of nature. Kant is adamant that the reflective judgement does not produce any cognitive explanation of the world. Science "explains" the world according to the laws of nature. Practical reason supplies a different principle of interpreting the world -- the transcendent standpoint of free causality. For that reason "the union of both principles [in the concept of purpose] cannot rest upon a ground of explanation (Erklärung) of the possibility of a product according to given laws, for the determinant judgement, but only upon a ground of its exposition (Erörterung) for the reflective judgement." CJ, p. 261. Schriften, V, 412. The reflective judgement simply expounds or discusses (erörtern) the world. That is, it provides us a way of talking about the world in its complex forms without making theoretical claims. We can talk about a concept of Nature without identifying it with the laws of "nature." Such a Nature is a regulative idea. This Nature cannot be discovered, simply by induction or by the deductions of pure reason (neither wholly a priori nor a posteriori) but serves only as a kind of pictorial assumption guaranteeing the "logical compatibility" between the ideas of nature and practical reason. Cf. S. Körner, Kant (Baltimore: Penguin Books, 1955), p. 176ff.

[1] CJ, p. 34. Schriften, V, 197.

peculiarity of man's purposiveness.[1]

Human purposiveness, for Kant, is thus the model for natural purposiveness. It is by recognition of the intricate structure of his own purpose-making that man ascribes purposiveness to natural entities with a connate complexity. That a high degree of complexity in the form of action of a natural entity (the characteristic which Kant terms "self-organization") cannot be reduced to linearity makes it mandatory for the investigator of life in general (of which human life is the culmination) to interpret his data using the principle of purposiveness.

In fine, Kant summons the principle of purposiveness to explicate how man through his practical reason comes by the power to transcend his givenness as a natural being, while at the same time preserving that givenness. From the standpoint (the standpoint which denies the possibility of a "science" of moral agency, though not a "metaphysics" with a practical interest), the relationship between nature and morality appears a contradiction or "antinomy."[2] Kant's "solution" to the antinomy in the first Critique does not wholly abrogate the contradiction, as moral spontaneity and the mechanism of nature still stand as diametric counters to each other; the attempt at "harmonization" through the postulate of noumenal causality does not achieve a complete synthesis of terms in a higher concept. Thus the "dialectic" which Kant claims to undertake in this section is not a true dialectic. No mediating term is set forth to unify the contrarieties. Nonetheless, in the third Critique Kant offers what can be taken as such a mediating term. The mediating term is human purposiveness. The concept of human purposiveness, though only a regulative idea, nonethe-

---

[1] "Purposes have a direct reference to reason, whether it be our own reason or an alien one. Specifically, in order to attribute them to an alien (fremd) reason [such as that of non-human things], we must take as a basis our own reason for an analogy of them, since they could not be represented at all without our reason." Gebrauch: Schriften, VIII, 180.

[2] K_rV (B): Schriften, III, 308ff.

less serves to locate moral causality within the field of nature. This is done by postulating (provisionally) noumenal status for certain events in the natural order. Thus, "now the principle common to the mechanical and teleological dirivations is the supersensible, which we must place at the basis of nature, regarded as phenomenon."[1] Similarly, the regulative idea of a supersensible foundation for the natural order provides a conceptual matrix for looking upon man as if he himself, qua moral agent, were not transcendentally abstracted from natural life, but intimately involved therewith. "The effect in accordance with the concept of freedom is the final purpose which (or its phenomenon in the world of sense) ought to exist, and the condition of the possibility of this is presupposed in nature (in the nature of the subject as a sensible being, that is, as man)."[2] Man as final purpose, that is, of "creation" or Nature, implies a concept of humanity whose moral reason can be explained by the reflective judgement a priori "without reference to the practical," and thus can "furnish the mediating concept between the concepts of nature and that of [moral] freedom."[3]

The ramifications of this view that man can be viewed as a citizen of the two worlds of nature and freedom at one and the same time will be worked out later in our discussion of Kant's philosophy of history. We should note, furthermore, that, in introducing his "mediating concept" of human purposiveness, Kant does not want to abolish the noumenal/phenomenal, practical/theoretical distinctions altogether. He only desires

---

[1] CJ, p. 261. Schriften, V, 412.

[2] CJ, p. 33. Schriften, V, 195-6.

[3] Ibid. "...because of the constitution of our (in part sensuous) nature and faculty it is, so far as we can represent it in accordance with the constitution of our reason, for us and for all rational beings that have connection with the world of sense, a universal regulative principle (allgemeinen regulativen Princip)." CJ, p. 252. Schriften, V, 404. "Now of this we can have no concept but the indeterminate concept of a ground, which makes the judging of nature by empirical

to find a heuristic mode for comprehending the two terms of
these polarities under a single concept. Thus we find him
moving beyond the terminological dualisms of the first two
Critiques toward a synthetic picture of human agency. This
synthetic picture Kant finds necessary, perhaps, because of (1)
the insufficiency of mechanistic explanations for moral behavior; (2) the need to square, on the other hand, the metaphysical overtones of his practical philosophy with an all-
encompassing world view that takes into account events that
happen in nature. The "two standpoints" theory proves inadequate to the task. Thus Kant's idea of recasting the scope of
teleological interpretation arises. He, however, demands that
teleology be fenced within the limits of heuristic constructions
rather than making the same claims as scientific theory.

E. Moral Agents in a Moral Universe

   1. Ultimate and Final Purposes

The fact that man's purpose-making provides the basic analogue for conceiving Nature as a system of purposes underlines
the pre-eminence of the human species within such a system.
Man stands as the nodal point, Kant informs us, for this system.
Without his purposive activity, "the whole creation would be a
mere waste (Wüste), in vain, and without final purpose (Endzweck)."[1] Amid a system of purposes man rises in relief as the
"ultimate purpose" (letzte Zweck). "He is the ultimate purpose
of creation here on earth, because he is the only being who can
form a concept of purposes and who can, by his reason, make out
an aggregate of purposively formed things (zweckmässig gebil-

---

laws possible but which we cannot determine more nearly by any
predicate. Hence the union of both principles cannot rest upon
a ground of explanation (Erklärung) of the possibility of a
product according to given laws for the determinant judgement,
but only upon a ground of its exposition (Erörterung) for the
reflective judgement. CJ, pp. 260-1. Schriften, V, 412. Man
cannot be explained, but he can be discussed (erörtert) as part
of nature.

[1] CJ, p. 293. Schriften, V, 442.

deten Dingen) as a system of purposes."¹ All other purposes are subordinate to his purposiveness. That is because man uses all the things of nature as means to attain the ends which he has in mind.² Vegetable life, for instance, does not have an "ultimate purpose" in the sense that its existence as end for itself (for the vital reproduction of itself in conformance with a definite generic pattern -- what today we would call its "genetic code") cannot be extended as an instrument for some further end. Man utilizes the growth of vegetable life to feed and clothe himself. The same is true with the animal kingdom, even with those species like lions whose mastery of his surroundings has earned him the title of "king of beasts." If men did not exist, lions might appear in the world as a kind of ultimate end, since they would have no use-value for any other beings. But men kill lions to use their skins as clothing. The king of beasts, therefore, is merely one of many subjects in man's technical dominion.

The view that man is an ultimate purpose hangs on his

---

¹CJ, p. 276. Schriften, V, 426-7.

²"...we have sufficient cause for judging man to be, not merely like all organized beings a natural purpose, but also the ultimate purpose of nature here on earth, in reference to whom all other natural things constitute a system of purposes according to the fundamental proposition of reason. If now that must be found in man himself which is to be furthered as a purpose by means of his connection with nature, this purpose must either be of a kind that can be satisfied by nature in its beneficence, or it is the aptitude and skill for all kinds of purposes for which nature (external and internal) can be used by him." CJ, p. 279. Schriften, V, 429-30. Kant is here refuting obliquely the Enlightenment's conception of what Lovejoy has called "the great chain of being" in which nature is seen as web of purposes with man as only an incidental link, a conception replaced the Middle Ages' anthropocentric view that "Tout est cree pour l'homme." Cf. A. O. Lovejoy, The Great Chain of Being (New York: Harper & Row, Torchbook Edition, 1960), p. 186f. Kant, in a sense, restores the Medieval view, albeit not by any appeal to God's choice, but by showing that the entire concept of a purposive arrangement does not reflect any inherent structure of things, but the way man alone shapes the world with his mind and action.

ability to subject the world to his purpose-making. Kant labels man's general aptitude for purpose-making his "culture" (Kultur).[1] As the German term in its conventional usage connotes, Kultur can mean the process of "cultivating" (or "husbanding") crops, animals, or any other natural things for our use, as in the sense of "agriculture." Culture is technics, in the sense that it may represent man's manipulating and controlling the means of life to meet his own needs. However man acts upon the world and shapes it to his will goes into the process of culture.

The fact of human culture places man at the vital center of the whirl of purposive activity which whoever reflects on the world as a total process ends up reading into nature. "Man is then," Kant observes, "always only a link in the chain of natural purposes, a principle certainly in respect of many purposes, for which nature seems to have destined (bestimmt) him in her disposition and to which he sets himself, but also a means for the maintenance of purposiveness in the mechanism of the remaining links."[2] Kant's phrase here "a means for the maintenance of purposiveness in the mechanism of the remaining links" (Mittel zur Erhaltung der Zweckmässigkeit im Mechanism der übrigen Glieder) is telling. Apart from human intentionality, the operations of certain phenomena in nature would proceed with unbroken mechanical regularity that gave no hint of purposive significance. Rivers would flood their banks annually and the alluvion flushed on down to the sea. But man builds dams to trap flood waters and to harness its energy for electrical power. The seemingly "purposeless" raging of spring floods man converts into a purposeful bounty for his long-range use.

---

[1] "The production (Hervorbringen) of the aptitude of a rational being for arbitrary (beliebigen) purposes in general ...is culture." CJ, p. 281. Schriften, V, 431. Cf. also CJ, p. 279. Schriften, V, 430.

[2] CJ, p. 280. Schriften, V, 430-31.

In effect, man adds purposes to nature; he "teleologizes" the given constellations of cause and effect. Although his purpose-making is itself a fact of nature, that fact serves to identify him as the ultimate purpose of nature. Viewed from this angle, man seems to serve merely as a "means" for piloting nature on its correct and pre-ordained course.

But man's participation in nature, as we have seen, does not in the least indenture him to any "natural purpose" over and beyond his own. Man himself poses the upper limit of all purpose-making. Thus the concept of man as an ultimate purpose that must merge into the idea of him as a "final purpose" (Endzweck): "that purpose which needs no other condition of its possibility."[1] If man is a final purpose, his own purposiveness must not serve any other purposiveness, even the presumed purposiveness of nature. Man is a purpose or end only for himself. The final purpose that man is, Kant says, does not disclose itself in our probing of nature. Our notion of ourselves as an ultimate purpose derives from the concept we have of ourselves as our own purpose, or final purpose.[2] Man recognizes himself as final purpose, because he knows that he himself alone has the capacity constructing ends that transcend

---

[1] CJ, p. 284. Schriften, V, 434. If, Kant says, "the purpose of the existence of...a natural being is in itself...it is not merely a purpose but a final purpose (Endzweck). CJ, p. 275. Schriften, V, 426. "...if we go through the whole of nature we find in it, as nature, no being which could make claim to the eminence of being the final purpose of creation; and we can even prove a priori that what might be for nature an ultimate purpose, according to all the thinkable determination and properties (erdenklichen Bestimmungen und Eigenschaften) wherewith one could endow it, could yet as a natural thing never be a final purpose." Ibid.

[2] "...in order to find out where in man we have to place that ultimate purpose of nature, we must seek out what nature can supply...in order to be a final purpose, and we must separate it from all those purposes...that one can expect from nature." CJ, p. 281. Schriften, V, 431.

mere nature and of achieving them.[1] Man's culture or purpose-making directs itself to not only those ends which form his natural or animal constitution, but ends which define him as man.[2] These ends are moral ends.

Similarly, the final purpose of man incises a final purpose for the totality of existence which humanity and insentient beings share alike. Nature taken by herself can only have an ultimate purpose (not a final purpose), Kant suggests. Kant speaks of a final purpose strictly for the "world" (Welt) or "creation" (Schöpfung).[3] "Moral teleology," Kant writes,

> concerns us as being of the world, and therefore as beings bound up with other things in the world, upon which latter, whether as purposes or as objects in respect of which we

---

[1] "Now we have in the world only one kind of beings whose causality is teleological, i.e. is directed to purposes, and is at the same time so constituted that the law according to which they have to determine purposes for themselves is represented as unconditioned and independent of natural conditions, and yet is in itself necessary. The being of this kind is man..." CJ, p. 285. Schriften, V, 435.

[2] "As concerns the discipline of the inclinations -- for which our natural capacity in regard of our destination as an animal race is quite purposive, but which render the development of humanity very difficult -- there is manifest in respect of this second requirement for culture a purposive striving (Streven) of nature to a cultivation (Ausbildung) which makes us receptive of higher purposes than nature itself can supply." CJ, p. 283. Schriften, V, 433.

[3] Kant's use of the term "world" (Welt) here serves to describe the totality that earlier we designated by the locution "Nature" with a capital "N." In the Critique of Pure Reason Kant declares that "world, in the transcendental sense, signifies the absolute totality of the content (Inbegriff) of existing things, and we direct our attention alone to the completion of the synthesis..." K$_r$V (B): Schriften, III, 289. This conception is distinguished from that of "world" understood as "nature" or "the unity in the existence of phenomena" (die Einheit im Dasein der Erscheinungen). Ibid. It does, however, perhaps approximate the common-sense view of what "world" means, what Wittgenstein adroitly defined as alles was der Fall ist ("all that is the case"). Cf. Tractatus Logico-Philosophicus (London: Rouledge & Kegan Paul, 1961), p. 7. Kant, unlike Wittgenstein, however, does not take "all that is the case" to mean simply the composite of empirical facts

> ourselves are final purposes, the same moral
> laws require us to pass judgement. This moral
> teleology, then, has to do with the reference
> of our own causality to purposes and even to
> a final purpose that we must aim at in the
> world, as well as with the reciprocal reference
> of the world to that moral purpose and the ex-
> ternal possibility of its accomplishment.[1]

Our involvement as moral beings in the world, viewed heuristi-
cally as a totality of relationships between the sensible and
rational sides of us, confers on that world the final purpose
we are to ourselves. For our moral reason prescribes laws both
to ourselves and to nature as a whole.[2] And the imposition of
these laws inscribes a form for the world which constitutes its
final purpose. "The existence of a reason that can be for
itself the supreme law in the purposive reference (Zweckbezie-
hung), in other words the existence of rational beings under
moral laws, can therefore be thought as the final purpose of
the Being (Dasein) of a world."[3]

Nature moralized through man's rational will composes the
objective of all man's purpose-making. Because we cannot adduce
this objective from nature itself, but only from the "super-

(phenomena), but as a totality embracing "facts of reason" and
moral laws as well. The world of moral reason (mundus intell-
igibilis) is a possible natural world, and thus "world" in the
transcendental or regulative sense includes such a possible
world, together with the actual or perceptible world of nature.
Since the final purpose of man belongs to the moral world, nature
alone cannot have such a purpose; hence the term Endzweck applies
exclusively to the conception of world as a totality including
moral purposiveness.

[1] CJ, p. 298. Schriften, V, 446.

[2] Cf. above. Kant calls the system of laws constructed in
man's reasons "the archetypal world (natura archetype)" while
its "counterpart" in "the world of sense" is "the ectypal world
(natura ectypa), because it contains the possible effect of the
former as the determining ground of the will." CP_rR, p. 44.
Schriften, V, 43.

[3] CJ, p. 300. Schriften, V, 449-50.

natural" intentions of human reason, we call it a "final purpose" -- a purpose satisfying no other conditions than those which reason sets before itself. In that respect the concept of the world's final purpose falls strictly too within the scope and limits of man's praxis. The moral universe, moreover, is a presupposition of practical reason concerning what type of world is necessary as a meaningful frame of orientation for moral action. In such a world nature and morality would coincide. But what would yield this coincidence? The coincidence would arise when the contingent, or irrational forces within themselves and in external nature are subdued. Such control of man's natural life to suit his highest intentions would bring about the situation we might call a moral universe. How this moral universe actually comes into being we shall see later.

Control of nature life in general, however, without specific guidance by moral intentions, Kant terms "happiness" (Glückseligkeit). The question is whether, for Kant, happiness is possible apart from the direction of moral reason. To answer that question we must first examine what Kant means precisely by happiness. We must find out the limits of which man can have mastery over his natural destiny, or to what extent a moral universe seems likely.

2. Happiness

"Happiness," Kant says, "is the state of a rational being in the world for whom in all existence everything proceeds according to his wish and will."[1] It is "the satisfaction of all our desires..."[2] Furthermore, it is "a rational being's consciousness of the agreeableness of life which without interruption accompanies his whole existence."[3] The idea of happi-

---

[1] Beweis: Schriften, II.

[2] $K_r V$ (B): Schriften, III, 523.

[3] $CP_r R$, p. 20. Schriften, V, 22.

ness occurs to man, because he has an innate need to satisfy his numerous sense inclinations.[1] "Man is a being of needs, so far as he belongs to the world of sense, and to this extent his reason certainly has an inescapable responsibility from the side of his sensuous nature to attend to its interest and to form practical maxims with a view to the happiness of this and, where possible, of a future life."[2]

But the fulfillment of sense needs, we have shown, cannot possibly count for an objective law in the same way as the rational principle of the universalizability of maxims does. While men desire happiness, they desire it in so many private, sophisticated, and rarefied tones that the "formal" consistency demanded in all moral law-making escapes the person who tries to universalize the principle of merely making life "agreeable" to himself.[3] The concept of a totality of sense-satisfactions, therefore, does never assimilate to a clear rule of moral

---

[1] "...all men have already of themselves the strongest and deepest inclinations towards happiness, because precisely in this Idea of happiness all inclinations are combines into a sum total." GMM, p. 67. Schriften, IV, 399.

[2] CP_rR, p. 63. Schriften, V, 61.

[3] The satisfaction of all desires as the sufficient condition for happiness, Kant tells us, appeals to a complicated set of criteria. The satisfaction of desires must be "extensive as concerns their multiplicity (Mannigfaltigkeit), intensive according to their degree, and finally protensive in regard to their duration (Dauer)." K_rV (B): Schriften, III, 523. Such are the criteria which the utilitarian moral theorist insists must be weighed in order to ascertain the right course of action according to what Jeremey Bentham, for one, dubbed the "felicific calculus." Kant, however, insists that no felicific calculus is possible for men whose sole moral aim is to formulate a rational law of natural life valid for everyone. CP_rR, p. 24. Schriften, V, 25. "Where one places his happiness," Kant says, "is a question of the particular feelings of pleasure or displeasure (Lust oder Unlust) in each man, and even of the differences in needs occasioned by changes of feeling in one and the same man. Thus a subjectivity necessary law (as a law of nature) is objectively a very contingent practical principle which can and must be very different in different men. It therefore cannot yield any practical law, because in the desire for happiness it is not the form...but only the material which is decisive..." CP_rR, pp. 24-5. Ibid.

reason that "should determine an action by which we could attain the totality of a series of consequences which is in fact infinite."[1] Far from bestowing a logical pattern on the way we act, the desire for happiness only proliferates indefinitely the amount of fortuitous conditions that would have to be met in order to give our life order and purpose. "Happiness is an Ideal, not of reason, but of imagination (Einbildungskraft) -- an Ideal resting on merely empirical grounds."[2] Moreover, the imagination is forever concocting various new and tantalizing forms of enjoyment that cry to be tried. For experience, from which the imagination derives its power, is always widening our sense of concrete possibility, figuring out new permutations of conduct (or what today we might call "life styles"), beckoning us to experiment with new forms of pleasure.[3] Like Peer Gynt, the romantic character in Ibsen's play, the man who fixes happiness as his lone intention sadly discovers as his life draws to a close that he has had no inner integrity to his pursuits, that his existence has no stable foundations. Kant claims that only in commitment to the moral law can life gain coherence, while the quest for happiness only leads to confusion and despair.

The man who chases after happiness, moreover, tragically falls to the mercy of forces outside his own sway. Aristotle noted that every dose of real happiness depends to some degree on having "good fortune."[4] The history of the word "happiness" itself takes us back to the original morpheme hap, as in

---

[1] GMM, p. 86. Schriften, IV, 418.

[2] Ibid.

[3] Happiness of "sensuous contentment (Zufriedenheit)...which rests on the satisfaction of inclinations, however refined they may be, can never be adequate to that which is conceived under contentment. For inclinations vary; they grow with indulgence we allow them, and they leave behind a greater void (Leeres) than the one we intended to fill." CP_rR, p. 122. Schriften, V, 118.

[4] Aristotle Nichomachean Ethics, 1100b.

"happen" or "happenstance," which implies "luck" or some event of a contingent character. The man who sets happiness as his chief goal denies himself the prerogative of shaping the world in accord with nothing but his own rational purpose. With happiness we must rest content with "everything (and nothing more) than that which nature supplies (verschaffen) us with ..."[1] As the fulfillment of all our sense needs, it can be judged the ultimate purpose of nature. But such an ultimate purpose, we have noted, is not man's own peculiar purpose. Man's peculiar purpose consists in subjecting nature to the moral law.

Happiness only forms an ancillary purpose to what reason projects as the final aim of every moral agent. Only so far as men live upright lives can happiness possibly befall them. It is not Kant's position that happiness follows as an inevitable reward of right action. His point is that a serene and secure state of human life, which the notion of well-being or happiness calls to mind, must always be a product of the ordering of the moral will. The dream of happiness without morality must crumble into illusion. Only virtue can strike meaning and purpose into life. But what is this relationship between virtue and happiness? The idea of a possible world in which virtue conduces to well-being Kant calls the "highest good."

3. The Highest Good

The highest good (höchste Gut), for Kant, signals the total unification of all basic tendencies in man's life through the effects of moral action. The highest good is the general quality which moral reason ascribes to the best possible world it can conceive, viz., a world in which "virtue and happiness are thought of as necessarily combined."[2] The union of virtue with happiness in the concept of the highest good adds an unconditional value to the conditional goods which the man of sense

---

[1] Theor. Prax.: Schriften, VIII, 283n.

[2] CP_rR, p. 117. Schriften, V, 113.

has at heart.[1] What exactly Kant means by making the conditioned into something unconditioned (unbedingt) is not immediately obvious. But it begins to grow transparent when we remember that objects of sense, according to Kant, have validity for the most part when they satisfy a limited number of persons in a particular situation, and thus their worth is subject to these special conditions; whereas moral virtue does not depend on the conditions of any situation. When a man responds to the call of virtue, whose force of obligation is not restricted by the situation at hand, all his conditioned impulses and inclinations toward pleasure become subordinate to what he has in mind morally. His sensible wants are disciplined and transfigured by his primary intention to obey the moral law.

For example, to bet regularly on the horses is to do something which in itself provides merely a subjective pleasure. If the man bets compulsively, so far as to exhaust his weekly paycheck with no cash left over to support his family, his enjoyment of betting goes against the moral law as a rule applicable not simply to himself, but to his wife and children as well. Conversely, if the man's expenditures at the race track do not in any way interfere with his providing for his family, his betting, while not per se a moral action, is at least compatible with morality. His enjoyment of horseracing, moreover, is simply an emolument to his commitment to doing the right thing which constitutes his central purpose. It is not a question of having to choose between virtue and enjoyment so much as deciding their order of priority.

The example of the habitue of the race track represents a kind of microcosm of the problem of the highest good. The

---

[1] "As pure practical reason it likewise seeks the unconditioned for the practically conditioned (which rests on inclinations and natural need); and this unconditioned is not only sought as the determining ground of the will but, even when this is given (in the moral law), is also sought as the unconditioned totality of the object of the pure practical reason, under the name of the highest good. CP_rR, p. 112. Schriften, V, 108.

highest good identifies a world in which the sum of man's enjoyments (i.e., his happiness) are commensurate with his virtuous deeds. The notion that this harmony between pleasure and morality is a "highest good," however, carries with it a certain ambiguity which Kant attempts to clear up. Certainly the notion of this "good" is not a "highest good" in the sense that it can surpass moral action in itself as a desired end. How then can it be called "highest"? "The 'highest'," Kant notes by way of distinction, "can mean the 'supreme' (supremum) or the 'perfect' (consummatum). The former is the unconditional condition, i.e., the condition which is subordinate to no other (originarium); the latter is that whole which is no part of a yet larger whole of the same kind (perfectissimum)."[1] The supreme highest good is the genuinely moral good that cannot be qualified. It is the "good will" (guter Wille) which looks not to the subjective end to be attained, but to the character of the action itself.[2] Kant is saying that the good will stands for the "highest good" in the sense that it does not rank below other moral goods, even the good that is happiness. The good will, or virtue, is the "supreme condition (oberste Bedingung) of whatever appears to us to be desirable and thus of all our pursuit of happiness..."[3] It does not require any condition, such as the expectation that we should enjoy the sensible goods of the world, to be authentic.

Yet the very fact that man is a "being of needs" with ineradicable sense desires bars us from extolling moral virtue alone as the "perfect" good that expresses a rational being's complete range of intentions.[4] The German word for "perfection"

---

[1] CP_rR, p. 114. Schriften, V, 110.

[2] "It is impossible to conceive anything at all in the world, or even out of it, which can be taken as good without qualification (ohne Einschränkung), except a good will." GMM, p. 61. Schriften, IV, 393.

[3] CP_rR, p. 114. Schriften, V, 110.

[4] "But these truths do not imply that virtue is the entire and perfect good as the object of the faculty of desire of

(Vollkommenheit) means a "coming to fullness" or "completeness," just as the Latin term consummatum indicates a "summing up" of many things together. The perfect good of man, therefore, is that good which embodies the fullness of all men's powers and tendencies brought together into an optimal unity. It is the good of the "whole man" which takes into account his every form of participation in the universe -- his striving after happiness as well as his devotion to inner goodness.

Kant, of course, with this somewhat bizarre rendering of the term "highest," aims to mediate between what he perceives as the two rival paradigms of ethics: eudaimonism and Stoicism. Eudaimonism, resting on Aristotle's doctrine of the "function" of man, posits happiness as the ultimate good that all men desire. Stoicism, on the other hand, locates the good largely in the consciousness of virtue itself. According to the Stoic theory, happiness (thought it does not have the same precise meaning with them as in the sense of eudaimonia) is found in the "self-contentment" a man feels when he has done what he knows he ought. Were the options limited to either the eudaimonistic or Stoic positions, Kant would choose the latter.[2]

---

finite rational beings. For this, happiness is also required, and indeed not merely in the partial eyes of a person...but even in the judgement of an impartial reason." Ibid.

[1]"It is true that the upright man cannot be happy if he is not already conscious of his righteousness (Rechtschaffenheit) in each action, since with such a character the moral self-condemnation to which his own way of thinking would force him in case of any transgression would rob him of all enjoyment of the pleasantness which his condition might otherwise entail." CP_rR, p. 120. Schriften, V, 116. Also: "Do we not have a word to denote a satisfaction with existence, an analogue of happiness which necessarily accompanies the consciousness of virtue, and which does not indicate a gratification (Genuss), as 'happiness' does? We do, and this word is 'self-contentment' (Selbstzufriedenheit), which in its real meaning refers only to the negative satisfaction with existence in which one is conscious of needing (bedürfen) nothing. Freedom and the consciousness of freedom, as a capacity for following the moral law with any unyielding disposition, is independence from inclinations, at least as motives determining...our desiring; and, so far as I am conscious of freedom in obeying my moral maxims, it is the exclusive source of an unchanging contentment necessarily connected with it and resting on no particular feeling. This may be called intellectual contentment." CP_rR, p. 122. Schriften, V, 110.

If man must experience sensible feeling at all, in Kant's estimate, he should only come by it when he has been faithful to his conscience. This derivative kind of sensible feeling, we saw earlier, constitutes the specifically moral feeling of "respect." Nevertheless, Kant is a shrewd enough observer of human nature to recognize that such pleasure at any rate is not just accidental, but is necessary in some way. Virtue for virtue's sake alone does not attend to the real aspirations and needs of a moral agent. The agent's sensible desires irremediably encroach upon his choice of how to act, and thus the dilemma of the moralist does not consist in recommending cures for sensuality, but in advising how to bring these desires under the discipline of reason. When discipline at an integral level of the moral life is achieved, the question then does not concern whether a man has a right to be happy, but whether he is allowed "happiness in exact proportion to morality (as the worth of a person and his worthiness to be happy)..."[1] Striking a proper balance between happiness and morality would create a moral universe. And such a balance would make up for the apparent defects in the "goods" of happiness and pure willing taken singly.[2]

The highest good as perfect justice[3] (as giving every man

---

[1] CP_rR, p. 115. Schriften, V, 110.

[2] "Happiness alone is, in the view of reason, far from being the complete good (vollständige Gut) for us. Reason does not sanction it as such (so far as inclinations may wish for it), unless it is the worthiness (Würdigkeit) to be happy, that is, it is united with good conduct (Wohlverhalten). Morality alone, together with the worthiness to be happy, is however a long way from the complete good. In order to complete it, he who conducts himself in a fashion not unworthy of happiness must be able to hope for the latter's possession (theilhaftig)..." K_rV (B): Schriften, III, 527-8.

[3] Whereas Kant does not talk about "justice" in the particular context of the highest good, it is evident that he implies such a notion. The highest good, for Kant, represents a sort of cosmic justice in which every man, as in Plato's ideal state, receives the goods of life according to his merit. It is what is commonly called "distributive justice," or what Justinian termed "the firm and continuous desire to render to everyone that which is his due."

the happiness he deserves in reward for virtue), is a notion
<u>derived</u> from the primary consideration that every man must act
morally. The highest good in this form constitutes the ideal
of a moral world.[1]

But such a world, though it may strike our rational preference for justice as the genuine context in which human morality proves to have value not only as a private expression of perfection, but as the ultimate arbiter and regulator of the natural order, nonetheless does not give any clear evidence, from the way we experience the world at hand, of having any immanent reality. The very absoluteness of the moral imperative suggests that nature in its givenness will conflict somehow with the workings of man's practical reason. Kant's conviction of the efficacy of reason does not entail a belief that the world as we know it is completely pliant to man's bidding. The life of reason is itself an unremitting struggle with the irrational forces of nature and the immoral fillips of inclination. Our conscious effort to forge a moral universe is forever thwarted by the evils of hunger and disease, natural calamities, human aggression and malice, as well as by radical evil in our own natures. The moral law, if we as rational beings purpose it with all our energy, is still impaired from becoming a universal law of nature by the immoral acts of other men. I may never do anything to countermand the moral law during the whole span of my lifetime; yet if some petty criminal should happen to assault me some dark night on the streets, the causality of my reason in apportioning virtue to happiness is cancelled out in that instance. The highest good, Kant warns us, does not eventuate simply when one, two, or three men are scrupulously moral. It continues to elude the righteous man. Then what warrant does such a conception of justice have for our moral reason? The highest good, set before us a moral

---

[1] "Pure reason can, only in the ideal of the highest <u>original</u> (ursprünglichen) good encounter the ground of the practically necessary connection between both elements of the highest <u>derived</u> (abgeleiten) good, namely an intelligible moral world." K_rV (B): <u>Schriften</u>, III, 526. Cf. also Wood, <u>op</u>. <u>cit</u>., p. 91f.

universe, while not a current fact of experience, still beckons us to purpose it in some way. By purposing it we come to anticipate its reality. But how can we anticipate it without indulging in only wishful thinking? It is in the face of this dilemma that Kant poses the religious question. The highest good is possible, Kant says, because there is a God who guarantees it. But how does God guarantee the highest good? That is the subject we shall now focus on.

CHAPTER II. God as Moral Agent

A. God as a Postulate of Practical Reason

1. Willing and Hoping

In the last chapter we saw that to be a moral agent, for Kant, does not mean that a man must insulate himself in his own personal conscience with no heed to the moral significance of the world around him. The moral agent needs a moral universe in which to perfect all aspects of his life, to do justice to his inclinations as well as his reason. Such perfection can only come about in a world embodying the "highest good" which matches happiness with virtue. If we could not conceive of this highest good, then "the moral law which commands that it be furthered must be fantastic, directed to empty imaginary ends, and consequently inherently false."[1] The impetus of the moral law is to bring under a "discipline of reason" (Disciplin der Vernunft) not only one's maxims, but the tangled skein of external circumstances that thwart or advance one's inner purposiveness, that provide him pleasure or pain, depending on how a man is affected by outward events. If one could not anticipate some tangible satisfaction in his moral efforts, those efforts would soon seem quixotic and devoid of lasting meaning.

On the other hand, the kind of world in which we might expect rewards for our moral labors seems to elude our grasp. This is because we perceive no innate necessity that our individual moral actions will lead to a moral system of nature.[2]

---

[1] CP_rR, p. 118. Schriften, V, 114.

[2] "...every practical connection of cause and effect in the world, as a result of the determination of the will, is dependent not on the moral intentions (Gesinnungen) of the will, but on knowledge of natural laws and the physical capacity of using them to its purposes; consequently, no necessary connection, sufficient to the highest good, between happiness and virtue in the world can be expected from the most meticulous observance of the moral law." CP_rR, p. 118. Schriften, V, 118.

Certainly we may draw a link between the causality of the will and a variety of concrete effects; but the link, Kant repeatedly stresses, lies predominantly in the realm of possibility. The "necessary" connection between the causality of reason and sensible effects is a connection in terms of obligation, that is, in terms of the <u>unconditional</u> imperative constraining us to behave in a way we think we <u>ought</u> to behave: not in terms of the <u>actual</u> relation obtaining in the world between thought and action in general. I may, moreover, continually and unflinchingly do what I know is right, but I have no guarantee from the actions themselves that they will cause other persons to do the right thing, or for the universe as a whole to treat me as fairly as I think is proper. As Kant says,

> ...the acting rational being in the world is not at the same time the cause of the world and of nature itself. Hence there is not the slightest ground in the moral law for a necessary connection between the morality and proportionate happiness of a being which belongs to the world as one of its parts and as thus dependent on it. Not being nature's cause, his will cannot by its own strength bring nature, as it touches on happiness, into complete harmony with practical principles.[1]

For "the moral law does not of itself promise happiness..."[2] How, then, does Kant proceed from the concept of moral acts to a moral universe?

In the final pages of the first <u>Critique</u> Kant lays out for the first time the conditions under which a rational being may look to a moral universe as possible. According to Kant, a rational being always sizes up the character and possibilities of his life within the parameters of inquiry contained in three main questions: "1. What can I know? 2. What ought I to do? 3. What may I hope?"[3] Knowledge (<u>Erkenntnis</u>), as

---

[1] CP_rR, p. 129. <u>Schriften</u>, V, 124.
[2] CP_rR, p. 133. <u>Schriften</u>, V. 128.
[3] K_rV (B): <u>Schriften</u>, III, 522.

we have seen, is nothing more than an account of appearances
revealed through the senses. Knowledge reports merely how
things seem without further reference to what is only possible
or unrealized. Kant's first question, therefore, in contrast
with the second, is inadequate if one wants to discover whether
there can be a moral universe. For the knowledge we have of
the familiar world of sense persuades us, for the most part,
that the emergence of a moral universe is not very likely, in
view of the enormity of human wickedness. The only knowledge
we could possibly have of a moral universe would be an inductive
knowledge of its probability based on calculation and extrapolation from perceived effects; and the betting here would be
that the probability would be small indeed. To ask about the
possibility of a moral universe is not a theoretical question.
Any pretense that we can know something about the moral universe betrays a metaphysic that is "purely speculative."[1]

On the other hand, the second question regarding how one
ought to act does not suffice either to grapple with the main
problem at hand. Preoccupation merely with what one should do
informs us nothing concerning what will happen when he does it.
The second question is "purely practical." The third question
is decisive. "If I act as I ought, then what may I hope?"
Such a question, Kant maintains, is "at the same time practical
and theoretical"; for "all hoping aims for (geht auf) happiness,
and has the same intention (Absicht) for the practical and the
moral law, as knowing and the natural law have in respect to
theoretical knowledge."[2]

Kant's insight is that to hope for the appearance of the
moral universe in the future provides the necessary context
for meaningful action in the present. To hope for something
does not assure that it will come to pass. But neither is hope
reducible to fancy or idle wishing. These are what we might
call "false hopes." The contemporary German philosopher Ernst

---

[1] Ibid. Schriften, III, 523.

[2] Ibid.

Bloch has described hope as the discovery of possibilities found within the world itself, possibilities that signify "a not yet completely determined universe."[1] The view toward a possibility that is not yet a reality comprises, for Kant, the "practical" dimension of hoping; for the possibility which hope projects is given *a priori* in the legislation of pure reason. The understanding, however, that this possibility is not "wishful thinking," but is a real possibility insofar as it can be known to come about in some sense, constitutes the "theoretical" aspect of hoping. For every man always has some objective reason or "cause" (Ursache) to hope for happiness.[2] The ground of hope, Kant tells us, lies not so much in any certainty we might have that our finite moral wills are competent to attain happiness, but in a special kind of assumption we must make. We have to "assume" (annehmen) the coming of the moral universe "as a consequence (Folge) of our conduct in the sensible world, since the latter does not offer any such connection..."[3] But *a fortiori* we have to assume the existence of a God whose omnipotence is responsible for the being of that universe. The moral universe guarantees the purposefulness and integrity of our moral acts; the existence of God guarantees the reality of the moral universe. To assume God along with the moral universe is to open a horizon of meaning for all our moral purpose-making. We can act morally with only the pure incentives of reason in mind, but we cannot account for those actions outside of themselves unless we "know" somehow that our deeds have just consequences.

---

[1] Ernst Bloch, *Das Prinzip Hoffnung* in *Gesamtsausgabe*, Bd. V (Frankfurt/Main, Suhrkamp Verlag, 1955), p. 258f. and *passim*.

[2] "I say therefore that, just as moral principles and reason are necessary in their practical use, so it is necessary according to reason (in its theoretical) use to assume that everybody has cause to hope for happiness in the same measure as he has in his conduct made himself worthy, and that the system of morality is bound inextricably with happiness, though only in the idea of pure reason." K_rV (B): *Schriften*, III, 52

[3] K_rV (B): *Schriften*, III, 526.

In the process of assuming God and the moral universe, we come to "know" something which aids our action. Knowledge in the form of an assumption, however, is not the same as empirical knowledge obtained through comparison and analysis of the given data of the senses. Nor is such knowledge merely an a priori intention to realize something within our power, such as in the case of moral ideas. An assumption tells us about an existing state of affairs irregardless of whether we are capable of producing or preventing that state. An assumption is a sort of quasi-knowledge about things that affect me. Thus, if I say, "I assume that Fred is coming to pick me up for our dinner engagement," I am speaking with a certain degree of authority that my friend is planning to drop by. This is not the same as saying, "I intend for Fred to pick me up," because I cannot intend what Fred does. Fred, contrary to my expectations, may have in mind to leave me waiting all night. Yet, from what I know of Fred and the situation in question, it is possible to claim that in some real sense I know my friend will not leave me in the lurch. I cannot know with unimpeachable certainty that my friend will pick me up insofar as I can verify his intentions, but the evidence at hand, including the trust I hold in him, makes me believe without question in his reliability. The reality of an assumption, therefore, is lodged in an expression of belief about a state of affairs. We must now examine more closely what Kant means by an assumption of, or belief in, God.

2. Believing

In Section III of the "Canon of Pure Reason" in the first Critique Kant classifies the idea we entertain of a God who authorizes the reality of the highest good a "belief" (Glaube). At the outset of this section, Kant distinguishes holding a belief from merely having an "opinion" (Meinen) about something. "Opinion is to hold insufficiently (unzureichendes) as true (Furwahrhalten) something consciously, subjectively as well as objectively."[1] To "be of the opinion" that something is truly the case implies that, neither have we ample evidence to warrant a proposition which has been put forth, nor are we able to convince even ourselves, in the fact of a recognized dearth of supporting data, that it is at least "true for us." If pressed, we are bound to tergiversate concerning its truth. Thus Plato was right in dismissing "opinion" (doxa) or "what seems right" as one of the lowest modes of cognition, as a "knowledge" only of the mutable and fleeting impressions of the world, impressions that often contradict each other.[2] Belief, on the other hand, does not recoil at the insufficiency of confirming evidence, but assets to the truth of something in spite of its inability to be verified. In contradistinction to an opinion, a belief is "subjectively sufficient" (subjektiv zureichend) in the sense of a "conviction (for myself)" (Überzeugung [für mich selbst])."[3] Both opinions and beliefs, however, do not have the public and repeatable character of empirical knowledge which enjoys "objective sufficiency" or "certainty (for all)" (Gewissheit [für jedermann]).[4] Still, a belief specially provides a person with a "practical" knowledge which, although "theoretically insufficient," can suffice as a frame of orientation for action.[5] The practical function of belief, indeed, interests Kant more than its epistemic content; and thus the question of belief in God boils down to how our con-

---

[1] K_rV (B): Schriften, III, 533.

[2] Plato Republic 474B-477.

[3] K_rV (B): Schriften, III, 533. "Belief...on account of its merely subjective reasons does not give a confiction that can be communicated to others, or command universal assent, like the confiction that comes from knowledge. Only I, myself, can be certain of the validity... of my practical belief." Log., p. 60. Schriften, IX, 70.

[4] Ibid.

[5] K_rV (B): Schriften, III, 533f.

viction of his existence might help direct our lives. But the practical aspect of believing in God also depends on our consideration of the peculiarly moral elements in experience. How Kant arrives at the necessary relation between moral claims and theistic belief we shall have to trace out. But first we must examine the concept of belief in the broad sense of the term.

Beliefs, Kant recognizes, do not necessarily have a moral role to play. The inward conviction which passes in a man for belief serves as a kind of shortcut for reaching a certainty closed to the methods of induction. The practicality of beliefs, therefore, only provides a provisional kind of surety. David Hume, for instance, regarded most claims of certitude, in science or religion, as concealed "beliefs." A belief, Hume said, is a "feeling" of the mind that a given representation is connected with certainty to another impression. Belief operates even at the level of common perception and helps us distinguish the "truth" of certain relations in experience from bald illusions or hallucinations.

> ...in philosophy we can go not further than assert that _belief_ is something felt by the mind, which distinguishes the ideas of judgement from fictions of the imagination. It gives them more weight and influence, makes them appear of greater importance, enforces them in the mind, and renders them the governing principle of our actions. I hear at present, for instance, a person's voice with whom I am acquainted, and the sound comes as from the next room. This impression of my senses immediately conveys my thought to the person, together with all the surrounding objects. I point them out to myself as existing at present, with the same qualities and relations of which I formerly knew they possessed. These ideas take faster hold of my mind than ideas of an enchanted castle.[1]

Belief arises as the cognitive cachet of "the relation of cause and effect," "as a general law which takes place in all the

---

[1] David Hume, _An Inquiry Concerning Human Understanding_ (New York: Bobs-Merrill, 1955), p. 63.

operations of the mind."[1] A belief couples neatly together our train of observations which, when analyzed in its separate components, does not show that one event in experience invariably follows upon the other.

John Henry Newman, whose theological cast of mind was quite at odds with Hume, viewed belief -- or what he termed "real assent -- as higher than processes of inference which can never afford us the complete and reliable knowledge about the world which we might demand in order to make a reasonable decision in life. The function of belief, therefore, for Newman, was to provide a structure of firm meanings which aid us in our acting.[2] A contemporary student of Newman in the analytic tradition is H. H. Price. Price sees beliefs as cognitive reference points that obviate confusion when we cannot judge for certain what is right in a given set of circumstances. He compares beliefs to "posts which we plant in the shifting sands of doubt and ignorance." They are

> fixed points or stable landmarks; and once they are there, we are able to make short journeys into the surrounding wastes planting another post or two as we go. That is why the loss of a belief can be such a serious matter for us. We have lost something which we have been using to find our way about a wilderness.[3]

Beliefs are maps of action which we value not for their intrinsic truth or falsehood, but for their serviceability.

In this sense, they are really _suppositions_, rather than conclusions, about reality. These suppositions, for Kant, may

---

[1] Ibid., p. 64.

[2] "life is for action. If we insist on proof for everything we shall never come to action..." John Henry Newman, An Essay on the Grammar of Assent (New York: The Catholic Publication Society, 1870), p. 92.

[3] H. H. Price, Belief (London: George Allen & Unwin, 1969), p. 293. For a good summary of contemporary literature on the problem of belief, see also Anthony Quinton, "Knowledge and Belief," The Encyclopedia of Philosophy, vol. ii, 345-52.

be used, among other ways, as a method of locating and putting
in perspective various courses of action to secure a desired
end. Kant advances the example of a doctor who, not knowing
the exact nature of a disease in his patient, nevertheless seeks
to restore his health. The doctor has no tested prescription
for the patient, because he does not know all the causes of
his malady that would warrant a definite prognosis. Yet this
ambiguity in the patient's condition does not bar him from
trying a remedy. The doctor merely relies on a belief, or "best
judgement," that the disease is "phthisis," and thus orders a
possible cure.[1] If he insisted on knowing for certain what was
wrong with the patient, the latter might die. A belief or
assumption entertained in the face of any given exigency of
life Kant terms "pragmatical belief" (pragmatischen Glauben).
Pragmatical beliefs each have a certain "degree (Grad) according to the different interests...which can come into play (im
Spiel)."[2] The doctor's interest in saving the patient is
strong. The interest of the man on the street, however, in believing that his neighbor has been visited by intelligent beings
from outer space is not as great as in believing, for instance,
that American democracy is better than Communism, or that his
wife loves him more than she loves the Fuller Brush salesman.
Whether his neighbor has really had such an extraordinary
visitation does not impinge upon his most intimate life concerns
that much.

On the other hand, there are certain types of belief which
carry a sense of urgency, which indeed we could hardly live
without. We cannot waive these beliefs, because they tend to
certify in some manner our most deep-felt intentions -- in
point of fact, our _moral_ _intentions_. Moral beliefs, for Kant,
are grounded in an impregnable conviction that reflects the
gravity of the moral concerns themselves. They are compelling
in some sense, because we are compelled by the moral "ought" in

---

[1] K_rV (B): Schriften, III, 534.
[2] Ibid.

our conscience.¹ If, instead of merely believing, we had first to gather enough relevant evidence to make these beliefs theoretically plausible, the burden of the moral claims on us might prove insufferable. William James has eloquently described how moral situations oblige a sense of certainty that cannot wait until "all the results are in."

> Moral questions immediately present themselves as questions whose solution cannot wait for sensible proof. A moral question is a question not of what sensible exists, but of what is good, or would be good if it did exist. Science can tell us what exists; but to compare the worths, both of what exists and of what does not exist, we must consult not science, but what Pascal calls our heart.²

The option of taking a moral belief, thus, according to James is "living" or "forced" upon us in virtue of the momentousness of the issue at stake.³ We find ourselves obliged to believe because, in light of our perception of what would happen if we did not believe, unbelief becomes very difficult indeed. The argument adduced by Kant and James resembles Pascal's "wager." The benefits to be gained if our belief is true dwarf proportionally what is lost if it is false.

Kant formulates the necessity of belief in God on the basis of the unthinkability of living in a world not morally

---

¹"For [with moral belief] it is absolutely necessary that something must happen, namely, that I follow the moral law in all aspects (Stücken). The purpose is inevitably (unumgänglich) established, and there is only a single condition possible according to all my insight, under which this purpose accords with all of my ends taken together (gesammt), namely, that there is a God and a future world...and so I am ineluctably (unausbleiblich) forced to believe in the existence of God and a future life, and I am sure that nothing can make this belief waver (wankend), since if that happened my moral principle would be overturned..." K_rV (B): Schriften, III, 536.

²William James, "The Will to Believe" in Essays on Faith and Morals (New York: The World Publishing Company, Meridian Books, 1962), p. 53.

³Ibid., p. 33f.

governed to some end. "I am morally certain. That is, belief in a God and another world is so interwoven (verwerbt) with my moral disposition (Gisinnung) that I run very little risk of forfeiting (einzubüssen) the latter, moreover, that I hardly fear that former can be torn away (entrissen) from me."[1] The unshakable quality of a moral belief rests on its apparent necessity for the life of a rational being. Such necessity, according to Kant, can be deduced through a priori reasoning about the requirements of the moral life. On that account, however, the simple term "belief," connoting any incidental presumption about a state of affairs, does not always bear the force of necessity which "moral beliefs" have. In consequence, Kant must have an expression designating more aptly this necessity. In the second Critique Kant develops, therefore, the notion of a "postulate."

3. Postulation

"A need of pure reason," Kant writes, "in its speculative use leads only to hypotheses; that of pure reason, to postulates."[2] Hypotheses supply a principle or "ultimate ground" for organizing a system of empirical cognitions. In the field of metaphysics, a hypothesis, instead of lending "objective reality" to these cognitions, serves "completely to satisfy my inquiring reason with respect to them."[3] Thus a "hypothesis is an assent (Fürwahrhalten) of the judgement to the truth of a principle on account of the sufficiency of the consequences (Zulänglichkeit der Folgen); or more briefly, assent to a supposition as a principle (Vorausetzung als Grundes)."[4] A hypothesis "can never attain to apodictic certainty, but only to a degree of probability (Wahrscheinlichkeit) sometimes greater, sometimes less."[5] In metaphysical speculation, God

---

[1] K_rV (B): Schriften, III, 537.
[2] CP_rR, p. 147. Schriften, V, 141-2.
[3] Ibid. Schriften, V, 142.
[4] Log., p. 75. Schriften, IX, 84.
[5] Ibid.

is never anything greater than a hypothesis. The inference from a perceptible design in nature to "a definite cause, especially to one so exactly and perfectly defined as we have to think God to be, is always uncertain and fallible," and "such a presupposition cannot be brought to a higher degree of certainty than the acknowledgement that it is the most reasonable opinion for us men."[1] Hypotheses thus do not lay adequate grounds of certainty for moral action. Again, according to James, a hypothesis is "anything that may be proposed to our belief."[2] A hypothesis points only to a likelihood that something is true, or, to play on an idiom in common parlance, a hypothesis is merely "hypothetical."

Yet a postulate, while it cannot be demonstrated as theoretically sufficient, nevertheless furnishes a definite rationale why we should behave or think in a particular fashion. A postulate is a presupposition or belief which we know "must be true" if we are to apply certain rules to our life. A postulate is not the same as a rule itself, but it at least fixes the conditions for putting these rules in effect. Consider the example of "pure geometry," which "has postulates as practical propositions, which, however, contain nothing more than the presupposition that one *can* do something and that, when some result is needed, one *should* do it."[3] A postulate in mathematics represents a necessary assumption that such and such is definitely the case, if we want to carry out a further operation or construction. A postulate establishes the possibility of following a whole series of rules which we know will achieve the desired result within the context prescribed. We postulate, for instance, that two parallel lines can never intersect, even if extended to infinity. We cannot demonstrate conclusively this postulate in the way we can demonstrate

---

[1] CP_rR, p. 147. Schriften, V, 142.

[2] James, op. cit., p. 33.

[3] CP_rR, p. 30. Schriften, V, 31.

theorems, for to do so we would have actually to make an infinite extension of the lines which would be impossible. Yet we must presuppose that parallel lines do not intersect if, say, we want to show that certain angles formed by a straight line cutting across the parallel lines are equal in magnitude, in conformance with the rules of a geometric proof in general.

As far as moral postulates are concerned, such assumptions are tailored to making the rules of practical living viable. Apart from the use of moral postulates, we could not meaningfully persevere in attempting to realize the moral law, as the categorical imperative calls for.[1]

The necessity of a practical postulate, therefore, has to do with the fact that it is indispensable as a standpoint for moral action. From the cognitive perspective, a practical postulate gives the semblance of "objective reality" to an idea such as God, which cannot be confirmed or denied by the usual empirical criteria.[2] Unlike hypotheses, moral postulates have their truth-value not solely in any theoretical application, but in the practical office they perform in providing a context for action. A practical postulate intends to convince us the universe *exists* in such a way that takes consideration for our moral intentions, though no scientific experiment could ever produce public evidence for our conviction. That God is a practical postulate means, whenever we behave morally, we must at the same time *think* God as real to us in some manner of speaking. Thinking God as real bolsters moral action, because it validates the consequential end of such action -- the attainment of the highest good.

---

[1] "The postulates of pure practical reason all proceed from the principle of morality, which is not a postulate but a law by which reason directly determines the will. This will, by the fact that it is so determined, as a pure will requires these necessary conditions for obedience to its precept." CP_rR, p. 137. Schriften, V, 132.

[2] Ibid.

The necessity with which we think God mirrors the necessity with which we feel obliged to obey the moral law. Whereas moral obligation is a fact of reason that presents itself a priori to human conscience, God's existence is a necessary belief that makes possible the discharge of that obligation from reflection on what is required to be a moral agent in any concrete sense.[1] It is not legitimate to reflect in any other way: we cannot reason from God to morality, but only from morality to God. Kant rejects all "theological ethics" which derives moral principles from a metaphysical conception of the divine nature. The divine nature must be conceived in concert with the canons of morality laid down by pure reason alone.[2] Speculative theology is a mere imposture when paired with "moral theology."

The need to think God, we have seen, occurs with the recognition that happiness does not always accrue to virtue, even though "it is not impossible that the morality of intention (Gesinnung) should have a necessary relation as cause to happiness as an effect in the sensuous world..."[3] The contra-

---

[1] "...there are practical laws (moral ones), which are absolutely necessary, and we must, if these laws necessarily presuppose the existence of something (irgend ein Dasein) as the condition of the possibility of their obligatory force, postulate such an existence. For the conditioned, from which the process of inference (Schluss) proceeds to the determined condition, is recognized as itself a priori absolutely necessary. We will show later that the moral laws not only presuppose the existence of a supreme (höchste) being, but moreover freely (albeit only practically) postulate it, since the laws are absolutely necessary in a different respect..." K_rV (B): Schriften, III, 421-22.

[2] K_rV (B): Schriften, III, 421n. "Not theological ethics, for they contain moral laws which presuppose the existence of a supreme World-ruler (Weltregierer); whereas moral theology, to the contrary, is a conviction of the existence of a supreme being, which is grounded in moral laws." Beck notes that Kant's repudiation of "theological ethics" "secularized" the previous understanding of Sittengesetz which was theonomic and had nothing to do with the a priori in pure reason itself. Op. cit., p. 280

[3] CP_rR, p. 119. Schriften, V, 115.

diction between the empirical fact of injustice in the universe, and the practical possibility of a relation between virtue and happiness, disappears when we postulate God, because the "relation is indirect, mediated by an intelligible Author of nature."[1] This Author of nature, or "supreme cause," in himself

> ...must contain the ground of the agreement of nature not merely with a law of the will of rational beings but with the idea of this law so far as they make it the supreme ground of determination of the will. Thus it contains the ground of the agreement of nature not merely with actions moral in their form but also with their morality as the motives to such actions, i.e., with their moral intention.[2]

"Therefore," Kant adds, "the highest good is possible in the world only on the supposition of a supreme cause of nature which has a causality corresponding to the moral intention."[3]

God is a "postulate" of practical reason, because he is as vital to the consistency of our moral reasoning as any assumption in a geometric proof. Kant spells out how God serves as a frame of orientation for moral reasoning[4] in the preface to the Religion Within the Limits of Reason Alone (1792). "So far

---

[1] Ibid. "... the existence is postulated of a cause of the whole of nature, itself distinct from nature which contains the ground of the exact coincidence of happiness with morality." CP_rR, p. 129. Schriften, V, 125.

[2] Ibid.

[3] CP_rR, p. 129-30. Schriften, V, 125. Similarly, "...we must assume (anzunehmen) the existence of God, if we want to judge concerning the first cause of all contingent factors, especially the order of existing purposes in the world. Far more important is the need of reason in its practical employment for this concept, since...the use of pure practical reason is to formulate the moral law." Orient.: Schriften, VIII, 139

[4] The idea of a postulate as somehow "orienting" man's reasoning is implied in the title of Kant's little essay of 1786, "What is called orientation in thinking?" Here Kant discusses in detail how the God-postulate provides a general frame of reference for the moral life.

as morality is based on the conception of man as a free agent (eines freies)," Kant begins, "who, just because he is free, binds himself through his reason to unconditioned laws, it stands in need neither of the idea of another Being over him, for him to apprehend his duty, nor of an incentive other than the law itself, for him to do his duty."[1] Man does not act primarily for the sake of getting his just deserts; he need have no end in mind as a maxim of his will, when he does the right thing, other than right action itself. "But although for its own sake morality needs no representation (Vorstellung) of an end which might precede the determining of the will, it is quite possible that it is necessarily related to such an end, taken not as the ground but as the sum of inevitable consequences of maxims adopted as comformable to that end."[2] If moral willing did not have an end in the sense of an ultimate consequence to one's right action, his action itself would appear a mere charade in an indifferent universe.[3] Morality, for Kant, is not some ideal point in a space of measurable action and reaction, but is an active force with vectors extending outward and meeting resistance as a play of concrete purposes. In our role as moral agents, we do not merely ask -- What should we do? -- but "What is to result from this right conduct of ours?"[4]

Kant emphasizes how the moral agent is compelled by his own reasoning to have an eye, not merely for the immediate results of his deeds, but for their long-range consequences. The moral agent is concerned about "what sort of world he would create" were his agency altogether effective in his purposing.[5]

---

[1] RWL, p. 3. Schriften, VI, 1.

[2] RWL, p. 4. Schriften, VI, 2.

[3] "Without an end of this sort a will envisaging to itself no definite goal for a contemplated act (vorhabende Handlung), either objective or subjective (which it has, or ought to have, in view), is indeed informed as to how it ought to act, but not whither (wohin), and so can achieve no satisfaction." Ibid.

[4] Ibid. Schriften, VI, 5.

[5] RWL, p. 5. Ibid.

The moral agent wants a world in which happiness and the pure will exist alongside each other. The concept of this world is the highest good, "the absence of which would be a hindrance to moral decision."[1] But for the highest good to come true, "we must postulate a higher, moral, most holy, and omnipotent Being which alone can unite (vereinigen) the two elements of the highest good."[2] The act of postulating God as guarantor of the highest good as an act of "faith" (Glaube), more precisely, a "rational faith" (Vernunftsglaube).[3] It is a rational faith, because "pure reason alone (by its theoretical as well as practical employment) is the source from which it springs."[4]

Rational faith, as we may gather from our previous discussion, is not "belief" in the weak sense: a merely pragmatic way of looking at things in order to reach an arbitrary end. Nor does rational faith pose as a surrogate for scientific knowledge of the world. If it did, the act of faith, so far as it is a free assent to certain conditions of truth not confirmable by the testimony of the senses, would seem quite otiose.[5] Rational faith yeilds a "knowledge of God, but only

---

[1] Ibid.

[2] RWL, pp. 4-5. Ibid.

[3] "But in reference to the comprehensibility (Verständlichkeit) of an object (the highest good) placed before us by the moral law, and thus as a practical need, it can be called faith and even pure rational faith..." CP_rR, p. 130. Schriften, V, 126.

[4] CP_rR, pp. 30-1. Schriften, V, 31-2.

[5] "Rational belief (Vernunftglaube), then, can never reach to theoretical knowledge; for in theoretical matters an objectively inadequate assent is merely Opinion. It is only a supposition of the reason in a subjective but absolutely necessary practical point of view. The mental disposition (Gesinnung) which accords with moral laws leads to an object of elective will, determinable by pure reason. The assumption of the feasibility of this object, and therefore, also of the actuality of its cause, is a moral or free belief, and in the moral point of view of the fulfillment of its end it is a necessary assent." Log., p. 60n. Schriften, IX, 69n.

in a practical context."[1] The knowledge of God gained in rational faith has no value per se, but serves to keep our reasoning about the moral life internally consistent, or "self-maintaining"; so that we do not have to choose between irreconcilible antinomies or contradictions in moral experience, while in the same breath we remain certain that the knowledge we have is "true" in some profound sense.[2] Borrowing the expression Collingwood has devised for identifying the basic principles of metaphysics as a whole, we may say that faith in God, for Kant, is an "absolute presupposition" of the moral life. This absolute presupposition is the bedrock assumption undergirding the whole structure of moral inferences. An absolute presupposition cannot be verified (the way logical positivists today regard verification, i.e., submitting a proposition to possible empirical criteria which would either confirm or falsify it), because the demand for verification is not germane to presupposing.[3] A "presupposition" (in German Voraussetzung) is merely something "placed" or "set out" "in advance" of a process of inference. Having a starting point that is already established

---

[1] CP_rR, p. 142. Schriften, V, 137. Similarly, "rational faith...is that which is grounded in no other data than what is contained in pure reason. All belief is a subjectively sufficient, although for consciousness objectively insufficient, assent (Fürwahrhalten); thus it is set in opposition to scientific knowledge (Wissen)." Orient.: Schriften, VIII, 141. "...rational faith, which rests on a need of reason in its practical use, can be called a postulate of reason: not as if it were an insight (Einsicht), which satisfied all logical demands of certainty, but because this mode of assent is inferior to (nachsteht) no degree of knowledge, though it is at the same time completely different from such knowledge." Orient.: Schriften, VIII, 141.

[2] "The principle of the self-maintenance (Selbsterhaltung) of reason is the fundamental element in rational faith, in which the mode of assent (Fürwahrhalten) is of the same degree as in knowledge yet of a different kind; inasmuch as it is not derived from the ground of the object, but from the genuine need of the subject regarding the theoretical, as well as from the practical use of reason." Nach. 2446: Schriften, XVI, 371.

[3] Cf. R. G. Collingwood, Metaphysics (Oxford: The Clarendon Press, 1940), p. 31f.

as valid in some sense is required for any sequence of reasoning, inductive and deductive alike.

The act of presupposing God as a starting point for moral reasoning about the consequences of action constitutes an act of "faith" in the classical theological sense of <u>fides</u>: an expression of "subjective trust (<u>Zutrauen</u>) in one another, that one will keep his promise to the other..."[1] "Speaking by way of analogy, the practical reason is, as it were, the <u>promiser</u>, man is the <u>promisee</u>, and the good expected from the act is the <u>promissum</u>."[2] Rational faith hence is not, as A. D. Lindsay rightly points out, a faith "that" something is true, so much as a faith "in" a divine will, higher than our own, which metes out happiness congruent with our merits.[3] In this regard faith is a kind of ironbound pact between God, who is postulated, and man. Faith observes the formula <u>do</u> <u>ut</u> <u>des</u>: God is obliged to give to man the moral universe on the condition that he follow the moral law. Thus, in light of this pact, morality "leads <u>ineluctably</u> (<u>unumgänglich</u>) to religion, through which it extends itself to the idea of a powerful moral Lawgiver (<u>Gesetzgeber</u>), outside of mankind, for Whose will that is the final end (of creation) which at the same time can and ought to be man's final end."[4]

God's moral "will," therefore, represents a sort of archetype for man's willing. To postulate God means to assume a superior will, of which ours is a mere shadow, that can fill in for our deficiencies. God, in short, is the perfect moral agent. But does "postulating" the existence of such a will mean that, when we speak of it, we are indeed using agential language in the same sense as when we talk about human moral

---

[1] <u>Log</u>., p. 60n. <u>Schriften</u>, IX, 69.

[2] <u>Ibid</u>.

[3] A. D. Lindsay, <u>Kant</u> (London: Ernest Benn, 1934), p. 210. Faith "in" the efficacy of the divine will, however, entails belief that such a will indeed exists.

[4] <u>RWL</u>, pp. 5-6. <u>Schriften</u>, VI, 6. Italics mine.

agency? We shall deal with this question shortly, but first we must take close stock of the instances in which Kant seems to refer to God as a moral agent. We must examine the "grammar" of divine agency.

B. The Grammar of Divine Agency

1. God as World Cause

In the "Transcendental Dialectic" of the Critique of Pure Reason Kant delivers his well-known refutation of the familiar arguments for the existence of God. It is not our objective to recapitulate these criticisms; but we should remember that Kant largely succeeds in denying that a Supremely Perfect Being, or ens realissimum, can be demonstrated by rational proof alone a la Aquinas, Descartes, Leibniz, and others who had made contributions to the field of metaphysics. Although much has been said about Kant's demolition of the ontological argument, his general pre-occupation seems to have been with those arguments (which Kant terms the "cosmological" and "physico-theological" or "physico-teleological" arguments) alleging to prove God's existence through metaphysical exploitation of the category of causality. Speculative metaphysics, Kant claims, topples into illusion when it tries to deduce the existence of a Being as First Cause beyond the world from the empirical chain of causes within the world. Here Kant accedes to Hume's objection that we cannot infer a necessary First Cause from any regress of known causes. We cannot use our knowledge of the world to give an account of the nature of a Being who lies outside the region of this knowledge.[1]

The cosmological argument, according to Kant, works back to a "supreme cause" of the existence of the world as a whole.

---

[1] Hume's quarrel with arguments for God based on causal inference is pronounced by Philo in the Dialogues. Philo takes as an epistemological principle that "like effects arise from like causes." Thus "where several known circumstances are observed to be similar, the unknown will also be found similar." Dialogues Concerning Natural Religion, edited by Normal Kemp Smith (New York: Thomas Nelson and Sons, 1947), p. 170.

105

The physico-theological or "teleological" proof, on the other hand, begins with taking cognizance of the complete perceptible scheme of "effects and causes, of ends and means" in nature as its primary datum, and not only argues for an abstract prima causa or rational ground of things, but for that which, "as the cause of [perceptible thing's] origin secures its continuing existence (Fortdauer)."[1] In a word, the teleological argument tries to establish a First Cause in the person of a Designer, while the cosmological argument makes no reference to design.

On the whole, the comological argument, Kant observes, remains the property of the "Deist." The Deist "allows that we know in every instance by pure reason the existence of a Primal Being (Urwesen)..which one cannot, however, come close to defining."[2] The teleological argument, on the other hand, serves as the manifesto of the "theist." The theist "asserts that reason is in a position (im Stande) to define closely its object according to analogy with nature, namely, as a Being that contains in itself the primal ground (Urgrund) of all things through understanding and freedom."[3] Whereas the Deist view God simply as World Cause without further specification, the theist looks upon this Being as "an Author of the world (Welturheber)."[4] Nevertheless, the claims of both Diest and theist that a World Cause can be definitely verified as an existing fact, just as we can verify the existence of causal series in the natural order, are misguided. Claims of this sort mistake the a priori for empirical principles of argument. A priori or purely deductive arguments, which metaphysical proofs in essence constitute, fail to answer questions arising out of experience, questions such as those concerning the "whence" or

---

[1] K_rV (B): Schriften, III, 414-5.

[2] K_rV (B): Schriften, III, 420.

[3] Ibid.

[4] Ibid.

the cause of a perceived event. Like all categories of understanding, the category of causality can never help to adduce any information surpassing the bounds of sense-knowledge.[1] Thus Kant avers that "all efforts of a merely speculative use of reason in respect to theology are wholly fruitless...and thus...there can be, in general, no rational theology (Theologie der Vernunft), unless one bases it upon the moral law as a guide (Leitfaden)."[2]

Kant's addition of the qualifier "unless" (wenn nicht) in the above sentence is telling. His suggestion that rational theology, while a sorry standby for science, is yet able to come into its own when used to validate moral claims, previews his whole program for defending God as a practical postulate. Regarding the language of theology, Kant's stance seems to be that talk about God in the theoretical vein (as language purporting to describe the origins of the world at the same level of discourse by which we describe the world itself) is conceited and empty. On the contrary, talk about God in a practical context (as the "language of faith" that begs interpretation, not in reference to the world at hand, but in light of a possible or ideal world consonant with moral intention) is perfectly admissible. Granted, we may speak of God "theoretically" as First Cause, so long as we understand our notion to be nothing more than a regulative principle for ordering empirical concepts;[3] but regulative ideas are merely abstract ciphers for the unity of empirical relations. We need not even call

---

[1] "...all synthetic principles of the understanding are of immanent use; for a knowledge of a Supreme Being, however, one demands a transcendent use of reason, for which our understanding is not at all equipped (ausgerüstet)." K_rV (B): Schriften, III, 423.

[2] Ibid. Cf. also, "the concept of God is onw which belongs originally not to physics, i.e., to speculative reason, but to morals." CP_rR, p. 145. Schriften, V, 140.

[3] Kant's notion of regulative ideas or "ideals" are given above. "The Supreme Being, therefore, remains for the merely speculative reason nothing but an ideal (Ideal), though a faultless (sehlerfreies) one; it is a concept which closes and

the sort of regulative idea mentioned above "God" at all in order to express the same relations. Aristotle's Unmoved Mover would have the same meaning. For Kant, God language comes into play, because men have an interest, not so much in the notion of a "Cause of causes" in the abstract, as in the idea of a denominated and concretely working cause that somehow guarantees the causality of man's moral behavior. Talk about God as "Cause" has significance only so far as His causality resembles the causality of moral agents.

Kant can hardly be said to take up the language of moral causality in reference to God as an occasional metaphor. In the "Canon" of the first Critique, Kant mentions God as "an efficient cause" (wirkende Ursache) that "corresponds exactly to our highest purposes."[1] In the second Critique we find the same figure of speech. Here Kant speaks of God as "a supreme cause of nature which has a causality corresponding to the moral intention" of men.[2] Similarly, in the Groundwork God is the "beneficent Cause" of nature who gives man his moral aptitudes.[3] In the third Critique, He is "an intentionally operating cause" (absichtlich wirkende Ursache)[4] or intentionally operating "highest cause" (oberste Ursache).[5] At the same He is "highest cause of nature" (oberste Ursache der Natur)[6] or "World Cause" (Weltursache),[7] not merely in the sense of a rational ground of existing things, but of an intentional

---

crowns all human knowledge, though its objective reality cannot be proven in this way..." K_rV (B): Schriften, III, 426.

[1] K_rV (B): Schriften, III, 527. Cf. also "cause of the whole of nature" that brings forth the highest good. CP_rR, p. 129. Schriften, V, 125.

[2] CP_rR, p. 130. Schriften, V, 125.

[3] GMM, p. 63. Schriften, IV, 395.

[4] CJ, p. 271, 284. Schriften, V, 422, 434.

[5] CJ, p. 247. Schriften, V, 399.

[6] CJ, p. 291, 286, 287. Schriften, V, 441, 436, 437.

[7] CJ, p. 287, 294, 298, 307. Schriften, V, 437, 444, 447, 456.

Being or Agent with a rational plan for ordering the universe. Elsewhere, the terms Kant employs to designate God's agency are "Author of the World" (<u>Welturheber</u>),[1] "Author of Nature" (<u>Urheber der Natur</u>),[2] and "Author of All Things (<u>Urheber allen Dingen</u>).[3] Earlier we linked Kant's use of the term "Author" with the theistic contention that the First Cause is purposive in character. However, we also saw that the divine purposiveness can only be understood as <u>moral</u> purposiveness.[4] God's authorship of the world does not admit of demonstration; it is simply an assumption "in which a free interest of pure practical reason is decisive."[5] God's causality only has meaning ultimately as a presupposition of reason considered necessary because of the finite capacity of man's will to realize the highest good. God is viewed as the cause which realizes the highest good. The language of divine causality, for Kant, is rooted in the problem of stating man's inability to accomplish his deepest moral intentions. Thus the grammar of divine agency corresponds with the grammar of moral agency in general, including the grammar of <u>willing</u>.

2. God as Supreme Will

In the first Critique Kant denotes God as "Supreme Will (<u>obersten Willen</u>), which takes into (<u>befasst</u>) itself or under itself all private wills (<u>Privatwillkür</u>)."[6] God is the Supreme Will, because his will is the vehicle for realizing the moral universe, a "system of self-compensating (<u>sich selbst lohnen-</u>

---

[1] CP_rR, p. 145, 151, 133, 134. <u>CJ</u>, p. 288. <u>Schriften</u>, V, 140, 145, 128, 129, 438.

[2] CP_rR, p. 119. <u>Schriften</u>, V, 115.

[3] CP_rR, p. 143. <u>Schriften</u>, V, 138.

[4] Cf. above, p. 107, n. 3.

[5] CP_rR, p. 151. <u>Schriften</u>, V. 145.

[6] K_rV (B): <u>Schriften</u>, III, 526.

den) morality" in which "everyone does what he should."[1]
Several pages later Kant stipulates why we must believe in the
existence of such a will.

> ...if we consider from the point of view of
> moral unity as a necessary law of the world
> (Weltgesetz) the cause which alone can pro-
> duce the suitable effect and thus give this
> law obligatory (verbindende) force, there must
> be a single Supreme Will which takes these
> laws into itself. For how would we among
> different wills find a complete unity of pur-
> poses? This will must be omnipotent (allge-
> waltig) so that all nature may be subject
> (unterworfen) to it in reference to morality
> in the world.[2]

The "omnipotence" of the divine will remedies the impotence of
finite wills in their effort to make nature comply with morality.[3] Apart from the concept of a divine will, the ideal of
the highest good would evaporate; since the highest good,
according to Kant, if it can have practical reality, must be
attainable by some agent, and human agents, we have seen, lack
the power to attain it. One reason they are incapable of
reaching the highest good is the recalcitrance of nature; but
another reason is the presence of radical evil in the maxims
of men. The immoral acts of men result in a state of injustice
that blocks the proportioning of virtue to happiness. This
inveterate defect in man's will cannot, however, be said to
represent the limits of willing, if the moral law, as a counsel
of rational perfection, is to make any sense. It must be
possible to conceive of a will not subject to the limitations
man discerns in himself. Hence, Kant comes to speak of a
divine will containing a moral capacity that man natively lacks.
God is what Kant terms a "holy will" (heilige Wille).

A holy will, or the state of "holiness," is "complete fit-

---

[1] K_rV (B): Schriften, III, 525-6.

[2] K_rV (B): Schriften, III, 528-9. Italics mine.

[3] Cf. "the supreme cause of nature" which is God's "will."
CP_rR, p. 130. Schriften, V, 126.

ness of the will to the moral law."[1] But holiness is "an idea which can never be fully reached by any creature."[2] Broadly speaking, therefore, only the divine will is holy. The emblem of a holy will is that it needs no constraints to morality. "Hence for the _divine_ will, and in general for a _holy_ will, there are no imperatives: 'I ought' is here out of place, because '_I will_' is already of itself necessarily in harmony with the law."[3] Similarly, the divine will or holy will needs no "incentives" (Triebfeder) to action. By "incentive" Kant means "a subjective determining ground of a will whose reason does not by its nature necessarily conform to the objective law." A divine will inherently and without force of obligation acts according to moral principles. In consequence, "absolutely no incentives can be attributed to the Divine will."[4]

Kant's use of the expression "divine will," as with the phrase "world cause" and its synonyms, serves largely to articulate precisely what men with finite wills must postulate in order to find a frame of meaning for their own agency. The divine will embodies what men's wills lack; yet men cannot attribute to this will any reality in itself. This will has reality only _for_ the moral consciousness. All other kinds of claims for the reality of this will Kant puts out of court as "idolatry."[5] Language about God's will, for Kant, is meaning-

---

[1] CP_rR, p. 126. Schriften, V, 122. A holy will is "a perfectly good will." GMM, p. 81. It is "a will incapable of any maxims which conflict with the moral law." CP_rR, p. 32. Schriften, V, 32.

[2] CP_rR, p. 128n. Schriften, V, 124n.

[3] GMM, p. 81. Schriften, IV, 414.

[4] CP_rR, p. 74. Schriften, V, 72. "The moral law is, in fact for the will of a perfect being a law of holiness. For the will of any finite rational being, however, it is a law of duty, of moral constraint, and of the determination of his actions throug respect for the law and reverence for its duty." CP_rR, pp. 84-5. Schriften, V, 82.

[5] "...the concept of a will of the Supreme Being, as a reality inhering in itself...is either an empty or, worse

less if divorced from the language of morals. God, therefore, has a will, but his "willing" is always equivalent to what man cannot morally will. The inadequacies of man's will specify the circumstances in which God must be believed to exist. Man's will can never in itself achieve all that it intends, but we must believe God's will can. Man's will is corrupted, inconstant, unholy; but God is holy. In fine, God's will encapsulates what man's will would be if it were all that the moral ideals of virtue and the highest good urge that it should be, i.e., omnipotent. To think of "divine will" is "to think of our morally necessary purposes as at the same time his purposes."[1] Purpose is that which we aim for in all our acts of will. Thus we must examine Kant's description of God as a moral purposer to clarify the conception of him as a will.

3. God as Moral Purposer

In the "Methodology of the Teleological Judgement" of the third Critique, Kant analyzes why it is necessary to talk about God as a Being with the moral universe as his purpose. Language about God as moral purposer grows out of the need of practical reason to view nature somehow as harmonizing with moral ends. Formerly we saw how Kant explodes the claims of natural theology (or "physico-theology") to infer a purposive cause of nature from an experience of design in the strands of visible events. Natural theology, Kant further argues in the Critique of Judgement, can only "infer the supreme cause of nature and its properties from the purposes of nature (which can only be empirically known)."[2] Its "date, and so the principles, for determining that concept of an intelligent (verständlich) world causes (as highest artiest) are merely empirical" and "do not enable us to infer any of its properties

---

still, an anthropomorphic concept...which ruins all religion and turns it into idolatry." Neuer.: Schriften, VIII, 400n.

[1] Los. Bl. (SF) G 19: Schriften, XXIII, 438.

[2] CJ, pp. 286-7. Schriften, V, 436.

beyond those which experience reveals in its effects."[1] Hence, its "purposive reference therein is and must be always considered only as conditioned in nature, and it consequently cannot inquire into the purpose for which nature itself exists."[2] "Moral theology," however, can adduce that purpose. For moral theology infers "that [purposive] cause and its properties from the moral purposes of rational beings in nature (which can be known a priori)."[3] Moral theology alone discloses the "final purpose of creation" which is inaccessible to natural theology"[4] -- the moral universe, or "man under moral laws."[5]

Moral theology harbors the concept of a highest good in which nature is teleologically subordinated to human morality. Such a theology teaches us that nature, if we want to think of it as designed at all, must appear morally designed. Only in recognition of "the inner moral purposive destinations of man's being" are we allowed to think "the supreme cause [as endowed] with properties whereby it is able to subject the whole of nature to that single design (for which nature is merely the instrument), i.e., to think it as a deity."[6] The acknowledgement of man's moral purposiveness leads to the conception of a cause with a similar, though perfect, purpose for the world. Were there no higher purpose consonant with the moral law, our own moral purposing would come to nought.

As a result, Kant argues, our moral reason presupposes a "cause" that "is capable of representing purposes to itself, and consequently is an intelligent Being; at least it must be

---

[1] CJ, p. 288. Schriften, V, 438.

[2] CJ, pp. 287-8. Schriften, V, 437.

[3] CJ, p. 287. Schriften, V, 436.

[4] Ibid. Schriften, V, 437.

[5] CJ, p. 296. Schriften, V, 445.

[6] CJ, p. 298. Schriften, V, 447.

113

thought as acting in accordance with the laws of such a Being."[1] In the sublunary sphere, such a purposive cause of events resides in man's moral will. But, in order for the moral will to be able to effect invariably what it intends (i.e., the moral control of nature), an all-sufficient purposive cause must mediate this efficacy. Such an efficacy is impossible so far as finite wills are left to their own means. One can "never think if any other principle of the possibility of the unification of nature with its inner ethical laws than a supreme cause governing the world according to moral laws."[2] The teleological unity of nature with morality Kant in the third Critique buds man's "final purpose."[3] But this final purpose melts into illusion, unless we assume a Being who not only has the same purpose for the world in mind, but is able to accomplish it in deference to our native inability to do so. Thus we assume a God.

Kant calls this type of argument "the moral proof of the existence of God" (moralischen Beweise des Daseins Gottes).[5] It should be noted, however, that by "proof" (Beweise) Kant

---

[1] CJ, p. 299, 448. Schriften, V, 448.

[2] CJ, p. 310. Schriften, V, 458.

[3] "...reason takes for final purpose the furthering (Beförderung) of happiness in harmony with morality." CJ, p. 302. Schriften, V, 451. Elsewhere, Kant calls this teleological unity the highest good.

[4] "Consequently, we must assume a moral world cause (an author of the world) in order to set before ourselves a final purpose consistently with the moral law, and in so far as the latter is necessary, so far...the former must be necessarily assumed, i.e., we must admit that there is a God." CJ, p. 30. Schriften, V, 450. By the same token, if one "wishes to remain dependent upon the call of his moral internal destination (Bestimmung) and not to weaken the respect with which the moral law immediately inspires him, by assuming the nothingness of the single, ideal, final purpose adequate to its high demand...he must assume the [existence] of a moral author of the world, that is, a God." CJ, pp. 303-4. Schriften, V, 452-3.

[5] CJ, p. 298. Schriften, V, 447.

means a metaphysical demonstration combining both a posteriori and a priori premises, as we have in the physico-theological argument. "Proof," for Kant, consists in any method of reasoning that reaches certainty. The non-moral "proofs" could not generate the certainty of God's existence. "The moral ground of proof (Beweisgrund) of the existence of God," Kant declares, "properly speaking, does not merely complete (ergännzt) and render perfect the physicotelelogical proof, but it is a special proof that supplies the conviction which is wanting in the latter."[1] In this sense, it is a "special proof": it has little to do with the formal philosophical proofs for God's existence at all. The "moral proof" does not demonstrate the existence of God per se. For "our knowledge of existence," Kant shows in his refutation of the ontological argument, "belongs entirely to the domain of experience."[2] And since experience cannot divulge what lies beyond experience (that is, a First Cause), we cannot prove God's existence as glibly as we can confirm the existence of objects in the empirical world. The "moral proof" only proves that we must believe in God's existence.[3] The "moral proof" "supplies the conviction" absent in the physico-theological proof, because from it we see why we must ascribe a reality to what we perceive as a purposiveness in nature. This purposiveness, however, has meaning only as moral purposiveness, and we cannot impute reality to it so long as we are bent on immediately proving the proposition "God exists," instead of the qualified construction, "If there is to be morality, God must be real." We do not prove directly the existence of a supreme moral purpose; only that, in order to act morally ourselves, we must somehow think such an existence. Kant never insists we try to verify

---

[1] CJ, p. 331. Schriften, V, 478.

[2] K_rV (B): Schriften, III, 402.

[3] This interpretation of the moral proof is set forth by Eugene Peters, Descriptions of God in the Later Writings of Kant (Harvard University, Unpublished Doctoral Dissertation, 1968), p. 167.

God's existence. He only argues we must <u>assume</u> the existence
of God. To argue for the necessity of making an assumption
differs from arguing for the truth of what is not assumed.
Formally, a moral argument, in the standard sense of "argument,"
for God's existence might look something like this:

    The moral universe is possible

.˙.God exists.

But Kant is not arguing in this fashion. For the chief assumption here would be: "the moral universe is possible." But
that is what Kant wants to demonstrate! <u>Per contra</u>, the argument appears as follows:

    God exists

.˙.The moral universe is possible.

Here "God exists" is the assumption. The former type of argument represents in abbreviated form an instance of the classical "argument for God's existence." The latter shows Kant is
arguing for two things: 1) that the moral universe is possible
2) that if the moral universe is possible, our first premise
or assumption must be the existence of God. Thus the locution
"moral proof," notwithstanding Kant's dependence on it, seems
to belie the critical philosophy's own intentions.

In exploring the grammar of God in the passages cited, we
have incurred the striking impression that, while Kant deliberately leans on the use of the language of moral agency (employing such terms as "cause," "author," "will," "purpose,"
among others to which we have called attention), he is not
using that language univocally. For the "reality" attached to
the concepts which this language articulates is a quite different reality from that of other types of concepts. We cannot
say God's moral actions are real at the same level of meaning
as man's actions are real, since the latter can be observed
and attributed to their proper subject, while the former are
not cognizable in this way. The lack of identity between man's
actions and God's actions from the moral point of view is
twofold: (1) God's moral agency is always the "perfect"
corollary to our imperfect agency. Thus the truth of the

proposition, "God acts," never quite has the same value as the statement, "man acts." God's perfection can be found in the mode of actuality, while man's "perfection" in general seems a distant possibility.[1] (2) We always <u>postulate</u> God's reality in order to secure the reality of moral obligation. Reasons can be adduced for believing in God. God's reality, therefore, is not an elementary datum of reason, as is the moral law. We never adduce reasons for moral obligation. Reasons can be adduced for believing in God. God's reality, therefore, is not an elementary datum of reason, as is the moral law. We never adduce reasons for moral obligation.

In all events, we must take a hard look at why Kant uses the language of God in this way. So far our account of the grammar of divinity in Kant's writings has aimed merely to describe a situation. We shall now deal with some possible solutions to the ambiguities in this kind of grammar. In investigating the relationship between Kant's use of agential language about God, and his implication that such language is faith-language, we shall have to take under consideration some possible modes of discourse which help clarify Kant's aims. These modes we shall call the language of analogy, the language of limitation, and the language of intention.

C. Postulation and Agency

  1. The Language of Analogy

In the third Critique Kant offers some suggestion that his talk about God is one of analogy. "The objective reality of

---

[1] The whole question whether it is possible for man to attai perfection, as far as Kant is concerned, appears highly problem atic. Kant makes it clear, by his prohibition of human holines that man on his own can never bring a perfect harmony of his wi with the moral law. The possibility of perfection in the sense of the highest good is stated by Kant more ambiguously. Kant distinguishes two senses of "possibility": "possibility perceived with respect to what is immediately in our power, and secondarily in that which is beyond our power but which reason holds out to us as the supplement to our impotence." CP_rR, pp. 123-24. Schriften, V, 119. Thus man's "possibility" of achievi the highest good is only a real possibility so far as it is God

the idea of God," Kant says, cannot "be established by physical purposes alone"; yet "if the cognition of these purposes is combined with that of the moral purpose, they are, by virtue of the maxim of pure reason, which bids us to seek unity of principles so far as is possible, of great importance for the practical reality of that idea, by bringing in the reality which it has for the judgement in a theoretical point of view."[1] No theoretical knowledge of God is permitted, yet it is still possible to "think" certain "properties of the highest Being (höchsten Wesens)," and this "according to analogy" (nach der Analogie).[2] Later in the same section Kant tenders a definition of analogy:

> Analogy (in a qualitative signification) is the identity of the relation between reasons and consequences (causes and effects), so far as it is to be found, notwithstanding the specific difference of the things or those properties in them which contain the reason for like consequences, i.e. considered apart from this relation. Thus we conceive of the artificial constructions of beasts by comparing them with those of men, by comparing the ground of those effects brought about by the former, which we do not know, with the ground of similar effects brought about by men (reason), which we do know, i.e. we regard the ground of the former as an analogon of reason.[3]

Analogy enables us "to think one of two dissimilar things, even in the very point of their dissimilarity (Ungleichartigkeit)," even though we cannot "conclude from the one to the other."[4]

In consequence, we may think God as a purposive cause of nature on analogy with the various purposes recognized in

---

possibility. "With God all things are possible." But this does not clarify the meaning of "possibility" sufficiently.

[1] CJ, p. 307. Schriften, V, 456.

[2] Ibid.

[3] CJ, p. 315n. Schriften, V, 464n.

[4] CJ, pp. 315-6. Schriften, V, 464.

nature,[1] although "the causality of the beings of the world... cannot be transferred to a Being which has in common with them no generic concept save that of thing in general (eines Dinges überhaupt)."[2] The "theoretical point of view" that analogy takes (which is not, however, theoretical knowledge in the strict sense) Kant further elaborates elsewhere. If, for instance, we should account for what we mean by an "act" of love on God's part, as contained in Scripture, we must resort to "the schematism of analogy, with which (as a means of explanation) we cannot dispense."[3] "Knowledge" from analogy, about which Kant speaks, smacks distinctly of the knowledge which, we saw previously, is accessible to the believer in God. Such knowledge is neither empirical knowledge, nor the vacuous speculative knowledge which Kant disowns. How, then, can it be knowledge at all?

Kant consciously employs such terms as "explanation" and "knowledge" in a two-edged sense. Likewise, his language about God has the same double valency. The concept of analogy Kant puts forth, while disclosing this double valency, nonetheless gives us little clue as to the precise meaning of terms used analogically. It is one thing to say we can talk about God's agency on analogy with human agency; it is quite another thing to show how we are correct in ascribing significance to analogical words or phrases. Analogy lets us think "two dissimilar things"; but, when all is said and done, is the analogical statement we make about God's nature meaningful according to any criteria other than the fact that such is the way one thinks or talks about God? Does the language of analogy authenticate itself, or must it be amenable to external criticism?

---

[1] "Just so we can indeed conceive of the causality of the original Being in respect of the things of the world, as natural purposes, according to the analogy of an understanding, as ground of the forms of certain products, which we call works of God..." CJ, p. 316. Schriften, V, 464-5.

[2] CJ, p. 316n. Schriften, V, 464n.

[3] RWL, p. 58n. Schriften, VI, 65n.

Frederick Ferre distinguishes two main types of analogical comparison: the analogy of attribution and the analogy of proportionality.

The *analogy* *of* *attribution*, according to Ferre, compares properties of two widely different things, predicating of the second term or concept the literal (or "univocal") meaning of the first in a non-literal fashion. Thus, to use Ferre's example, we call both a man and a resort "healthy." Only a man can be literally "healthy." The "healthiness" of a resort derives from this literal meaning.[1] Extending this example to the problem under study, we conclude that the analogous attribution of moral agency to God derives from the literal ascription of such agency to man. The question that occurs, if this be the case, is whether we can attribute moral agency to God in the first place. Ferre points out that "no analogy of attribution can be manufactured out of thin air."[2] There must be some agreement in meaning between the two different subjects "God" and "man," according to which we assign the single predicate "agent." Moreover, Ferre says such agreement exists if the second term of the analogy (or "analogue") can be said to *produce* the properties ascribed to the first term (or "analogate"). A resort is "healthy," because it produces health in whoever visits it. Likewise, we call God a moral agent, because he is said to produce moral actions in the world.

The above interpretation of analogy, especially in reference to Kant, however, merely begs the question. For attributing moral agency to God is a habit of Kant's language we are trying to justify. The analogy of attribution informs us nothing about why Kant, or anyone else, is permitted to attribute reality to God to begin with. Granted, Kant's use of attribution may possibly be explained from his demands that we must think a supreme moral agent who produces effects corresponding to the

---

[1] Frederick Ferre, *Language*, *Logic* *and* *God* (New York: Harper Torchbooks, 1961), p. 70.

[2] *Ibid*.

possible effects of our own moral agency. But "thinking" a
supreme moral agent is a far different matter from comparing the
relations between, and properties of, known agents as subjects
to whom the predicate "moral" might mutually apply. We know
something definite about the analogates "man" and "resort."
Hence we proceed, in virtue of our understanding of our own
language as to when it is appropriate to apply certain words to
certain relations or things, to add the predicate "healthy" to
both subjects. On the other hand, we do not know something as
definite about God as about a resort. We know there are moral
acts in the world, and we know there are (human) agents, but we
do not know offhand that there is something extra-human to whom
it would be appropriate to ascribe moral agency, even derivative-
ly. The analogates "man" and "resort" have a pre-determined
noetic value as objects in the knowable universe which the term
"God" lacks.

We do not know God in the same fashion as we know moral
agents. Moral agency is known directly whenever we ourselves
act. God is "known" only indirectly, qua belief or postulate.
Our knowledge of God is not empirical or object-knowledge, but
a "practical" knowledge that is only knowledge per se in a highly
qualified sense. Thus we do not attribute moral agency to God
as easily as we attribute "healthy" to a resort, because we do
not know anything about him that would warrant our doing so.
The analogy of attribution falls apart when the dissimilarity
between the analogates has to do, not only with their properties
as subjects, but with the very means of cognizaing these properties.[1] When talking about God, the analogy of attribution is

---

[1] In the final analysis, the "analogy of attribution" seems
to be little more than a sophisticated explanation of the use of
a particular variety of metaphor. A metaphor is a construction
that emphasizes a resemblance between two things, or relation between the meanings of two terms, which was not apparent before.
Thus we call a man with expressionless countenance "stoney faced."
Literally, the adjective "stoney" only applies to such things as
granite or feldspar. But there are certain characteristics of
an expressionless face that invite us to attribute this adjective to it, even though there is nothing literally "stoney"
about a face. The same is true if I say, "This beer hall is a

no longer an analogy, because there exists no real basis for making a comparison.

The analogy of propertionality furnishes a second prospective interpretation of Kant's aims. This type of analogy is Thomas Aquinas' -- the analogia entis or "analogy of being." The analogy of proportionality, or analogy of being, in contrast with the analogy of attribution, refuses a distinction between the "literal" and "derived" meanings of the separate analogates. The meaning of the common predicate in this analogy is "literal" for both analogates, albeit with two different significations that are "proportional" to each other be reason of their mutual relation to a third term. Thomas poses this definition of analogy more laconically than Ferre:

> Whenever a word is used analogically of many things, it is used of them because of some order or relation they have to some central thing. In order to explain an extended or analogical use of a word it is necessary to mention this central things.[1]

In other words, two things are analogous by propertion when they bear some of the generic characteristics of a third thing. We should remember here Wittgenstein's account of generic filiation as one of "family resemblance." A whale is analogous to a shark because both have streamlined bodies, live in the ocean, eat sea life, etc. Thus, for a long time it was proper (and still remains so if one does not depend on the taxonomy of a zoologist) to call both whales and sharks "fishes;" although the mammalian characteristics of a whale make it a "fish" in a different sense than a shark. By the same token, though it is stretching the point, we can say a man is analogous to a hyacinth, because both share the condition of "life." Aquinas claimed God is analogous to some degree with every animate and inanimate creature,

---

happy place." Literally, a beer hall is not happy, but it produces a feeling of happiness in me and others. Thus the adjective "happy" is short-hand for describing a state of affairs which produces mirth.

[2]St. Thomas Aquinas, Summa Theologica la, 13, 16. English translation by Blackfriars (New York: McGraw-Hill, 1963), vol. iii, p. 69.

because God and creatures, though they do not have anything else in common, at least share the state of existence or "being." The predicate "being" is the mediating term allowing us to think of God on analogy with anything in the world. The proportionality between God's properties and the properties of created entities varies considerably; but even the smallest amount of proportionality allows us to compare God with creatures.

The trouble with the analogy of proportionality, however, is that it works only in special instances. We can say a house cat that hunts mice is analogous to a lion, which also hunts its prey. By extention, we might call both animals "predatory," although the literal meaning of this term when applied to a house cat and to a lion has different significations. A tame kitten that consumes mostly canned cat food and homogenized milk is not predatory in the same sense as is a lion. By the same token, the Thomist, citing the "analogy of being" between man and God, claims he may call the latter "wise" or "good," which are also human characteristics, because of a basic proportionality between the two subjects. But the choice of the predicates "wise" or "good" to illustrate the analogy between man and God seems fairly arbitrary. Why would the predicates "green" or "feathery" not suffice just as well? Both illustrate the property of "being" as precisely as "wise" and "good."

Dorothy Emmett notes that "when Thomist theologians speak more descriptively of the attributes of God, their analogies are drawn in a selective way from relations which are in some way judged to be appropriate."[1] The advocate of the analogy of proportionality comes to a pretty pass trying to justify his reasons for selecting the appropriate relations. His only touchstone is the conventions of theological discourse. Ferre concedes as much. The "analogy of proportionality," he says, contains the rule that a certain term may enter discourse about God "in the manner (unimaginable to us) permitted by the funda-

---

[1] Dorothy Emmett, The Nature of Metaphysical Thinking (London: Macmillan and Company, 1946), p. 180.

mental axioms and entailment-rules governing the entire system of theistic talk about God."[1] But who sets the ground rules for theistic talk? Again, the analogy of proportionality merely calls attention to the patent fact that theologians customarily attribute certain predicates to a Supreme Being. These predicates are meaningful within the grammar of theology, but are they meaningful in the strong sense that Kant's account implies: that it is necessary a priori to speak of God in such a way? So far the examples cited have not presented a model of language about God that can be measured by any other yardstick than the fact that there exists a conventional syntax for God-talk.

The difficulties unravelled heretofore give some inkling that Kant's language about God may not really be the language of analogy at all. We have seen Kant does indeed claim to make use of analogy, but our analysis of what actually goes into analogical comparisons discloses that, when Kant talks about "thinking God by analogy," he really has in mind something quite different. For Kant, we only talk about God so far as moral reasoning compels us to assume his existence. This compulsion of reason accounts, in some measure, for why we have to talk about God instead of, as in the case of analogy, how we may in fact do so. Analogy, in Austin Farrer's approved definition, is simply "a relation between objects, capable of being classified as a species of likeness."[2] But analogies about God, apropos of this definition, simply take for granted that there is a relation of likeness between the divine and the human. The existence of such a relation is the first premise of all analogical argument.

Returning to Kant's argument, we cannot presume a likeness between the two available terms. We cannot even say this likeness is one of "being," since God's being or "existence" is not given without question. It is a "postulated" existence

---

[1] Ferre, op. cit., p. 77.

[2] Austin Farrer, Finite and Infinite (Glasgow: The University Press, 1943), p. 48.

that is different from the "existence" of empirical objects to which such a predicate properly or formally applies.

In analogies, the subjects compared each have an independent meaning separate from the meaning of the predicated added to them by way of analogy. "Man" and "resort," "whale" and "shark," as individual terms have a distinct significance before the predicate of analogy is added. But the term "God," for Kant, has no independent significance. Kant's argument sets about to show how analysis of the concept of human morality leads to a dilemma which can only be solved by introducing a correlative concept (God's existence as a moral agent); this second concept qualifies the meaning of the first, and vice-versa. The term "God" possesses meaning only as the correlative of man in his capacity as a moral agent. Even the appelation "He who is" does not have meaning in itself, since the predicate of "existence" acquires precise value exclusively within the syntax of moral terminology. But moral terms are the very terms which are supposed to be compared with the term "God."

In sum, the idea of God, for Kant, is unique, inasmuch as it is generated by the moral consciousness, yet refers to no cognizable object alongside that consciousness. Analogy, we have seen, cannot generate in purely ideal form any of the terms or items which it compares, but must locate both items within some pre-given field of signifiers. The idea of God cannot be so located. On the other hand, the idea of God which the moral consciousness creates does bear a certain analogy with familiar concepts of moral agency. The notion of the divine moral agent is _something_ _like_ the human moral agent, but the analogy in this case represents a deliberate anthropomorphism contrived in order to meet the needs of human reason. For example, I propose to my young son the idea of Santa Clause in order to clarify in an imaginative way why gifts for him appear under the tree every Christmas morning. It is permissible to say the idea of Santa Clause bears an analogy with other human beings - an analogy which encapsulates traits of human personality which my child readily comprehends and finds appealing, traits such as generosity, jucundity, etc. Yet I cannot say that I definitely <u>know</u> something about Santa Claus <u>via</u> this analogy. The idea of Santa Claus is generated intentionally with the aim of making coherent the child's experience; it is not itself an object of immediate experience. Similarly, the moral consciousness generates the idea of God to lay moorings for moral experience of the world, though God does not appear within the world. Thus we must select a grammatical form beside analogy to elucidate the language of God as moral agent.

2. The Language of Limitation

Analysis of the language of analogy, we saw, fails to illumine adequately Kant's use of the term "God" because of (1) the virtual unknowability of the subject God; (2) the fact that the term "God" has no independent meaning <u>comparable</u> with the meanings of other terms. This second point of failure, while crippling the claims of analogy, nevertheless forms the basis for a further possible understanding of what Kant is doing. Since "God" has meaning in terms other than those of the dialectic of morality, we may gather that the term performs the function of setting bounds for the development of the dialectic somehow. The dialectic may by synopsized as follows:

<u>Thesis</u>: Man finds it necessary, in order to give his moral labors an ultimate meaning, to strive to create a moral universe in which all reasonable beings do the right thing and are compensated for their virtue. Because the moral universe is necessary, it must at least be possible.

<u>Antithesis</u>: Due to man's basic finitude -- his impotence in the face of the universe and the presence of radical evil in his own person -- he lacks the power to create the moral universe his reason deems necessary. Thus the moral universe appears impossible.

<u>Synthesis</u>: The moral universe, which man deems necessary, becomes possible, if one postulates the existence of an omnicompetent power or agent reconciling the natural order to man's highest moral intentions.

If God is not postulated, the interest of reason in the creation of a moral universe eventuates in a paradox: what moral reason judges necessary must prove impossible. If God is postulated, on the other hand, necessity becomes a _real_ possibility, and we succeed in allaying the presumed conflict between the demands of moral reason and man's perception of his actual place in the universe. God, therefore, serves as a kind of "limiting" concept that restricts how far we can push the claim that a moral universe is necessary without stumbling into a paradox or antinomy. Without this limiting concept, we would have to conclude that man must realize the moral universe on his own. But the more man tries to realize it, the more difficulty he encounters. If he attempts to create the conditions for the moral universe in part, his obstacles will not be too great. If he wants to create these conditions in nearly all their entirety, he will run up against stubborn resistance both in his own will and the laws of nature. If he persists in attempting to realize the moral universe in its perfect form, he will have an insurmountable problem. If, in aiming for the highest good, he thinks, "I must make sure justice is done in every conceivable case," he will inevitably confront the contradiction that he cannot make justice a universal rule of human affairs. But if he assumes the existence of God, he will recognize the limits of his ability, and thus see how the demand of reason to promote the highest good is possible.

When we call "God" a limiting concept, we do not mean that in itself the concept marks out how far we can progress in the moral life. Experience of our own finitude and of the failures of the race throughout history suffice to call attention to these limits. Experience, indeed, gainsays the proposition that man shows himself competent to forge toward moral goodness. The "history of all times cries out too loudly against it."[1] By a "limiting concept," we mean one which designates a state of affairs that we know cannot be reached, merely approximated.

---

[1] RWL, p. 15. Schriften, VI, 20.

God is not the "limit" of morality in the sense that he represents everything man is finally capable of achieving. He is a limit in the mathematical sense of limit: a mode of perfection that one, by an indefinite series of steps, can draw close to, though never actually attain. On the other hand, this limit adds the idea of "completion" to the indefinite series. Apart from such a limit, the series would appear a never ending succession or regress and hence, paradoxically, as incomplete. Let us take as an example the familiar algebraic function $f(x) = 1/x$. If we gradually increase the value of "x," the value of "$f(x)$" grows smaller and smaller without attaining a definite quantity, no matter how miniscule, so that there is no possible value of "$f(x)$" less than such a quantity. Ideally, however, we can assign a definite and insurpassable value to the changing function "$f(x)$" in terms of an ever increasing value of "x"; that is, we can designate it as a limit. Thus $\lim 1/x = 0$. We can never say that the value of "$f(x)$" ever actually attains nullity, even if we enlarge the value of "x" so far as our numbering system allows. As "x" increases, however, the actual value of "$f(x)$" approaches closer and closer to the ideal value of 0, although it is always the case that $f(x)$ 0. If we lay out the decreasing values of $1/x$ as a series ($1/1$, $1/2$, $1/3$, $1/4$, $1/5$....etc.), we see that the value "0" constitutes the ideal "end" of the series; in a sense, it completes the series.

Likewise, God's will signals the ideal limit of man's will, inasmuch as it "completes" in conceptu the cumulative improvement of man's capacity to create a moral universe which is never actually, but always potentially perfect. The possible perfection of man's moral capacity depends on two ineradicable conditions: a holy will and the consistent apportionment of happiness to virtue.

The first or "supreme" condition Kant says can be obtained through the postulate of immortality. The accomplishment of the moral universe or "highest good" is the necessary object of a will determinable by the moral law," and "in such a will... the complete fitness (völlige Angemessenheit) of intentions to

the moral law is the supreme condition of the highest good."[1]
But, for a finite being, such a "fitness" can come about only
through "endless progress" (Unendliche gehende Progressus).[2]
This "infinite progress is possible...only under the presupposition of an infinitely enduring existence (fortdauernden Existenz) and personality of the same rational being; this is called
immortality (Unsterblichkeit) of the soul."[3] Aside from the
concept of infinite progress, the "hoped-for complete attainment
(verhofften völligen Erwerb) of holiness of will," required by
both ideas of the moral law and that of the highest good,
appears only "an unattainable destination" (unerreichbaren Bestimmung).[4] Still, infinite progress alone does not ensure that
man will reach the condition of moral perfection. The notion of
a ceaseless advance from bad to good to better implies that
"complete fitness" or holiness transcends the dynamics of human
willing as such. Holiness "is never reached," as we have seen,
"by any creature."[5] Every finite stage on the road to perfection that is infinitely long composes merely an increment of
the full distance to be traversed. The final goal of the
pilgrim's journey forever beckons him onward as a mirage on
the horizon. This situation compares with what Bernard Bolzano
has levelled a "paradox of the infinite." For the concept of
the "infinite" itself signifies a perpetual "negation" of what
is finitely described or attained.[6]

The idea of holiness, therefore, means, on the one hand,
the "limit" of man's will in the negative sense of that which,

---

[1] CP_rR, p. 126. Schriften, V, 122.

[2] CP_rR, pp. 126-7. Ibid.

[3] CP_rR, p. 127. Ibid.

[4] Ibid. Schriften, V, 122-3.

[5] Cf. above, p. 111, n. 4.

[6] Cf. Bernard Bolzano, Paradoxes of the Infinite, trans. Fr. Prihonsky (New Haven: Yale University Press, 1950), p. 75ff.

after unending struggle, he can approximate but never reach. On the other hand, the limit means something more than the merely unattainable. It is in the face of the paradox of infinity that Kant introduces the idea of a divine will which "completes" the infinite quest for holiness. "The Infinite Being," Kant says, "sees in his series, which is for us without end, a whole (<u>Ganze</u>) conformable to the moral law; holiness, which His law inexorably commands in order to be true to His justice in the share He assigns to each in the highest good, is to be found in a single intellectual intuition (<u>Anschauung</u>) of the existence of rational beings."[1]

We thus see how, for Kant, the concept of God as holy will functions as the perfect correlate to man's imperfect will, how, in fact, his will represents the "limit" of finite willing as such. Man "cannot hope here or at any foreseeable point of his future existence to be fully adequate to God's will";[2] yet this perfect will "sees" or attributes to the infinite progress of the human will a completed totality or "whole" that is virtually "holy."[3] The concept of God's will is akin to the value of "0" as the limiting term of the function $f(x) = 1/x$. It completes an infinite series that otherwise would turn out incomplete.

The same holds true with regard to Kant's understanding of God as sponsor of the "perfect" highest good. Kant argues that reason requires happiness to be the reward of our moral activity.

---

[1] CP_rR, p. 127. <u>Schriften</u>, V, 123.

[2] CP_rR, p. 128. <u>Schriften</u>, V, 123-4.

[3] "According to our mode of estimation...conduct itself, as a continual and endless advance from a deficient to a better good, ever remains defective. We must consequently regard the good as it appears in us, that is, in the guise of <u>an act</u> (<u>Handlung</u>), as being always inadequate to a holy law. But we may think of this endless progress of our goodness towards conformity to the law, even if this progress is conceived in terms of actual deeds, or life-conduct, as being judged by Him who knows the heart...as a completed whole (<u>vollendetes Ganze</u>)." <u>RWL</u>, pp. 60-1. <u>Schriften</u>, VI, 67.

Deserved happiness is the second condition of the highest good. But man's innate impotence precludes rewards consistent with good acts. Through political and social legislation, for example, groups of men may create a system of distribution of just rewards, but even in such a system there will arise exceptions and shortcomings. Besides the distortion of justice within a community, men will always have to content with the blind calamities of nature. The effectiveness of men's will, individual as well as social, in creating the highest good as perfect justice will always remain incomplete. As a result, "we can hope for the highest good (to strive for which is our duty under the moral laws) only from a morally perfect (holy and beneficent) and omnipotent will" that determines every man's just deserts.[1] The adjective "beneficent" and "omnipotent" betoken the limits of man's unending labors to achieve justice in the universe. A "beneficent" being, or one who dispenses happiness, supplies the "completion" of man's flawed ability to attain happiness. An "omnipotent" being possesses "all" or complete powers to carry through his intentions, while man only enjoys this power partially.

We find a similar interpretation of God-language as the language of limitation in Ian Ramsey. Generally speaking, the notion of God as a perfect being unites or "completes" "diverse strands of language" that specify different grades of "goodness," "knowledge," etc. The notion of God's perfection thus functions like a "limit word in mathematics." It is a "word presiding over and unifying the languages of empirical imperfections."[2] The word God is related to other terms like the relation of a circle to a polygon with numerous sides. No polygon, even if we add to the number of its sides indefinitely, can ever be a circle;[3] yet the shape of a polygon, as the number of its sides

---

[1] CP_rR, p. 134. Schriften, V, 130.

[2] Ian Ramsey, Religious Language (New York: The Macmillan Company, 1957), p. 57.

[3] Ibid., p. 79f.

tends toward infinity, comes to approximate a circle. A circle may be "called" an infinitely-sided polygon, though a circle differs qualitatively from a polygonal figure. Similarly, the language we use about God also denotes something qualitatively distinct from any of the countless proximate "perfections" discernible in man. God's goodness is always different from the goodness of even the most saintly man we might conceive. His attributes radically transcend all human superlatives; yet the terms we employ to paraphrase God's superlatives have meaning as the "completing" term of the gradation of human superlatives.

In one sense, our examination of the language of limitation reveals how Kant is licensed to talk about God in the way he does. It has often been noted, perhaps _ad nauseam_, that the critical philosophy itself consists of a philosophy of limitation. The concept of God as supreme moral agent defines the limits of man's moral agency both positively and negatively: 1) _positively_ insofar as it provides a completeness or unity to man's moral experience; 2) _negatively_ insofar as it shows how far moral intentions can be realized. On the other hand, the language of limitation on the whole says essentially that man _lacks_. In that respect, the language of limitation only explains in part the usage of the term "God" in Kant's writings. Why, for instance, is God seen solely as the limit of our moral powers? He could just as well be the limit of our ability to cook a perfect stew or to raise prize-winning dahlias. The language of limitation fails to do justice to Kant's critical pre-occupation with the moral element in human experience. For that reason, we must still designate a type of language that accounts for this preoccupation. This type of language is what we shall call the language of intention.

3. The Language of Intention

The language of intention translates talk about God into talk about the fulfillment of human purposes. It cannot be said, of course, that Kant's God is simply man turned inside out. That would oversimplify the meaning of God-language in

the critical philosophy. The curious fact of the grammar of
God in Kant, however, is that the predicates of divinity invariably collate with the terms used to designate the final end
of human projects. The clue to this interpretation of Kant's
God-language lies in his assimilation of religious to ethical
categories. The a priori certainty of moral obligation stands
as the inexpungible fact of reason in the conscience of any man.
The meaning of the concept God hangs on the meaning of man's
moral predicament as a whole. Were man not in this predicament,
the notion of God would lose significance for him. The one true
religion, Kant reiterates again and again, is moral religion.
The value of the term "God" gets expressed in terms of moral
intention. Previously we documented some of the words and
phrases Kant banks on to depict God as moral agent. We shall
now appraise the wider import of these constructions.

Religion -- that is, belief in God -- for Kant, "is the
recognition of all duties as divine commands, not as sanctions,
i. e, arbitrary and contingent ordinances of a foreign will,
but as essential laws of any free will as such."[1] The salient
phrase here is "foreign (fremden) will." The divine will is
not foreign or alien to man's own will. God's will is "the
final end (of creation) which...can and ought to be man's final
end."[2] The divine intention embodies, in a sense, the perfection of man's moral intention. "Mankind (rational earthly
existence in general) in its complete moral perfection is that
which alone can render a world the object of a divine decree and
the end of creation."[3] The divine decree is a concept deriving
exclusively from the concept of man's highest moral purpose
manifested a priori through his reason. "Perfection," in fact,

---

[1] CP_rR, p. 134. Schriften, V. 129. Cf. "the heart's disposition to fulfill all human duties as divine commands..." RWL,
p. 79. Schriften, VI, 84.

[2] Cf. above, p. 105, n. 2.

[3] RWL, p. 54. Schriften, VI, 60.

133

is pre-eminently a moral perfection from which we adduce the idea of divine perfection. Any attempt to reverse this inference and begin with some prior idea of divine perfection contravenes the sovereignty of morality itself.[1] The notion of a divine will, therefore, has hardly any meaning if it appears as a "foreign" will instead of a *possibility* (in a certain sense) of man's own will. The continuity between God's will and man's intention to conform to that will, the latter of which is an *a priori* construct of his own reason, emerges into clear focus in Kant's exposition in the *Religion* of the dogma of the Incarnation.

The idea of Christ, the God-man, Kant says, is nothing more than the "personified (*personificiert*) idea of the good principle" which is "completely real in its own right, for it resides in our morally-legislative reason."[2] The ideal of the God-man is an "archetype" of our purest moral intention. It represents an ultimate possibility of man's will. "We *ought* to conform to it; consequently we must *be able* to do so."[3] The archetype finds "no empirical example," such as the personality of the histor-

---

[1] The concept of rational moral perfection "is better than the theological concept which derives morality from a divine and supremely perfect will; not merely because we cannot intuit God's perfection and can only derive it from concepts, among which that of morality is the most eminent; but because, if we do not do this (and to do so would be to give a crudely circular explanation), the concept of God's will still remaining to us...would inevitably form the basis for a moral system which would be in direct opposition to morality." *GMM*, p. 110-11. *Schriften*, IV, 443. Also, "The supreme perfection in substance, i.e., God (hence external), when regarded practically, is the sufficiency of this Being to all ends in general. Only if ends are already given can the concept of perfection in relation to them (either internal perfection in ourselves or external perfection of God) be the determining ground of the will. An end, however, as an object which precedes and contains the ground of determination of the will by a practical rule...is, if taken as a determining ground of the will, only empirical..." CP_rR, p. 42. *Schriften*, V, 41.

[2] *RWL*, p. 55. *Schriften*, VI, 62.

[3] *Ibid*.

ical Jesus. It is "already present in our reason."[1] It is "sought in ourselves (even though we are but natural men),"[2] and thus we find it "our universal duty as men to <u>elevate</u> ourselves to this ideal of moral perfection, that is, to this archetype of the moral disposition in all its purity -- and for this idea itself, which reason presents for our zealous emulation (Nachstrebung), and give us power."[3]

Kant seems to have previewed Hegel's insight that the Incarnation did not involve the supernatural presence of the divine in one particular historical figure, but was simply the initial moment for the possible realization on a universal scale of the Godhead immanent within all men. The ideal of a God become man, for Kant, becomes evident on inspection of one's own "power" as a moral agent. It is the archetype of which our finite rational agency is the <u>ectype</u>. For "an appropriation of this righteousness for the sake of our own must be possible when our own disposition is made at one with that of the archetype."[4] Granted, our own defective wills pose "the greatest difficulties" which "stand in the way of our rendering this act of appropriation comprehensible."[5] Yet these difficulties do not cleave the significance of the idea of perfection in the archetype from the significance of our own moral purposing. The archetype bespeaks what we as rational agents "have in mind," in a word, what we ultimately intend. The theological doctrine of the God-man expresses the intimate correlation between the divine and human. The concept of God is not intelligible as a "thing" apart from man, only as an "idea" embodying the intentions of practical reason. That Kant's language about God symbolizes the intentions of man exhibits itself most pointedly when we study his unpublished drafts, jottings, and

---

[1] <u>RWL</u>, p. 56. <u>Schriften</u>, VI, 63.

[2] <u>RWL</u>, p. 57. <u>Schriften</u>, VI, 63.

[3] <u>RWL</u>, p. 54. <u>Schriften</u>, VI, 61.

[4] <u>RWL</u>, p. 60. <u>Schriften</u>, VI, 67.

[5] <u>Ibid</u>.

135

notes collected under the title of Opus Postumum.

Kant's Opus Postumum directs itself explicitly, as Erich Adickes observes, not only to the question "Is there a God" but "What is God."[1] This latter question is answered in the first and seventh Convolut of the Opus Postumum. "The concept of such a being [as God]," Kant says, "is not that of a substance (Substanz) -- that is, of a thing existing independently of my thought -- but of an idea (a self-creation), a thing of thought (Gedankending), an ens rationis..."[2] Similarly, "God must not be represented as a substance external to me (ausser mir), but as the highest moral principle within me (in mir)."[3] He "is not a substance, but the personified idea of justice and benevolence (Wohlwollen)..."[4] "God is not a thing existing outside of me, but my own thought (mein eigener Gedanke)."[5]

Kant's denial that God is a "substance" merely reinforces his implication in the earlier critical writings that God is any sort of "thing-in-itself" (Ding an sich).[6] Since God surpasses any knowledge we might have about him as a thing subsisting in his own right, he can only "exist" in the sense that we possess an idea of him as existing. In that respect, He is a "self-creation" (Selbstgeschöpf) of our own thought, since our reasoning about the moral life produces him in order to impart reality to our moral intentions. For that reason Kant warns, "it is absurd (ungereimt) to ask whether there is a God."[7]

---

[1] Erich Adickes, Kants Opus Postumum (Berlin: Reuther und Richard, 1920), p. 776.

[2] OP: Schriften, XXI, 27.

[3] OP: Schriften, XXI, 144.

[4] OP: Schriften, XXII, 108.

[5] OP: Schriften, XXI, 153.

[6] "A substance is the thing-in-itself, the subsistent (Selbständig)..." OP: Schriften, XXII, 121.

[7] OP: Schriften, XXI, 153.

Such a question implies a facticity about God as an object independent of one's conception. The "existence" of God is contained exclusively within thought. In keeping with the spirit of his criticisms of the ontological argument, Kant would maintain that we cannot proceed from the _idea_ of an _ens realissimum_ to the "most real thing" itself. Since we can have no experience of the _ens realissimum_, the "reality" of God must remain on the ideal level.

In other places in the Opus Postumum, moreover, Kant seems to indicate that the very consciousness of moral obligation through the categorical imperative certifies God's reality to us. "The categorical imperative represents all human duties as divine commands, not as though certain injunctions (_Befehle_) had been issued to men in history, but as though reason had been subjected to them by the highest power of the categorical imperative..."[1] "For the moral law-giving reason pronounces through the categorical imperative duties which are at the same time like a substance in which the laws of nature are fulfilled. "The categorical imperative realizes the concept of God, though only in a practical respect and not in regard to objects of nature."[3] _Prima facie_ these passages, because their language departs notably from that found in the main critical treatises, lend themselves handily to the interpretation that Kant in the Opus Postumum has shifted his earlier position. According to this interpretation, the notion of God as an "objective reality" is here reduced to a merely "subjective idea." Such an interpretation, indeed, found a champion in Adickes and it was long held that Kant's posthumously published papers evidenced a major turning in his thought. However, as we have shown, even in the critical writings Kant maintains that God's "objectivity" exists only from the practical point of view and that, as an

---

[1] OP: _Schriften_, XXII, 51-2.

[2] OP: _Schriften_, XXII, 122.

[3] OP: _Schriften_, XXI, 55.

object of belief and not of knowledge, he is only "subectively" certain. Thus no shift has actually occurred.

George Schrader, stressing basically the same point in his effort to refute Adickes' claims concerning the uniqueness of the Opus Postumum, remarks that the wording of these passages merely uncovers Kant's own personal religious convictions which elsewhere are stated more discursively.[1] Kant's hint that the divine existence is revealed straightaway in the categorical imperative, is simply shorthand for the notion that the idea of God cannot be divorced from the fact of moral obligation. What remains crucial in the Opus Postumum is Kant's attempt to adjust the theological doctrine of divine law to the a priori law of morality in every human conscience. Indeed, by virtue of his insistence that we need not assume God at all to justify moral duties, Kant alchemizes the theocentric or Christian view of morality into a rationally self-consistent morality for which God is a secondary consideration. God enters into the picture as a projection of the idea of a will, perfect in disposition and power to produce natural effects, which human wills never seem able to match. In C. J. Webb's words, the revelation of God in the moral law

> ...was more truly revealed as personal than when imaginatively represented as external to our own inner and essential life; for he is now our own personality, confronting us as the ideal realized by us in so far as we exhibit the good disposition which alone constitutes any moral worth whereunto we can pretend.[2]

God can only be an idea, for Kant, because he represents the intention of the moral agent. To say that he "necessarily exists" apprises us nothing about the character of himself as an object but, like all modal terms such as necessity, possibility, and actuality, it indicates something about the attitude

---

[1] Cf. George Schrader, "Kant's presumed Repudiation of the Moral Arguments in the Opus Postumum: An Examination of Adickes' Interpretation," Philosophy 31 (1951): 235ff.

[2] C. J. Webb, Kant's Philosophy of Religion (Oxford: The Clarendon Press, 1926), pp. 199-200.

of the mind of the agent.¹ This attitude is one of intention -- commitment to achieve an ideal end. The necessity of God reflec[ts] the felt necessity of seeking to make real the moral "ought." Were morality unnecessary, the moral universe would not be necessary either, whereupon God would be superfluous.² Man, Kant seems to say, creates God in his own moral image -- the image of what he thinks he ought to do or be. Whether he can really _act_ like God is another question, however,

That the language of God in Kant is the language of intentio[n]

---

¹Cf. F. E. England, Kant's Conception of God (London: Georg[e] Allen & Unwin, 1926), p. 194.

²A comparison should be made here between ontological necess[]ity and moral necessity in light of Kant's argument for belief in God. It may be argued that Kant, while rejecting the claims of the traditional form of the ontological argument, is actually presenting a moral version of it. The traditional ontological argument usually is something like the following:
     A. I have an idea of God as a supremely perfect being.
     B. Something which does not exist is not perfect.
     C. Therefore, God exists.

Kant's argument may be schematized as follows:
     A. Because of the problem of the highest good, I construct in my mind the idea of a supremely perfect moral being.
     B. To be morally perfect, that is, to be able to effect the moral universe which moral perfection demands, such a being must exist (Otherwise, the moral universe becomes a chimera).
     C. Therefore, God must exist.

The similarity, however, pertains only to the forms of the two arguments and not their substance. The ontological argument co[n]cludes that God exists _in fact_. It contends that "existence," which is an _a posteriori_ concept, can be deduced analytically from the _a priori_ idea of God. Kant himself condemned this inference from the _a priori_ to the _a posteriori_ in his treatment of the ontological argument. Thus, consistent with his strictures in the first Critique, Kant does not insist that the predicate "existence" as it occurs in the moral argument has an _a posteriori_ status. God "exists" for the man of moral faith only in thought, i.e., as a necessary construct of reason. Thus, as we showed earlier, Kant does not argue for God's existence _per se_, but for belief in his existence. In this respect, moral necessity does not entail ontological necessity.

is illustrated by a second cluster of concepts describing the divine/human relationship which are located in the Opus Postumum. The axial concept in this set is that of man as a copula or "middle term" between God and world. By "world" in this context Kant means "The totality (Inbegriff) of all existence that is in space and time,"[1] the "entirety (Ganze) of sense-objects within as well as without us."[2] Set over against this world of sense-objects is God, and between God and world exists man. These three terms -- God, man and world -- form a triadic unity. "The all of being (universum) is God and the world" which "are both not objects of possible experiences but ideas."[3] These ideas spring from the mind of man who is the "unifying subject" which knits them together.[4] The "three principles of unity" are "God, the world, and the 'I'" or "the thinking being in the world which binds (verknüpft) them together."[5] "The medius terminus (copula) ...is here the judging subject (the thinking being of the world, man in the world.)"[6] "Man belongs to the world and is a part of it";[7] he is an "occupant of the world" (Weltinhaber)[8] or "world inhabitant" (Weltbewohner),[9] insofar as he is a sensible being; while at the same time he transcends the world with his powers of reason.[10] Through reason he is

---

[1] OP: Schriften, XXI, 36.

[2] OP: Schriften, XXI, 14, also 39.

[3] OP: Schriften, XXI, 43.

[4] OP: Schriften, XXI, 23.

[5] OP: Schriften, XXI, 36.

[6] OP: Schriften, XXI, 27, 34, 38.

[7] OP: Schriften, XXI, 53.

[8] OP: Schriften, XXI, 38.

[9] OP: Schriften, XXI, 27, 31, 36.

[10] "Man is, of course, a being of the world (Weltwesen) and an object of sense, but he is also free and thus not subordinate to nature." OP: Schriften, XXI, 57.

able to unite the concept of the world in which he lives with the concept of God. "God and the world are both united in a system by the indwelling (<u>einwohnende</u>) thought-principle of man as mind in the world."[1] God and the world join in "man as world-citizen (<u>cosmopolita</u>), as person, as moral being..."[2] In that sense "God, though not an inhabitant of the world, is however an occupant (Inhaber) also."[3] He is an "occupant," for he exists in the mind of man which creates the totality of intelligible objects, including the idea of the divine.

Kant's convoluted and far from limpid prose in the above-quoted fragments star this point: that both the world, as a totality of appearances, and God, seen as the moral governor of the same world, are concepts that depend on the judgement of the rational moral subject. Without the purposes of man's practical reason, the idea of a universe under the rule of a supreme will would lose its ballast. Man plays the starring role in Kant's drama; God is only a supporting actor. God and man, however, constitute discrete circles of meaning with a common center. The two concepts are intimately related to each other, for both God and man are moral persons with dominion over the world.[4] But God, for Kant, is a person, precisely because he stands for the perfection of human personality demanded in the idea of a morally flawless will. "This idea of God," Georg Antonoupolos notes, "which stands opposite to pantheism and to the deistic concept of an author of the world, guarantees and demands the moral vocation and spontaneity of man."[5] Kant's talk about God makes sense primarily as an expression of this vocation. The view put forth in the <u>Opus Postumum</u> underscores the fact that the language of God as agent is a language of moral intention. It does not, however, mark any broad departure

---

[1] <u>OP</u>: <u>Schriften</u>, XXI, 34.

[2] <u>OP</u>: <u>Schriften</u>, XXI, 31.

[3] <u>OP</u>: <u>Schriften</u>, XXI, 30.

[4] Löwith, Karl, <u>Gott, Mensch und Welt in der Metaphysik von Descartes bis zur Nietzsche</u> (Göttingen: Vandenhöck und Ruprecht 1967), p. 88.

[5] Georg Antonoupolos, <u>Der Mensch als Bürger zweier Welten</u> (Bonn: Bouvier, 1958), p. 48.

from the aim of Kant's talk about God in other contexts. Thus we are inclined to disagree with Antonoupolos that in the <u>Opus Postumum</u> "the Kantian metaphysic reaches its zenith."[1] Kant's practical philosophy is earmarked by its strict attention to the question of how man can realize himself as a moral agent in a universe that resists his intentions. All inquiries into God's existence are appurtenances to this key question.

---

[1] <u>Ibid</u>.

CHAPTER III. Autonomy and Theonomy

A. The Autonomy of the Moral Agent

1. Self-legislation

In the foregoing chapter we surveyed the concept of God appearing in Kant's writings and came to the realization that such a concept is tightly interlocked with the concept of moral purposiveness in man. From Kant's own words we inferred that the "idea" of God does not denote any sort of object or "thing" external to the idea, but is fundamentally a construct of the mind that fulfills a need of moral reason. God's existence or "objective" reality, therefore, is a "practical" reality of a different order of reality than that of objects in the world to which our senses give us access. The idea of God secures the reality of moral intentions, because the man of faith believes that God has the power to actualize completely these intentions. In that sense, God is equivalent to the intention in its objective satisfaction. Moral intentions exhibit the desire of practical reason to make the moral law immanent in human experience. Thus we must take more careful stock of what is involved in moral intentionality once more in order to refine our interpretation of the term "God" in Kant's thought more exactly than we have managed heretofore.

For Kant, a moral intention is descried by the fact that, as a project of man's action, it is directed toward the fulfillment of the moral law. The moral law is fulfilled as a law of nature so far as it is an _objectification_ of an intention in a moral act. Man does not passively "discover" laws already operative in nature, such as one must come across a law of physics by observation and experiment. Nor is the moral law revealed from on high in the way Moses is said to have received the Decalogue from God. The moral law subsists primordially as a datum of man's reason. In this respect the moral law does not

have its source in a realm of reality "other" than the mind of
man. Man gives to himself this law; he legislates it for himself. The moral law, then, is exclusively man's own law. So
far as morals are concerned, man himself is the primary law-
giving or nomothetic being. That the moral law is "self-legislated" renders it a law of auto-nomy. The notion of autonomy
thus affords the key to understanding how Kant can subordinate
the moral intentionality of God to that of humanity. God's
purpose or law can never be a norm for man unless it is, first
and foremost, man's purpose or law.

In the Groundwork Kant reckons "autonomy of the will" as
"the property the will has of being a law to itself (ihm selbst)
(independently of every property belonging to objects of
volition."[1] Antithetical to autonomy is what Kant calls
"heteronomy" (Heteronomie). Heteronomy occurs if "the will
seeks the law that is to determine it anywhere else than in the
fitness of its maxims for its own making of universal law -- if
therefore in going beyond itself it seeks this law in the
character of any of its objects."[2] An autonomous will becomes
a "law to itself," because it establishes a law of action in a
choice affected by no power other than the conviction of one's
own reason, according to the idea of doing what is right in
itself, or what Kant calls "duty for duty's sake." A heteronomous will, on the other hand, seeks a law of action in "objects,
in external ends to be attained rather than in the bare pres-
criptions of reason. The formula of heteronomy says, "'I ought
to do something because I will something else.'" The "basis"
for this "something else"

> must be a further law in me as a subject whereby
> I necessarily will this 'something else' --
> which law in turn requires an imperative to impose
> limits on this maxim. The impulsion supposed to
> be exercised on the will of the subject, in accord-
> ance with his natural constitution, by the idea
> of a result to be attained by his own powers be-

---

[1] GMM, p. 100. Schriften, IV, 440.

[2] Ibid. Schriften, IV, 441.

> longs to the nature of the subject -- whether
> to his sensibility (his inclinations and taste)
> or to his understanding and reason, whose
> operations on an object is accompanies by sat-
> isfaction in virtue of the special equipment of
> their nature...[1]

The "objects" of a heteronomous will do not reside in the reason of the subject or agent, but in a world external or "alien" to him. The world alien or "objective"[2] to the reasoning subject, as we have seen, Kant calls "nature."[3] "This law, as a law of nature...is always merely heteronomy of the will," for "the will does not give itself the law, but an alient impulsion (<u>fremder</u> <u>Antrieb</u>) does so through the medium of the subject's own nature as tuned to its reception."[4] This "alien impulsion" emanates from objects in the natural world which man desires in order to satisfy the inclinations of his animal nature. The law of a heteronomous will, therefore, conforms to the mechanical laws of stimulus-response affecting any living organism. A man's pattern of behavior is determined by the properties of the object desired instead of the imperative to act in a clear-cut manner regardless of whatever concrete satisfactions might be received. Let us take the example of a man with a craving for caviar. This craving may drive him to do virtually anything to appease his taste for the delicacy. He will "steal, beg, and borrow," as the saying goes, to keep himself supplied with caviar. By Kant's reckoning, the will of

---

[1] <u>GMM</u>, pp. 111-2. <u>Schriften</u>, IV, 444.

[2] "<u>ob-ject</u>-ive" as in the Latin etymology of the term: that which is "<u>thrown</u> <u>over</u> <u>against</u>" the subject. Cf. the German <u>Gegen-stand</u>, "standing over against."

[3] "...consequently, it is nature which would make the law [of heteronomy]." <u>GMM</u>, p. 112. <u>Schriften</u>, IV, 444.

[4] <u>Ibid</u>. Cf. <u>GMM</u>, p. 114. <u>Schriften</u>, IV, 446. Also, heteronomy is "natural necessity" which is "the property of being determined to activity by the influence of alien causes." Moreover, "all laws determined by reference to an object gives us heteronomy, which can be found only in laws of nature and can apply only to the world of sense." <u>GMM</u>, pp. 126-7. <u>Schriften</u>, IV, 458.

a man with such a craving is heteronomous, as it becomes subservient to circumstances outside its own power of pure rational choice. The chemical properties of cavier which make it pleasing to the palate are the actual determinants of the man's behavior. Without the acquisition of caviar which is an object external to the will, the will cannot rest content. The nomos of the heteronomous will depends on the presence of an "other" (hetero-); this nomos is the law of the object's effects on organisms, not a law of action intrinsic to the reasoning subject. The nomos of the will of the above mentioned man resides solely in the toothsome dualities of caviar. The heteronomous will, therefore, is wedded to attaining private gratifications in particular types of situations and resists the universal applicability which the law of practical reason contains. In that regard, the term "law of heteronomy" is something of a misnomer. For, as we have seen, a "law" generally represents a rule of action with universal validity. But if an act is heteronomous, the rule governing the will only pertains to subjective considerations.

There is a certain irony in the language Kant relies to discriminate autonomy from heteronomy. An autonomous will, Kant says, becomes a "law to itself"; yet this does not mean a private law of gratification binding only on the legislator.[1] Kant shrinks from the extreme voluntarism and individualism implicit in, for example, Nietzsche's conception of autonomous man -- the Übermensch. For a will to be a "law to itself" means it must legislate universally. Only a law properly "one's own" can be generalized as a maxim appropriate for the will of another and vice-versa. If such a law were not one's own as a product of self-legislation, it could only have universal

---

[1] "The autonomy of the will is the sole principle of all moral laws...The sole principle of morality consists in independence from all material of the law (i.e., a desired object) and in the accompanying determination of choice by the mere form of giving universal law which a maxim must be capable of having CP$_r$R, p. 33. Schriften, V, 33.

validity (if it were entitled to such validity at all) accidentally and without the force of necessity guaranteed by reason. A self-legislated law, however, is conceived to be a priori necessary for all rational beings in the mind of the agent; and thus without qualification it obliges universally, even though in actual fact (i.e., in the domain of nature) such universality may be missing.

This is essentially the irony of self-legislation: that man "is subject only to laws which are made by himself and yet are universal."[1] In addition, the irony lies in the fact that "he is bound only to act in conformity with a will, which is his own but has as nature's purpose for it the function of making universal law."[2] The law of nature does not determine the will, but the will as practical reason determines what should be the law of nature. Practical reason gives man in his autonomy power over nature. Rational values do not pre-exist in the natural order, but autonomous man imposes these values on nature as a whole. Because man, the self-legislator, serves as the source of all value, we may consider him the highest value among other values. For "the law-making which determines all value must for this reason have a dignity -- that is, an unconditioned and imcomparable worth -- for the appreciation of which, as necessarily given by a rational being, the word 'reverence' is the only becoming expression. Autonomy is therefore the ground of the dignity of human nature and of every rational nature."[3] In his autonomy man has "dignity" -- the right to be deemed by his fellows an absolute value within the total scheme of values. Thus we must advert to an additional group of concepts which Kant uses to explicate his view of rational autonomy. These are the concepts of man as "end-in-himself" or "person."

---

[1] GMM, p. 100. Schriften, IV, 432.

[2] Ibid.

[3] GMM, p. 103. Schriften, IV, 436.

2. Man as an End-in-Himself

The autonomy of man, as we have seen, grants to a law of human action the character of universality. That is because the reasoning subject alone (the self-legislator) can determine such a character. But we must explore further why only the reasoning subject can do so. A possible answer to this question is entailed in Kant's dictum that the reasoning subject, or moral agent, constitutes the lone power in the world capable of projecting purposes (ends). These purposes are constructed to advance the inner destiny or vocation (Bestimmung) of humanity. Moreover, if man's purposes serve to promote his inner destiny, we may conclude that the overall "purpose" to which these general purposes are directed is man himself. Consequently, the peculiarity of man consists in the fact that he is a purpose or end "in-himself" (Zweck an sich) without reference to further purposes. Kant states this principle apodictically: "Rational nature exists as an end in itself."[1] Kant adds, "This is the way in which a man necessarily conceives his own existence."[2] Every man conceives his own nature as such, because he is aware of himself as both subject and object of the purposive activity in which he is constantly engaged.

Rational agents endeavor to maintain themselves qua rational agents. Similarly, an autonomous being labors to preserve its native autonomy. On the other hand, rational autonomy cannot be preserved, if a man preoccupies himself with upholding his own autonomy at the expense of the autonomy of other agents like himself. "Ends that a rational being adopts arbitrarily as effects of his action (material ends) are in every case only relative; for it is solely their relation to special characteristics in the subject's power of appetite which gives them their value. Hence, Kant demurs, "this value can provide no

---

[1] GMM, p. 96. Schriften, IV, 429.

[2] Ibid.

[3] GMM, p. 95. Schriften, IV, 427.

universal principles, no principles valid and necessary for all rational beings and for every volition"[1] An end must have validity for all other rational beings; for without this validity, the principle of rational autonomy would be compromised. We have already seen how Kant's application of the rule of non-contradiction bars this compromise.[2] If in deeming myself, as a rational agent, an absolute value or end-in-itself, I look upon other rational agents merely as means for self-aggrandizement, I contradict the very principle of the end-in-itself, let alone the notion of what it means to reason correctly. Reason demands objective or law-like consistency in its maxims of conduct. But the supposition that I am end-in-itself only for myself breaches this consistency. If I am an end only for myself, then John, Paul, or Mary cannot be ends in themselves. At the same time, John, Paul or Mary may selfishly consider me nothing more than an instrument for their ends. They view me as much a means to their self-aggrandizement as I judge them. The concept of the end-in-itself, therefore, if it is not rationally inconsistent with itself, must apply to all beings endowed with reason.[3] "Humanity," therefore, and not just the isolated agent, must be conceived as an end-in-itself.[4]

Kant emphasizes that rational beings alone possess the ability to conceive their maxims as self-consistent rules of action; and thus to them alone does the notion of the end-in-itself specifically belong.

---

[1] GMM, p. 95. Schriften, IV, 427.

[2] Cf. above, pp. 26f.

[3] Kant gives the example of a man who makes a false promise to another. This man, Kant says, "will see at once that he is intending to make use of another man merely as a means (Mittel) he does not share." GMM, p. 97. Schriften, IV, 429. Italics mine.

[4] Thus, the second formulation of the categorical imperative: "Act in such a way that you always treat humanity, whether in your own person or in the person of any other, never simply as a means but always at the same time an end." GMM, p. 96. Ibid.

> Beings whose existence depends, not on our
> will, but on nature...if they are non-rational
> beings, [they have] only a relative value as
> means and are consequently called things.
> Rational beings, on the other hand, are called
> persons because their nature already marks
> them out as ends in themselves -- that is,
> as something which ought not to be used
> merely as means -- and consequently imposes
> ...a limit (einschränkt) on all arbitrary
> treatment of them...[1]

The demands of one autonomy are always limited by the demands of another autonomy. Like opposes like up to the limit that one subject's requirements for maintenance of himself no longer conflict with the other's requirements. If I regard another being akin to myself as a thing to be exploited for my own good pleasure, I deny his autonomy (in short, his innate humanity) and thereby enter into conflict with him. Practical reason, however, Kant stresses, aims to overcome such conflicts. Reason tries to make our ends "harmonize" with the ends of other men.[2] On that account, reason blocks out a social model of human relations embodying the fundamental moral precept to treat all men as persons or ends in themselves. In such a model of inter-personal relations, the autonomies of all agents are mutually limited and confirmed by the others without disruption or discord. Kant calls such a field of interaction in which different autonomies play upon each other the "kingdom of ends."

3. The Kingdom of Ends

Kant defines the kingdom of ends (Reich der Zwecke) as a "systematic union (systematische Verbindung) of rational beings under common laws."[3] The idea of a systematic union of ends represents a diagrammatic elaboration of the formula of universal law.

---

[1] Ibid. Schriften, IV, 428.

[2] GMM, p. 97. Schriften, IV, 430.

[3] GMM, p. 100. Schriften, IV, 433.

151

> Now since laws determine ends as regards their
> universal validity, we shall be able -- if we
> abstract from the personal differences between
> rational beings, and also from all the content
> of their private ends -- to conceive a whole
> of all ends in systematic conjunction (a whole
> both of rational beings as ends in themselves
> and also of the personal ends which each may
> set before himself); that is, we shall be able
> to conceive a kingdom of ends which is possible
> in accordance with the above principles.[1]

Moral action expands into a nexus of interaction in which the intention of a single agent is qualified by the intentions of other agents. Kant's point is that ethics concerns itself with more than just the "pure will" of the agent. The problem of right conduct turns directly on the problem of how to create a society of righteous men. Morality has no meaning in vacuo. In virtue of its demand for universalizability, morality always takes as its object the welfare of others.[2] In legislating for all men, the moral agent projects a scheme of interaction in which he both subjects others to, and is personally subjected by, the universal law he has chosen. Self-legislation, therefore, has a reflexive character. Kant describes this reflexivity in the following manner:

> A rational being belongs to the kingdom of
> ends as a member (als Glied), when, although
> he makes its universal laws, he is also
> himself subject to these laws. He belongs
> to it as its head, when as the maker of laws
> he is himself subject to the will of no other.[3]

The analogy comes from Rousseau. We are reminded of Rousseau's account of the social contract.

---

[1] GMM, pp. 100-01. Ibid.

[2] Schilpp, op. cit., p. 179. For a detailed discussion of the close relation between the idea of the end-in-itself in Kant's thought and the notion of a community of ends, see P. Chojnacki, Die Ethik Kants und die Ethik des Sozialismus (Freiburg/Schweiz: Studia Friburgensia, 1924), p. 140ff. Cf. also James D. Collins, The Emergence of Philosophy of Religion (New Haven: Yale University Press, 1967), p. 148f.

[3] GMM, p. 101. Schriften, IV, 433.

> ...each man, in giving himself to all, gives
> himself to nobody; and as there is no associate
> over which he does not acquire the same right
> as he yields others over himself, he gains an
> equivalent for everything he loses, and an
> increase of force for the preservation of what
> he has.[1]

In the kingdom of ends, so far as he enacts the moral law, every man recognizes the dignity and autonomy both of his own person and of all other persons with whom he might every enter into relationship. In legislating a universal rule for moral action, the agent confirms the possibility of moral action for all the various agents in the world. The possibility of moral action, as John MacMurray aptly puts it, "depends upon the Other being also agent, and so upon a plurality of agents in the field of action."[2] If one rational agent regards (MacMurray employs the term 'apperceive') another agent not as rational and autonomous like himself, but rather as a passive and pliable object for use as means, the moral action on the other's part is foreclosed. Thus a universal community of moral agents constitutes the supreme condition under which an immediate moral act can have the "objective" import which reason seeks.

It should be noted, moreover, that the idea of a kingdom of ends surpasses a mere "harmony of interests." Such a harmony of interests was the favorite model among social and political philosophers of the eighteenth century for representing the perfect form of communal life. A man's interest in protecting his property, for instance, may entail his denial of the interest in owning property on the part of a day-laborer. Only if a man's interest follows the interests of morality (that is, the interest in safeguarding the autonomy and dignity of all his fellow men) can a true harmony of interests emerge. Otherwise, the harmony is a spurious one. It becomes a harmony that is not innate to men's real interest, but one depending on

---

[1] Jean-Jacques Rousseau, *The Social Contract* and *Discourses* (New York: Everyman's Library, 1950), p. 14.

[2] John MacMurray, *The Self as Agent* (London: Faber and Faber 1954), p. 145.

repression of certain interests among the less powerful or less fortunate.

The kingdom of ends, as Kant expounds it, of course "is admittedly only an Ideal."[1] How the Ideal takes on visible shape in the actual course of human affairs is the subject which we shall treat in the last chapter. The insight to be culled from our analysis so far of the kingdom of ends is that the apriority of the moral law is a concept which only makes sense in light of the *a priori* idea of how much a law serves to represent in totality the interests of all reasonable beings whom it obliges. Autonomy, personality, and dignity become empty notions if abstracted from the total setting in which men affirm their common humanity through mutual give-and-take in social intercourse. To concentrate unduly on the supposed epistemological significance of the proposition, "man exists as an end-in-himself," as some commentators have done in a misguided attempt to clarify the "synthetic *a priori*" or transcendental status of such a statement, circumvents the fundamental importance of Kant's concept of personality.[2] For the ideal of the end-in-itself is part and parcel of the notion of a social unity of agents subscribing to that ideal and laboring to realize the end of humanity in their reciprocal dealings with one another. One cannot adduce the concept of an end-in-itself by mere analysis of the idea of man. Nor can one synthesize the concept by an appeal to our experience of how men do indeed treat other men. The "synthetic" aspect of the concept of personality is *a priori*. But it is not *a priori* in the sense

---

[1] GMM, p. 101. Schriften, IV, 433.

[2] Cf. particularly an article by Pepita Haezrahi, "The Concept of Man as End-in-Himself," in Robert Paul Wolff, Kant: A Collection of Critical Essays (Garden City: Doubleday and Company, Anchor Books, 1967), pp. 291-313. Haezrahi completely ignores Kant's discussion of the kingdom of ends in her analysis of the concept of human dignity in the Groundwork. Her efforts to explain, in part, the notion of the end-in-itself as a "regulative idea" for human conduct takes no account of the social dimension in all end-directed activity.

that we can make the connection between the terms "man" and
"end-in-itself" according to some kind of logical principle of
judgement, as we do with categoreal knowledge. The proposition,
"man exists as an end-in-himself," is of a different order than
"all events have causes." The synthesis of the principle of
personality derives from our elaborating as an experiment in
thought what it means to be a rational agent whose interests
are always limited by other persons in a social nexus. The
concept of man as end-in-himself is virtually unintelligible
apart from the idea of a kingdom of ends.

On the other hand, Kant seems to take the position that
one's person is limited not only by other persons in society,
but by a Supreme Person who stands over and above the field of
social interaction. The kingdom of ends is ultimately the
"kingdom of God" (<u>Reich</u> <u>Gottes</u>). On the face of it, a person
in the kingdom of ends would seem to be sufficiently limited
by other persons. But this limitation only takes place in a
kingdom which does not exist in fact. Since an actual harmony
of personal ends among all rational agents does not occur in
the world of experience, reason must recur to the <u>idea</u> of a
Supreme Person who performs the needed harmonization. In the
given system of nature one man's interests are not adequately
limited by other men's interests. The interests of all men,
however, are limited by God. This, at least, seems to be Kant's
suggestion. In order to understand, therefore, how Kant depicts the dynamics of the development of human personality in
concrete situations, we must inspect what he means when he
calls God a "person." For Kant, the concept of human autonomy
always goes hand in hand with the idea of a limiting power over
this autonomy -- what we shall call "theonomy."

B. Theonomy

1. God as Person

In Kant's words, "moral personality"

> ...is nothing but the freedom of a rational
> being under moral laws (whereas psychological
> personality is merely the capacity to be

> conscious of the identity of one's self in
> the various conditions of one's existence.
> Hence it follows that a person is subject to
> no laws other than those he (either alone or
> at least jointly with others) gives to
> himself.[1]

In the act of self-legislation, a person reckons or _imputes_ responsibility for what he does and thus affirms his own autonomy. If he did not own to responsibility for the act, the act would not be properly "his own." At the same time, his avowal of his own autonomy entails the recognition of autonomy in all other rational agents over whom the moral law has jurisdiction. Duty (_Pflicht_) to oneself as a person necessarily involves duty to a universe of persons. Duty to all persons, including oneself, gives concrete meaning to the demand of the moral law of acting "for the sake of duty." Duty as "the concept of a will estimable in itself (_an sich selbst hochzuschätzenden_) and good apart from any further end"[2] (i.e., "the good will") implies the agent's intention to treat humanity in every person as an end-in-itself. The formula of the end-in-itself, again, merely articulates in more pointed language the rudimentary principles of the system of morality (the motive of duty, the need for universalizability of maxims, etc.) which Kant erects in the _Groundwork_.

In the _Metaphysical Principles of Virtue_ (1797) Kant explains the concept of a person in terms of the internal sense of duty and the capacity to impute the moral law to oneself: to subject

---

[1] MEJ (MM: Intro.), p. 24. _Schriften_, VI, 223. Cf. also Kant's definition of "personality" (_Persönlichkeit_) in the second _Critique_: "the freedom and independence from the mechanism of nature regarded as a capacity of a being which is subject to special laws (pure practical laws given by his own reason)..." CP_rR, p. 89. _Schriften_, V, 87. "...man as person, i.e., as the subject of a morally-practical reason, is exalted above all price (_über allen Preis_). For as such a one (_homo noumenon_) he is not to be valued merely as a means to the ends of other people or even to his own ends, but is to be prized as an end in himself." MPV, p. 97. _Schriften_, VI, 434-5.

[2] GMM, p. 64. _Schriften_, IV, 397.

oneself to its constraints and judge oneself responsible for breaking these constraints.[1]

> Every concept of duty contains objective constraint through the law (as moral imperative restricting our freedom) and belongs to the practical understanding, which gives the rule. However, the internal imputation (<u>innere</u> <u>Zurechnung</u>) of a deed, as a case standing under the law (<u>in</u> <u>meritum</u> <u>aut</u> <u>demeritum</u>), belongs to the faculty of judgement (<u>judicium</u>), which, as the subjective principle of the imputation of the action, validly judges whether or not the action has taken place as a deed (as an action standing under law). Thereupon follows the conclusion of reason (the sentence), i.e., the connection of the lawful consequence with the action (the condemnation or acquittal). All of this takes place before a tribunal (<u>coram</u> <u>judicio</u>) called a court of justice (<u>forum</u>), as thought before a moral person who gives effect to the law.[2]

Consciousness of this "internal court of justice within man" (<u>inneren</u> <u>Gerichtshofes</u> <u>im</u> <u>Menschen</u>) Kant entitles "conscience" (<u>Gewissen</u>).[3] Conscience lies innate in every man; it binds every agent through a sense of duty to the moral law he has fashioned for himself. Conscience, in that sense, confirms what Kant calls "man's duty to himself" (<u>Pflicht</u> <u>des</u> <u>Menschen</u> <u>gegen</u> <u>sich</u> <u>selbst</u>).[4] On the other hand, Kant advises, duty to oneself as a person is impossible without a concomitant duty to another person.

---

[1] Cf. "A <u>person</u> is the subject whose actions are susceptible to imputation." <u>MEJ</u> (<u>MM</u>: <u>Intro</u>.), p. 24. <u>Schriften</u>, VI, 223.

[2] <u>MPV</u>, p. 100. <u>Schriften</u>, VI, 437-8.

[3] Ibid. <u>Schriften</u>, VI, 438. "...conscience might also be defined as follows: it is the moral faculty of judgement, passing judgement upon itself..." <u>RWL</u>, p. 174. <u>Schriften</u>, VI, 186.

[4] <u>MPV</u>, p. 100. <u>Schriften</u>, VI, 437.

157

> This original intellectual and (as a representation of duty) moral predisposition called conscience has the peculiarity that though this whole matter is an affair of man with himself, man sees himself, nevertheless, compelled to conduct this affair as thought at the bidding (Geheiss) of another person. For the business here is the conduct of a lawsuit (causa) before a tribunal. But if the man accused by his conscience is represented as one and the same with the judge, then such a mode of representation is absurd in a court of justice; for in that event, the accuser would certainly lose every time. Therefore, as far as all man's duties are concerned, his conscience will have to suppose someone other than himself to be the judge of his actions, if his conscience is not to contradict itself.[1]

In the perfect socio-ethical order, or kingdom of ends, there would be no need for any judicial court of conscience. In such an order every man's intention would conform to universal law, and hence the need for a "judge" of other persons' misdeeds and evil intents would disappear. Law courts have no place where virtue is uniquitous and habitual. The court of conscience, however, exists, because the motive of respect for other persons is not a habit of the will for finite rational agents. An assize to limit men to virtue or respect has to be imposed. This assize takes place in conscience. The "person" who performs the assize "may be a real (wirkliche) person" like oneself.[2] Conscience taken as a sense of duty to a real person or "other," who by judging our motives and deeds restrains our own self-interest to the interest in mankind as an end in itself, reflects a possible scheme of moral obligations which one member of a community may express toward other members who know him and have definite influence over his activity. This is what we might call the "social" function of conscience. In this view conscience serves as the internalization of normative constraints fostered on a man by his social peers or what George

---

[1] MPV, p. 101. Schriften, VI, 438.

[2] Ibid. Schriften, VI, 438-9.

Herbert Mead called the "generalized other."[1] On the other hand, no actual society, for Kant, consistently imposes the norm upon its members represented in the formula of the end in itself. More likely than not, conscience of duties to mankind does not reflect the norms which real persons conventionally practice and revere among themselves. Real persons are easily given up to the moral perversity that thwarts the realization of the moral law in society. The generalized other, therefore, who presides over the tribunal of conscience and admonishes us with the moral law, cannot be a personification of a real being, of the man we meet at church, behind a store counter, or in the stock exchange. This "other" is "an ideal one which reason creates for itself."[2]

Moreoever, real persons cannot be the model for the judge of conscience, because as finite beings they are incapable of knowing the true intentions of men. Such a moral scrutiny and clairvoyance is necessary, however, if a person shall succeed in judging whether another's demeanor exhibits a true inward sense of duty or the mere pharasaical pretense of virtue. Because real persons lack this clairvoyance, they cannot hold other persons accountable to themselves. Thus reason posits an "ideal person" presiding over men's consciences who "must be a searcher of hearts, for the court of justice is set up in our inmost selves." Furthermore, this ideal person "at the same time...must be all-obliging (allverpflichtend): he must be, or be conceived as, a person in relation to whom duties are to be regarded as commands by him, because conscience is the internal judge of all free actions."[3] Only an ideal person,

---

[1] Cf. G. H. Mead, "The Genesis of the Self and Social Control" in Selected Writings, Andrew Reck (ed.) (New York: Bobbs-Merrill, Library of Liberal Arts, 1964), pp. 267-93.

[2] Ibid. Schriften, VI, 439.

[3] MPV, p. 102. Schriften, VI, 439. God must be "'one who knows the heart,' in order to see into the innermost parts of the disposition of each individual..." RWL, p. 91. Schriften, VI, 99.

having the strictest moral probity, can regulate a man's conscience a mere idol contrived in the image of ordinary men with their vices and failings. Such persons are pale shadows of the moral archetype of what man ought to be. Thus they cannot obligate us to virtue. The ideal person alone commands a genuine sense of duty. Unlike real persons, this ideal person "must at the same time possess all authority (over heaven and earth), for otherwise he could not give proper effect to his laws." This "moral being possessing power over all is called God." By the same token, "conscience must be conceived as the subjective principle of being accountable to God for one's deeds."[1]

Broadly speaking, Kant's account of God as an ideal person constitutes a variant on the moral argument for belief in God's existence. Man's capacity as a self-legislating person is diminished by his own imperfections. Because of these imperfections, man requires a conscience to reprove him for his shortcomings and to inspire him to right living. However, this reproof and correction must have its source in a person other than the man of conscience himself, in a person who does not share the latter's moral ineptitude. Such a person does not correspond to any empirical person. In consequence, the moral agent must posit in thought a supreme person with the keenest faculty for scrutinizing and judging the former's intentions. The supreme person must be thought to have incorporated the moral law into his will sufficiently and to have perfected his autonomy as a person. God's autonomy, therefore, is in a manner of speaking an idealization of the autonomy necessary to be an independent and righteous judge of other persons. If God did not possess this autonomy, he would fail to exemplify the moral law in its pure form and thus would be a poor arbiter of men's consciences. Every person possesses a sense of his own accountability. Through conscience he projects the existence of an "other" person to do the accounting. This "other" must

---

[1] MPV, p. 102. Schriften, VI, 439.

not have the ability to lapse in his office as a just accountant, if conscience is to hold a man accountable in every instance of willing. Since no real men have ever attained this _ne plus ultra_ of autonomous personality, the "other" who does the accounting must be an ideal being. Kant calls this ideal "other" God. The possibility of human autonomy, therefore, presupposes God's autonomy (theonomy),[1] which is really nothing more than man's autonomy without blemish or defect.

Theonomy, however, is only an idea. And "this is not to say that by the idea to which his conscience inevitably leads him, man is entitled to suppose that such a supreme being actually exists outside himself; and even less, that man is bound by his conscience to assume such existence."[2] The idea of a supreme person to whom we make ourselves accountable in conscience is given "only subjectively by practical reason."[3] In that respect, our duty to such a being does not equal duties to real beings. This is because the concept of duty itself takes as its primary point of reference _real_ relationships among men, and only by some peculiar refinement of the concept do we entertain the notion of a duty to God. "To judge by mere reason, man has no duties to men (himself or others), for his duty to any subject at all is the moral constraint by his will."[4] A duty to God is essentially a "duty regarding that which lies completely beyond the limits of our experience" and "is not to be met within our ideas."[5] Yet the idea of a duty to God "is not the conscious-

---

[1] Our use of the term "theonomy" should be distinguished from the special connotation given to it in the writings of Paul Tillich. The term should be rendered simply according to its literal meaning: "law of God" or "law-making" activity of God. Theonomy is always contrasted here with autonomy or "self-legislation."

[2] MPV, p. 102. Schriften, VI, 439.

[3] Ibid.

[4] MPV, p. 105. Schriften, VI, 442.

[5] MPV, p. 107. Schriften, VI, 444.

ness of a duty to God."[1] We cannot exercise a duty per se to a being existing only in thought. Kant denies, therefore, that a man can enjoy a real personal relationship with God. God's personality and autonomy are not real objects of duty in the sense that the personality and autonomy of my next door neighbor are such objects. In what sense, then, do men have a duty to God?

In a "practical" sense, according to Kant, "to have religion," or an awareness of duty to God, "can be asserted to be a duty of man to himself."[2] With the concept of God to whom we feel duty-bound "we do not hereby have before us a given being to whom we are obligated; for the actuality of such a being would first have to be proved (disclosed by experience)."[3] Duty to God consists mainly in duty to an ideal construct engendered in the mind of the agent. On that account duty to God is essentially a kind of duty to oneself. But obviously it is not a duty to one's everyday moral self. Duty to God is duty to man's genuinely autonomous self imprisoned in the perversity and contradictions of his conventional self. Man's duty to God, therefore, signifies a relationship of the agent not to a real person of flesh and blood, but a reflexive relationship to one's own intention to become an autonomous agent, to become "like God." This intentional self is human autonomy freed from the limitations of self-interest and heteronomy.[4] It is what man

---

[1] Ibid. Schriften, VI, 443.

[2] Ibid. Schriften, VI, 444.

[3] Ibid.

[4] The "double-self" interpretation of Kant's view of the relationship between man and God is illustrated in a footnote from the Tugendlehre. "This double self (on the one hand, having to stand trembling at the bar of a court of justice entrusted to one, but, on the other hand, possessing the judgeship by innate authority), this two fold personality in which the man who in his conscience accuses and judges himself must think of himself, requires an explanation. I, the accuser and likewise the accused, am the very same man..." Tugend., p. 101. Schriften, Vi, 439. Italics mine.

intends, or what he thinks he ought to become. The intentional
self functions as an Other; it checks man's actual self from
transgressing the rule of universality in his maxims, from divesting himself of accountability for his actions and surrendering to one heteronomy or another. The intentional self
disciplines and exhorts the everyday self to progress in virtue
and become a genuninely autonomous self. The idea of God as
person thus serves to develop in man his consciousness of himself as a person. Kant, of course, rarely uses language that
expressly designates God as man's perfect alter ego; but such
a designation can be made in virtue of Kant's denial that God
is "substance" and his earnest insistence that the divine exists
only in thought.

2. Divine Grace

In the second portion of the Religion Kant tackles the
question of how man can come to possess an authentically good
will. The answer to this question, for Kant, rides incontestably on the demand for autonomy in morality. Only "man himself
must make or have made himself into whatever, in a moral sense,
whether good or evil, he is to become."[1] He "is to be adjudged
morally good only by virtue of that which can be imputed to him
as performed by himself."[2] So far as the achievement of virtue
is concerned, therefore, Kant would seem to regard man as the
sole actor. But the state of virtue which the categorical
imperative exacts from man is a well-nigh impossible demand.
The categorical imperative requires holiness, yet holiness
represents an unattainable asymtopic limit of man's moral
progress. Earlier we saw how Kant devises the postulate of a
God who reckons the entirety of a man's progress as a virtual
holiness. The postulate then bridges the gulf between the

---

[1] RWL, p. 40. Schriften, VI, 44. For "duty bids us to do
this, and duty demands nothing of us which we cannot do." RWL,
p. 43. Schriften, VI, 47.

[2] RWL, p. 50. Schriften, VI, 50.

demand for holiness and man's finite capacity for attaining it.

In the Religion Kant interposes a second means of resolving the difference: the notion of "grace" (Gnade), or supernatural cooperation with man's will in the struggle for moral perfection. Basically grace is, for Kant, that action of God which creates in man a holy will, an action that the latter cannot carry off by his own efforts.[1] What man is unable to do, therefore, God does for him.

Nonetheless, Kant is adamant in his view that God's action in bringing man to holiness and rational autonomy can never totally supersede man's endeavors. False religions are those "which are endeavors to win favors (mere worship)"; they substitute for the conviction that man himself must achieve the good the idea that "God can make him eternally happy (through remission of his sins) without his having to do anything more than to ask for it."[2] These false religions scorn "the basic principle that each man must do as much as lies in his power to become a better man, and that only when h has not buried his inborn talent (Luke XIX, 12-16) but has made use of his original predisposition (Anlage) to good in order to become a better man, can he hope that what is not within his power will be supplied through cooperation (Mitwirkung) from above."[3] By this account, grace supplements man's moral achievements; it does not displace them. God's action upon the will of man simply closes the gap between man's actual will and perfection. But this action "from above" does not in any fashion figure in man's knowledge of what must take place if he is to make a moral improvement. "'It is not essential, and hence not necessary, for every one to know what God does or has done for his salvation;' but it is essential to know what man

---

[1] ..."faith in good life-conduct, as being effected through a higher agency (Einflüss) would be reckoned to [man] as grace." RWL, p. 109. Schriften, VI, 118.

[2] RWL, p. 47. Schriften, VI, 52.

[3] Ibid.

himself *must* *do* in order to become worthy of this assistance."[1] Since the only "knowledge" required for right action consists in consciousness of the moral imperative, any knowledge of how God might compensate through grace our native inability to do what we think we ought turns out to be superfluous. Indeed, such knowledge is impossible, since we must "admit a work of grace as something incomprehensible (Unbegreifliches)."[2] For that reason the concept of grace as supernatural cooperation Kant dubs a mere "*parerga* to religion within the limits of pure reason,"[3] that is, an unnecessary accretion to genuine piety. "Works of grace" are "aberrations and cannot be adopted into the maxims of reason."[4] Like the notion of God, that of grace has no theoretical significance; yet, too, "even the hypothesis of a *practical* application of this idea is wholly self-contradictory."[5] For

> the employment of this idea would presuppose a rule concerning the good which (for a particular end) we ourselves must *do* in order to accomplish

---

[1] Ibid.

[2] RWL, p. 49. Schriften, VI, 53. "Nor is it absolutely necessary for a man to know wherein this cooperation consists, indeed, it is perhaps inevitable that, were the way it occurs revealed at a given time, different people would at some other time form different conceptions of it..." RWL, p. 47. Schrifte VI, 52. Also, "As to these mysteries [such as grace] so far as they touch the moral life-history of every man -- how it happens that there is a moral good or evil at all in the world, and... how out of evil good could spring up and be established in any man whatever, or why, when this occurs in some, others remained deprived thereof -- if this God has revealed to us nothing and can reveal nothing since we would not understand it. It is as though we wished to explain and to render comprehensible to ourselves in terms of a man's freedom what happens to him; on this question God has indeed revealed His will through the moral law in us, but the causes due to which a free action on earth occurs or does not occur He has left in that obscurity in which human investigation must leave whatever...ought to be conceived of according to the laws of cause and effect." RWL, pp. 134-5. Schriften, VI, 144.

[3] RWL, p. 47. Schriften, VI, 52.

[4] RWL, p. 48. Schriften, VI, 53.

[5] Ibid.

> something, whereas to await a work of grace
> means exactly the opposite, namely, that the
> good (the morally good) is not our deed but
> the deed of another being, and that we there-
> fore can <u>achieve</u> it only by doing <u>nothing</u>,
> which contradicts itself.[1]

The concept of grace arises because "reason, conscious of her inability to satisfy her moral need, extends herself to high-flown ideas capable of supplying this lack without, however, appropriating these ideas as an extension of her domain."[2] Divine action, in the sense of what grants man the moral autonomy he has failed to achieve himself, is primarily a hollow notion. This is Kant's central point. Since, for Kant, one cannot say anything positive about the concept of grace, he must for all intents and purposes remain silent.

At this point the question arises why Kant raises the problem of grace to begin with. In all likelihood Kant poses grace as a limiting concept which marks the range of man's aptitude for eliminating radical evil from his maxims. Just as the notion of a divine ruler of nature proportioning virtue to happiness under the rubric of the perfect highest good compensates for man's <u>physical</u> impotence, so the idea of God's will as a gracious dispensation guarantees the supreme highest good by delivering man from <u>moral</u> impotence.

In his search for a term that aptly expresses the "completion" of the progress of the individual moral will, Kant lights upon the traditional theological idea of grace. Kant distinguishes grace from "nature," a term whose usage seems bizarre in comparison with how Kant employs it in other contexts, but one which nevertheless corresponds approximately to the Scholastic sense of the word.

> Whatever good man is able to do through his
> own efforts, under laws of freedom, in con-
> trast to that which he can do only with super-

---

[1] RWL, pp. 48-9. Ibid.

[2] RWL, pp. 47-8. Schriften, VI, 52.

> natural assistance, can be called <u>nature</u>, as distinguished from grace.¹

"Nature" in this instance does not signify, as it does in the other critical writings, the realm of sense-experience, but the world of moral willing which, though not evident empirically, at least is governed by regular laws similar to the laws of physics.

> Not that we can understand by the former expression a physical property distinguished from freedom; we use it merely because we are at least acquainted with the <u>laws</u> <u>of</u> this capacity (<u>laws</u> <u>of</u> <u>virtue</u>), and because reason thus possesses a visible and comprehensive clue to it, considered as <u>analogous</u> <u>to</u> (<u>physical</u>) <u>nature</u>.²

Grace, however, does not bear any analogy with either natural or moral laws. For "we remain wholly in the dark as to when, what or how much, <u>grace</u> will accomplish in us, and reason is left, on this score, as with the supernatural in general (to which morality, if regarded as <u>holiness</u>, belongs), without any knowledge of the laws according to which it might occur."³ Any claim that man can know under what conditions grace operates is sheer pretense; to arrogate grace to oneself Kant calls "fanaticism" (<u>Schwärmerei</u>).⁴

Although, on the one hand, Kant feels compelled to hold out the prospect of grace for all men because of their limited moral competence, on the other hand he plays down the notion of grace as a kind of surd. There can be no divine law of action (theonomy) that amply takes the place of the moral law as a maxim of man's will. Even the "practical" validity of such a theonomy is untenable, "since that which is to be

---

¹<u>RWL</u>, p. 179. <u>Schriften</u>, VI, 190.

²Ibid. <u>Schriften</u>, VI, 190-1.

³Ibid. <u>Schriften</u>, VI, 191.

⁴"The persuasion that we can distinguish the effects of grace from those of nature (virtue) or can actually produce the former within ourselves, is fanaticism..." <u>RWL</u>, p. 162. <u>Schriften</u>, VI, 191.

accredited to us morally as good conduct must take place not
through foreign influence (<u>fremden</u> <u>Einfluss</u>), but solely through
the best possible use of our own powers."[1] In respect to the
perfect highest good, the idea of divine action has greater
value, since there the question of man's autonomy does not
enter in. God's actions only affect the outward consequences
of man's deeds without interfering with the moral intention
itself. On the other hand, the notion of grace suggests that
the creation of the right intention in man comes <u>ab</u> <u>extra</u>, not
from the inner necessity of reason. "The best possible use of
our powers" therefore is foreclosed. The supreme highest good,
however, can only be attained by a Sisyphusian labor of human
will. Since "grace" has no real meaning -- practical or otherwise -- it virtually refers to nothing independent of the will
at all. That is the inference we may draw from Kant's remarks
on the subject. Kant, of course, does not expressly or consistently take the radical leap of reducing grace to "nature,"
divine action to human action, God's power to human intention:
his language sustains a functional distinction between man's
agency and that of the Deity. Yet the distinction begins to
break down when we see how language about divine action in
Kant's exposition is used. If divine action in the form of a
<u>donum</u> <u>gratiae</u> has no significance for formulating maxims of the
will, does it have any significance at all? If the conditions
under which grace operates cannot be "known" whatsoever, if
the very presumption of grace violates Kant's fundamental criteria of the worth of moral actions (inasmuch as theonomy is
thereby substituted for an authentic autonomy), does the concept
of grace make any positive sense for Kant? If we say grace is
clearly different from man's moral agency, yet refuse to make
any cognitive claims concerning it, even so far as to ground
such knowledge in the privileged insights of "faith," are we
not really consigning such statements to irrelevance? Do we
not kill the meaning of such statements, to paraphrase John

---

[1] <u>RWL</u>, p. 179. <u>Schriften</u>, VI, 191.

Wisdom, by an excess of qualifications?

In a little-known passage from the Strife of the Faculties, Kant seesm to surmount the difficulties just noted by taking the "leap" of setting grace in apposition with nature. Such a passage, however, cannot be considered representative of Kant's general approach. I quote the passage in full:

> If by nature is understood the chief principle in man of the advancement of his happiness, and by grace the inexplicable moral tendency in us -- that is, the principle of pure morality -- then nature and grace are not merely different from one another, but often conflict. Moreover, if by nature (in its practical signification) is understood the general capacity for accomplishing with one's own power a certain purpose, so is grace nothing more than the essence (Wesen) of man, insofar as he is destined for its performance by dint of his own inner, although supersensible principle (the concept of his duty); which, because we desire to explain it (yet we know of no further cause of it than of God working in us for the good to the extent that we have not established the same tendency in ourselves) is therefore regarded as grace.[1]

Regarded as divine action ab extra, grace becomes a factitious concept. In contrast, grace must now be viewed as a possibility of the human agent for accomplishing the highest (moral) purpose. Grace becomes the immanent "supersensible principle" enabling man to transcend by steps his given status as a moral agent. Grace in this sense, therefore, loses the stigma of a "parergon." Instead it expresses the ethical marrow of man's religious life. "Grace" is a more proper term than "nature," Kant suggests, because it betokens a power within us that seems to outstrip our "natural" or given abilities. We call this power "God working within us," yet introspection convinces us that this power is essentially our own, not that of another. If the power were not our own, we would suffer the heteronomy of an alien will.

The would-be concept of a theonomy in Kant's account of God, therefore, can be translated into man's potential for auto

---

[1] SF: Schriften, VII, 43.

nomy. One cannot say simply that Kant has deified human nature: for the power of grace understood as human intention concerns not what man is in himself at the current stage of development, but what he has the capacity to become. Man's undeveloped capacity, the "remainder" that results when his moral potential is divided by his actual accomplishments, has the value of "God." God in a sense represents the "not yet" of moral progress. How this "not yet" becomes an emergent reality we shall see in the last chapter. That grace, conceived as the volition of a superhuman being, is fundamentally "unknowable" for Kant merely points up the emptiness of any concept of moral action that does not entail an independent causality and accountability on the part of the agent. Divine grace, in the sense of God's independent causality, remains a parergon, because it subtracts from the concept of autonomous moral action.

Although grace in itself cannot serve as a viable substitute for autonomous moral action (the unconditioned character of the moral law enjoins man to act for himself and himself alone), it remains, however, for Kant a necessary construct of reason geared to resolving the opposition between man's limited powers as a moral agent and his intention to become perfect in virtue. The necessity of the concept of a limited divine action upon man owes to the latter's lack of maturity in the development of his powers of autonomy. Just as human society the moral authority and influence of adults serve to check the child's immoral impulses and to educate him in the growth of his own capacity for doing what is right, so the idea of grace (i.e., the notion of extra-human influence on man's will) is necessary so long as man languishes in his moral adolescence. This comparison provides us some insight into the meaning of the apparent contradiction in Kant's thought between his insistence of complete autonomy and his recognition that man yet needs to look for divine assistance to carry through his moral projects. There is an analogy here with Gotthold Lessing, a contemporary of Kant's, in the former's essay concerning "The Education of the Human Race." At the heart of Lessing's

Position is the idea that a positive initiative toward Man on God's part in the form of mysterious revelation (an initiative that seemingly would violate the principle of autonomy) must be understood as an educational tool for representing to a mankind still immature as a rational being certain inherent truths about his own nature. "Education gives man nothing which he could not also get within himself; it gives him that which he could get from within himself, only quicker and more easily."[1] By the same token, the concept of grace gives man, whose moral development is still puerile, a positive external impetus for harking to the categorical imperative.

Au fond divine grace, like revelation, signifies a capacity which man possesses within himself, but which is not yet fully developed. For Kant, it is man's capacity for moral action instead of, as for Lessing, his capacity for knowledge. Should man ever reach his genuine majority, the need for grace would vanish. But during the interim man finds himself unable to conduct his moral affairs without some sense of a higher power influencing him. On the other hand, such influence does not entail the outright co-ercion of man's will. That is why Kant eschews the concept of a God who forces man to act in a way that would negate his obligation to rely on his own innate powers wherever possible. God cannot have an over-arching plan of "justice" that cancels the sovereignty of the moral law itself. Kant is concerned to deny God absolute power in the rule of man's moral life.

C. The Inter-relation of Autonomy and Divine Action

1. The Failure of Theodicy

The question of God's justice is the question of theodicy. In a short essay composed in 1791 Kant endeavors to expose the "failure" of theodicy itself.[2] Kant attributes the failure of

---

[1] Gotthold Lessing, Theological Writings, trans. Henry Chadwich (Stanford: Stanford University Press, 1956), p. 83.

[2] The actual title of the essay is Über das Misslingen aller philosophischen Versuche in der Theodicee ("On the Failure of all Attempted Philosophical Theodicies").

theodicy to the overwhelming evidence meeting our eye that divine justice is absent from the workings of the world. But the real implication of this failure is that we are unable to speak of any sort of divine action superseding man's own free moral actions.

"By theodicies," Kant states, "one means the defense of the highest wisdom of the Creator against the complaints which reason makes by pointing to the existence of things in the world which contradict the wise purpose."[1] "Wisdom" (Weisheit), moreover, signifies "the ability of the will to coincide with the highest good as the ultimate goal of all things."[2] The divine wisdom represents the plan of the divine will to establish justice in the world. Theodicy is an attempt to account for the workings of this will.

The problem of theodicy, however, grows out of man's inability to perceive a plan of justice for the universe. The experienced order of events "contradicts" the thesis of a wise and beneficient Deity. The bulk of Kant's essay on theodicy runs through the sundry "complaints" filed against the doctrine of divine justice, together with the arguments often offered in defense of God's actions. But Kant finds none of these arguments satisfying. Each argument capsizes on its own antinomies. "The result of this trial before the tribunal of philosophy," Kant remarks in conclusion, "is that no theodicy proposed so far has kept its promise; none has managed to justify the moral wisdom at work in the government of the world against the doubts which arise out of our experience of the world."[3] The upshot is that "all further attempts of 'human wisdom' to fathom the ways of divine wisdom must be abandoned."[4]

---

[1] Theod., p. 1. Schriften, VIII, 255.

[2] Theod., p. 1n. Schriften, VIII, 256n. Cf. also "wisdom... is the harmony (Zusammenstimmung) of the will with the final purpose (the highest good)." Verkund.: Schriften, VIII, 418.

[3] Theod., p. 7. Schriften, VIII, 263.

[4] Ibid.

The opacity of the divine will to human sight makes the world, for Kant, "a closed book" (verschlossenes Buch). "It is a closed book when we want to read the ultimate intention (Endabsicht) of God (which is always a moral one) from a world which is only an object of experience."[1] God's moral activity in the world remains forever inscrutable to us. But if we are in want of any access to God's workings, does it make any sense to use concepts of divine action at all? Is total cognitive transcendence the same as nothingness? We may feel we have caught Kant in a dialectical snare; yet Kant at least has one avenue of escape with which we are already familiar. While Kant rejects theodicy, so far as it purports to reveal the divine intention from contemplation of the knowable universe, he nevertheless allows for a theodicy evident through conscience, a theodicy in which "God himself through our reason becomes the interpreter of his will as manifested in creation." Kant points out that "this interpretation we call authentic theodicy." Authentic theodicy "is not an interpretation set forth by ratiocinating (speculative) reason but by an authoritative (machthabenden) practical reason, which having in itself authority to legislate can be considered to be the immediate expositor and voice of God in charge of the interpretation of the book of creation."[2] "Authentic theodicy" here corresponds to what Kant elsewhere calls "practical faith." Kant's point is that, while forbidden to rely on metaphysics in giving an account of how God's will operates in creation, we are still permitted to talk about acts of God on the condition that we adhere to the language of faith. In essence, the language of theoretical metaphysics does a disservice to theodicy, because it seeks to descry a pattern of justice in the universe without concern whether it comports with the moral law. But a theodicy which does not keep in trust the moral law must always fail to provide a persuasive proof of God's justice. Such a theodicy

---

[1] Theod., pp. 7-8. Schriften, VIII, 264.

[2] Theod., p. 8. Ibid.

becomes mere conjecture or idle musing. Kant cites the example
of Job's comforters.

> Each side proposes his own theodicy for the
> moral explanation of [Job's] bad luck, each
> according to his opinion. The friends of Job
> accept the doctrine which explains all woes
> in the world by reference to divine justice;
> they are punishments for crimes committed.
> Although they are not able to name any crime
> with which to charge the unfortunate man,
> they nevertheless believe they can judge <u>a
> priori</u> that Job must have committed such a
> crime, or else divine justice would not have
> allowed him to become so unhappy.[1]

Job's comforters acclaim God's righteous justice is responsible for Job's sufferings. Still, Job knows in his heart that he has led an upright life -- that is, in Kant's parlance, he has obeyed the moral law to the hilt. Job's fidelity to the moral law not only makes a mockery of the actual deserts he has received, but indicates how vacuous are his friends' claims that God is in the right and not Job himself. The important factor in Job's plight is not how what happens can somehow be rationalized into a neat scheme of justice <u>de coelo</u>. What counts is "the uprightness of the heart, not the merits of one's insights."[2] Job -- the steadfast man of virtue -- not Liebniz with his cosmic spectacles merits Kant's applause. The question is not whether this is the best of all possible worlds; the best of all possible worlds is the moral world which lies beyond the horizon of understanding. The question is: how should one act here and now and what will be the possible consequences of one's action? We can only hope that a moral universe will come into being, but cannot know that such a universe is as sure a thing as the rising of the sun tomorrow morning.

Thus "theodicy is not a task of science (<u>Aufgabe...der Wissenschaft</u>) but is a matter of faith (<u>Glaubensache</u>). The

---

[1] <u>Ibid</u>.

[2] <u>Theod</u>., p. 9. <u>Schriften</u>, VIII, 266.

authentic theodicy has taught us that what matters in such affairs is not reasoning but honesty in the avowal of powerlessness of our reason..."[1] Knowledge of God's actions is pale in comparison with the certitude that a man can have of his own good will. Our good acts are all we can know with real satisfaction. To be sure, we can anticipate through faith (through a sort of theodicy of belief) that God will carry out a plan of justice consonant with the law of morality. "To be a creature," Kant writes in the essay on theodicy,

> and as such obeying the laws of its Creator, and yet to be also a freely acting being (who has a will independent of exterior influences and who can resist in many cases the will of the Creator); to be responsible, and yet to consider one's actions as the operations of a Superior Being, the unity between these two sets of concepts is a unity which we must postulate in the idea of a world that would be the highest good.[2]

The unity of human action and divine action is a moral universe, however,

> is a unity which can be understood only by the one who has obtained a knowledge of the supersensible (intelligible) world and has seen how this world lies at the basis of the world of experience. On this knowledge only can be based the proof of the moral wisdom of the Creator of the world..."[3]

But, Kant reminds us, "no mortal man...can attain to this knowledge."[4]

In the above quoted passages Kant reinforces the view of the second *Critique* that we can cognize divine action. We have only the "concept of a *moral* *wisdom* which could be realized in a world created by a perfect Creator," a concept which in its bare "apriority" lacks all possible analogues in a "world of

---

[1] Theod., p. 10. Schriften, VIII, 267.

[2] Theod., p. 7. Schriften, VIII, 263-4.

[3] Ibid. Schriften, VIII, 264.

[4] Ibid.

experience."[1] The notion of an independent divine agent acting upon the world, when all is said and done, is not the chief determinant in man's moral life. Men must struggle to live upstanding lives without antecedent pledge that God will reward them. That was Job's virtue. Job acted in obedience to his inner sense of right and wrong alone. His actions did not need validation by the commission of God's justice. For his actions were the prime condition of justice itself. Justice was only done when Job had been vindicated and his friends rebuked for their pretense to knowing that God had a "higher" justice than what would seem self-evident to the man of virtue.

The lesson of the tale of Job is that the divine will, for Kant, is bound just like man's will to the moral law. Theonomy must serve autonomy. God can never do merely as he "pleases." But if that is the case, what value may we assign to the notion of divine willing at all? As we have seen, the function of the concept of God's agency is not to pose a surrogate for man's willing, but to supply man with grounds for hope that the cultivation of his moral powers is progressing toward a meaningful consummation. The content of this hope ultimately must be translated into attainment of human autonomy itself. As man approaches moral maturity, the need for belief in divine guidance fades. The erstwhile power of God is progressively taken up as man's own. Thus God's actions gradually merge into a unity with human actions. The question of theodicy in the end must be turned on its head into the question of anthropodicy. Theology changes into moral anthropology. The idea of "faith in God," therefore, viewed now in light of moral progress, no longer simply points up a relationship between man and a cosmic Other, but rather the dialectical relationship of man to himself, the relationship of his current state of existence to his generic destiny.

---

[1] Ibid. Schriften, VIII, 263.

2. The Dilemma of Theism

The wraith haunting the heritage of Kant has been the figure of Ludwig Feuerbach. Feuerbach has been the "conscience" of Kant in his recognition that the latter's theism collapses under the weight of its own critical premises. In his *Principles* *of* *the* *Philosophy* *of* *the* *Future* Feuerbach takes Kant to task on this score. "Kant's idealism," Feuerbach writes, "is the idealism still bound by theism."[1] Kant's critical idealism, according to Feuerbach, grounds all discourse about God in the legislation of man's own practical reason. The norms of practical reason determine God's attributes. Feuerbach further notes,

> Kant has realized and negated theology in morality and the divine essence in the will. For Kant, the will is the true, original, and unconditional being originating in itself. In actuality, the predicates of the Godhead are claimed by Kant for the will; his theism still has, therefore, only the significance of a theoretical limit.[2]

In short, Feuerbach is arguing that the divine will merely expresses a magnification of the human will. God and man are ultimately one with each other. The difference is in degree of perfection, not in character. God thus becomes merely the "theoretical limit" of man as a moral agent.

The supposition that God and man compose a kind of unity -- a unity which Kant varnishes over with his theism -- finds some support in statements about God appearing in *Religion* *Within* *the* *Limits*. Kant, we remember, declines to ascribe any meaning to the concept of God as an independent entity or agent, as *Ding* *an* *sich*. "It concerns us not so much to know what God is in Himself (His nature) as what He is for us as moral beings..."[3]

---

[1] Ludwig Feuerbach, *Principles* *of* *the* *Philosophy* *of* *the* *Future*, trans. Manfred Vogel (New York: Bobbs-Merrill Company, 1966), p. 29.

[2] Ibid.

[3] RWL, p. 130. *Schriften*, VI, 139.

This sentence smacks a good deal of Luther's teaching that we can never know God in his self-existent majesty, but only in his relationship to men, as he is pro nobis.[1] Indeed, the Lutheran position, which Kant in his own way shares, is suscep tible to the anthropological reduction, as Karl Barth in his celebrated essay on Feuerbach has observed. We quote Barth here to illustrate the point.

> Luther himself urged us to seek deity not in heaven but on earth, in man, man, the man Jesus; and for him the bread of the Lord's supper had to be the glorified body of the Exalted One. This emphasis is crystallized in the orthodox Lutheran doctrine of the "communication of idioms" with its sovereign genus (genus majestaticum) according to which the predicates of the divine majesty belong to the humanity of Jesus as such and in abstracto. With great elation people triumphantly turned away (and are still turning away) from the Reformed Finitum non capax infiniti...All this clearly suggests the possibility of an inversion of above and below, of heaven and earth, of God and man -- the possibility of forgetting the eschatological limit.[2]

In Kant's case, as in Luther's, the terminus a quo for statements about God is the condition of man. Kant's God is a God who reflects this condition. For Kant, the condition of man to which God relates is the necessity of moral obligation. God is a being, therefore, who satisfies man's basic moral need.[3]

---

[1] Cf. Martin Luther, Werke, (Weimar: Herman Bohlhaus, Nachfolger, 1914), Vol. 40 III, 327f.

[2] Karl Barth, "An Introductory Essay," trans James Luther Adams, to Feuerbach's Essence of Christianity, trans. George Eliot (New York: Harper & Row, Torchbooks, 1957), p. xxiii. The German text of the essay appears as a chapter in Die Theologie und die Kirche (Zollikon-Zürich: Evangelischer Verlag, A.G., 1928), Vol. II, 212-39.

[3] "...each individual can know of himself, through his own reason, the will of God which lies at the basis of his religion; for the concept of the Deity really arises solely from consciousness of these laws and the need of reason to postulate a might which can procure for these laws, as their final end, all the results comformable to them and possible in a world." RWL, p. 95. Schriften, VI, 104.

But if God is principally a human construct intended to satisfy a basic lack or need -- what Feuerbach calls a "projection" or "objectification" (Vergegenständlichkeit) -- should we not reduce the illusion of God as an object to man into the self-objectifying act of the subject? This act of self-objectification expresses the subject's intention to be something it yet is not. In Kant's case, God becomes the symbol embodying man's desire to fulfill the moral ought. Yet the symbol does not exist apart from the act of self-objectification which created it.

According to Feuerbach, Kant suffers from a failure of nerve in refusing to press the logic of his critical idealism so far as to make the unity of God and man apparent. We have seen that the logic of Kant's position leads us to interpret his idea of God, not so much as an independent agent, but as a symbol of man's own inherent abilities. The unity of God and man must be seen as the end point of a project which the moral law bids man to undertake. The supposed division of wills between the divine and the human reflects the profound scissure in man's intention to do what he thinks he ought and what he conceives himself actually capable of doing. The distance between God and man, as Robert Tucker has noted, amounts to the fact that man himself is, for Kant,

> a divided being, a dual personality: homo noumenon and homo phenomenon. The former is the godlike self of man: the latter, his merely human self.[1]

The godlike self cries for realization in man's actions; "morality is the compulsion to become such a holy being in actual fact."[2] God, therefore, is nothing but a reification of this self. Kant denies, of course, that God is merely a res or thing; but his use of theistic phrasings commits him to his own peculiar manner of hypostatizing God.

On the other hand, Kant's very rejection of reifying God

---

[1] Robert Tucker, Philosophy and Myth in Karl Marx (Cambridge: Cambridge University Press, 1961), p. 34.

[2] Ibid., p. 33.

(indeed, his insistence that God is pre-eminently an "idea" in
our minds, as he spells out explicitly in the Opus Postumum)
uncovers a route for passage -- a passage which Feuerbach claims
Kant overlooks -- from the stance of theology to anthropology.
Kant, however, does not seem conscious of this transition. Yet
Kant's resort to the grammar of divine agency does not uphold
the principles of theistic discourse even as precariously as
one might surmise.

In our analysis of the "language of intention" we saw how
Kant's talk about God definitively expresses, not the notion of
a supreme and alien being, so much as man's own will and intention to rise above his given situation and to fulfill the
"moral law" to the limit of his powers. The putative transcendence of God, therefore, represents the inner self-transcendence of man. God's "holiness" is a projection of the moral
law as a possible dimension of human life. The problem of God
becomes the problem of how man, having failed in his own
personal and historical career to have realized the law of
holiness, can ultimately do so. So long as man remains imperfect,
he stands "outside" himself; he is compelled to alienate what
he needs to become in the person of an Other. But is man's
propensity for self-alienation constant and irremediable? Is
the concept of God as Other the invariably necessary postulate
Kant seems to suggest?

From our reading of certain portions of Kant's works,
particularly the Critique of Practical Reason, it seems clear
that such a concept cannot be dispensed with. Yet the necessity
of the God-concept, for Kant, is based on the perdurance of
man's alienation from himself in the form of a divided will.
The divided will is the bane of every man's personal life from
cradle to grave. Kant repeatedly stresses this point. Personal
progress toward moral perfection is slow and inconsequential,
in light of man's transient life span. On the other hand, the
historical progress of the human race opens a wider horizon
for the overcoming of man's alienation from himself than is
possible for the individual. While the isolated individual may

not complete his own apotheosis in his three score or more years, the human species itself enjoys seemingly endless time for advancement. The problem of God, therefore, to a large extent finds a solution in the philosophy of history. How Kant interprets the meaning and end of history is the topic we shall entertain now in the final chapter.

CHAPTER IV. HISTORICAL ACTION AND THE IDEA OF PROGRESS

A. The Foundations of the Idea of Historical Progress in Kant

1. The Paradox of Perfectibility

In the last chapter we concluded that the concept of God in Kant's philosophy derived from a fundamental state of alienation of man from himself -- a rupture within his will between his moral intention and his actual performance. The necessity of postulating God in the guise of a being set over against man, therefore, springs from the conflict between real and ideal, between man's desire to comply with the demands of his reason and his empirical inability to do so. The notion of a holy will belonging to God bespeaks a moral perfection which, albeit an ideal, still stands out as a genuine possibility for man in view of the fact that the categorical imperative enjoins him to attain it. Ought implies can! The meaning of the term God thus hangs on how we interpret the possibility of human perfection.

For Kant, human "perfection" (Vollkommenheit) consists in "the cultivation of one's capacities or natural endowments."[1] Generally speaking, the perfection of any existing thing in the world is "the concept of what sort of thing it is to be."[2] Now the concept of what man is meant to be includes rationality and morality. Thus the perfection of man consists in these characteristics.

Man's perfection is not given to him full-blown by nature; it must be pursued and cultivated over a period of time. In his Anthropology Kant notes that "man is capable of perfecting (zu perfektionieren) himself according to the ends which he assumes for himself whereby he, as an animal gifted (begabte)

---

[1] MPV, p. 44. Schriften, VI, 387.

[2] CJ, p. 63. Schriften, V, 227.

with the capacity for reason (Vernunftfähigkeit) (animal rationabile) he can make out of himself an actual rational (vernünftiges) animal (animal rationale)."[1] Rational perfection is basically a potential that man himself must strive to realize. In substance, "human perfection" is "one's duty to raise himself out of the crudity of his nature, out of his animality (quod actum) more and more to humanity, by which alone he is capable of setting himself ends."[2] Rational perfection is the inner telos of the human organism. In its latent form, human perfection constitutes what Kant calls the "disposition" (Anlage) to do what is morally good.[3] It is a nisus or drive within the human species for shedding its status as merely one organism in nature among other organisms and for achieving moral control over itself and the world at large.

Rational perfection is the limit of development for man in nature. It is man's innate intention to attain a condition of life surpassing his present experiences. In its explicit form, human perfection comprises man's actual fulfillment of his intention to attain the completely moral style of life. Perfection is thus, as the etymology of the German word itself indicates, a Voll-kommen or "coming to fullness" of all one's native powers as a human being. In that respect, the perfection of man is nothing more than the full and unhampered play of his

---

[1] Anthro.: Schriften, VII, 321.

[2] MPV, p. 45. Schriften, VI, 387. "...it is one's duty to push the cultivation of his will up to the purest virtuous disposition, in which the law is at the same time the incentive of one's actions which are in accordance with duty." Ibid. "The greatest moral perfection of man is to do his duty and to do it, of course, from duty (so that the law is not merely the rule, but also the incentive of his actions)." MPV, p. 51 Schriften, VI, 392.

[3] Cf. "This disposition which is inner morally-practical perfection..." MPV, p. 45. Schriften, VI, 387. Consider also what Kant in the Religion calls the "predisposition (Anlage) to personality in man, taken as a rational and at the same time an accountable (Zurechnung flähigen) being." This Kant calls a "fixed character and destiny (Bestimmung) of man..." RWL, p. 21. Schriften, VI, 26.

183

rational (i.e., his distinctly human) energies.

But the achievement of perfection, again, looms before man as a formidable project. One cannot lightly assume the task. Reason commands that man struggle to perfect himself.

> It is a duty of man to himself to cultivate his natural powers (of the spirit, of the mind, and of the body) as means to all kinds of possible ends. Man owes it to himself (as an intelligence) not to let his natural predispositions and capacities (which his reason can use some day) remain unused, and not to leave them, as it were, to rust.[1]

In moral terms the command of self-perfection represents an exhortation to become holy like God.

> "Be holy" is here the command...such perfection consists objectively in doing one's full duty and in attaining the completeness of one's moral end regarding himself. "Be perfect!"[2]

Yet moral perfection, while a determinate and transparent end of action which reason bids man to attain, remains for all practical purposes an elusive will-o-the-wisp. "For man, striving for this goal is always only in progression from one stage of perfection to another."[3] Perfection is always "more than the finite sum of an individual's attainments. There thus appears in Kant's account of the development of the human organism a curious antinomy: whereas man possesses the inbred capacity for moral goodness (as it were, the germ of his own perfection), he nevertheless is barred by some cosmic irony from realizing that capacity (his actual perfection). Au fond his capacity for perfection is an incapacity. In practice, his perfection becomes his imperfection! The idea of human perfection in Kant conceals a painful paradox.

By abjuring man's inherent perfectibility, Kant arrives at what has been called the doctrine of infinite progress. Any-

---

[1] MPV, p. 108. Schriften, VI, 444.

[2] MPV, p. 110. Schriften, VI, 446.

[3] Ibid.

where along the road to perfection man is liable to misdeeds, no matter to what length he may have bettered his moral character. Kant describes the constant tension between the urge to perfection in man and his congenital sinfulness which nips virtue in the bud.

> Virtue is always in progress and yet always begins at the beginning. The first follows from the fact that, objectively considered, virtue is an ideal and unattainable; but yet constantly to approximate it is nevertheless a duty. The second is founded subjectively upon the nature of man, which is affected by inclinations. Under the influence of these inclinations virtue, with its maxims adopted once for all, can never settle into a state of rest and inactivity; if it is not rising, it inevitably declines.[1]

Tucker labels this viewpoint the "Faust-theme" in Kant's philosophy.[2] Kant's Faust is the moral agent in his untiring quest for infinity, an infinity appearing before his gaze like a mirage on the desert, always seeming teasingly close yet actually miles away. Because of his latent aptitude for virtue, Kant's moral man finds himself compelled to struggle with a committed will to reach perfection. Yet man's own irremediably flawed character keeps the struggle going interminably.

It is the tragic fate of Kant's moral pilgrim that he must always plod forward without every coming to and entering the gates of the celestial city. The image of man that appears in much of Kant's writings is that of a lonely knight of virtue eternally in search of the Holy Grail that is the perfect moral life. But the motif of an endless solitary struggle for morality which suffuses so much of Kant's writings is not his first and last word on the "paradox of perfectibility." Man can ease the struggle by leaving behind his solitude and sharing the struggle with other men like himself. For the individual, virtue may be a laborious and well-nigh impossible chore; yet the collective pursuit of the same goal reduces the obstacles.

---

[1] MPV, p. 69. Schriften, VI, 409.

[2] Tucker, op. cit.

That is the thesis which seems to crop up in certain of Kant's writings -- particularly his essays on history. The problem of human perfection in this case enters into a new context; it no longer is concerned solely with the private ordeals of the individual, but with the evolution of human society. Progress in virtue, therefore, occurs along with man's social progress as a whole.

Kant's comments on society and history do not in themselves represent a conscious odyssey from moralism to humanism. They occur in scattered essays as well as in brief sections of his major works like the Religion Within the Limits which were composed at the different times and are contemporaneous with the development of the major themes in the critical philosophy. On the other hand, Kant's remakrs on history do identify an important strand in his thought which leads away from the more conventional interpretations of his moral philosophy. This new interpretation, therefore, sets the issue of moral perfection, and by extension the problem of God, in an entirely different light.

2. The Social Context of Moral Progress

In the Religion Kant designates the issue of moral progress in terms of man's struggle to eliminate radical evil from his maxims. Radical evil, for Kant, is the propensity of a will "not to adopt the moral law into its maxim."[1] Over and over again Kant stresses that radical evil, or the "evil principle," infects all human actions. The individual invariably suffers from this affliction. As the caption of the second section of the Religion implies, man's life is a constant "conflict" between the good and the evil principles in his constitution. His life is a "combat (Kampf) which every morally well-disposed man must sustain in this life, under the leadership of the good principles, against the attacks of the evil principle..."[2]

---

[1] RWL, p. 24.   Schriften, VI, 29.

[2] RWL, p. 85.   Schriften, VI, 93.

Yet the combat between good and evil in man does not inevitably wind up in a stalemate. The good principle, according to Kant, tends to gain finally the upper hand. The title of the third chapter of the Religion ("The Victory of the Good Over the Evil Principle") tells us as much. But how does man win the victory?

Most of Kant's writings convey the view that suppression of the evil principle demands severe discipline of man's will: a rigorous steeling of oneself against temptation. The individual must forge himself into what William James called the "moral athlete." On the other hand, Kant in the Religion displaces the burden of moral perfection from the individual alone and lays it on a society of men. Evil itself can only grow in a social matrix.

> When [man] looks around for the causes and circumstances which expose him to this danger [of acting immorally] and keep him in it, he can easily convince himself that he is subject to these not because of his own gross nature, so far as he is a separate individual, but because of mankind to whom he is related and bound...He is poor (or considers himself so) only in his anxiety lest other men consider him poor and despise him on that account. Envy, the lust for power, greed, and the malignant inclinations bound up with these, besiege his nature, contented within itself, as soon as he is among men. And it is not even necessary to assume that these are men sunk in evil and examples to lead him astray; it suffices that they are at hand, that they surround him, and that they are men, for them mutually to corrupt each other's predispositions and make one another evil.[1]

Moral evil does not occur in a social vacuum. It occrs only in the situation of one man interacting with another. The different formulae of the categorical imperative themselves imply that morality has distinct social vectors. The formula of universal-

---

[1] RWL, p. 24. Schriften, VI, 29.

[2] RWL, p. 85. Schriften, VI, 93.

[3] Ibid.

izability resolves itself into the formula of the end in itself and hence into the formula of the kingdom of ends. Violation of the moral law is essentially an infringement upon the rights of persons in communal relation to each other. Kant thus, in a sense, inverts Hobbes' view of the origins of human society. For Hobbes, social organization per se serves as an antidote to man's malevolence toward his fellow man. But, for Kant, wrongdoing may be a direct consequence of social organization (albeit the wrong type of organization) itself. The victory over evil, therefore, does not depend a la Hobbes on the establishment of a social order per se with its obligatory statutes and constraints, but on the creation of a universal society which has the moral reform and perfection of the person as its aim.

> As far as we can see, therefore, the sovereignty of the good principle is attainable, so far as men can work toward it, only through the establishment and spread of a society in accordance with, and for the sake of, the laws of virtue, a society whose task and duty it is rationally to impress these laws in all their scope upon the entire human race.[1]

The same sentiment appears in the Anthropology. Man, Kant says,

> ...is destined through his reason to be in society with other men and to cultivate himself therein through the arts and sciences, to civilize and to moralize himself, so far as his animal propensity (Hang) allows...[2]

Yet human society must not merely restrain man's anti-social impulses; rather, it should have a strong positive moralizing influence. On this score, Kant has adopted Rousseau's position that society must aim to inculcate virtue in the individual.

Human progress is possible only in society. "Man has an inclination to associate with others, because in society he feels himself to be more than man, i.e., as more than the devel-

---

[1] RWL, p. 86. Schriften, VI, 94.

[2] Anthro.: Schriften, VII, 324-5. Cf. also "Man is a being intended for society (even though he is also unsociable). In the social state he strongly feels the need to open himself up to others..." Tugend., p. 138. Schriften, VI, 471.

oped form of his natural capacities."[1] The state of being "more than man" is the self-transcendence with the moral law demands. Man becomes "more than man" when he gains control over his basic animal nature through expression of his rationality. But the possibility of self-transcendence depends on the presence and co-operation of other men forming "a society over extending itself, aiming solely at the maintenance of morality, and counteracting evil with united forces (vereinigte Kräften)."[2] Social pressure, mutual assistance and communication shared values and loyalties -- all these are required if the advancement of morality among men is to proceed unimpaired.

Men who try to conduct their moral affairs in isolation from others, Kant asserts in a kind of parody of Hobbes, exist in an "ethical state of nature" (ethische Naturzustande). In the ethical state of nature the "individual prescribes the [moral] law for himself, and there is no external law (öffentliche machthabendende Autorität) to which he, along with all others, recognizes himself to be subject."[3] Man, however, cannot be simply a "law to himself," because even the law of autonomy necessarily involves him with a common law of his fellows. The moral law ultimately finds embodiment in a concrete society. This it is an imperative that "man ought to leave his ethical state of nature in order to become a member of an ethical commonwealth (ethischen gemeinen Wesen)."[4] Man's call to abandon the ethical state of nature (what we might describe as the condition of moral self-sufficiency and Faustian willfulness championed in the second Critique) arises because of his frailty and powerlessness to do the good which is only made worse when he tries to act alone. For

> ...the ethical state of nature [is] one in which the good principle, which resides in each man, is

---

[1] OH (Idea), p. 15. Schriften, VIII, 20-1.

[2] RWL, p. 86. Schriften, VI, 94.

[3] RWL, p. 87. Schriften, VI, 95.

[4] RWL, p. 88. Schriften, VI, 96.

> continually attached by the evil which is found
> in him and also in everyone else. Men...mutually
> corrupt one another's predispositions; despite
> the good will of each individual, yet, because
> they lack a principle which unites them, they
> recede, through dissensions, from the common goal
> of goodness...and expose one another to the risk
> of falling once again under the sovereignty of
> the evil principle.[1]

In a manner of speaking, the ethical state of nature is only an abstract fiction. No man can truly live the moral life in the fashion of a Robinson Crusoe. For his moral (or immoral) involvements with other men are an irremovable fact of his human predicament. Mutual interdependence and interaction with other human beings are the natural condition of his species. Man is morally committed, nevertheless, not simply to take for granted life in society, but to participate actively in guilding better structures of voluntary association. The concept of morality itself takes on an eminently social meaning. The "universal law" becomes, In Hegel's terms, a "concrete universal."

The concept of the highest good, moreover, no longer refers to some nebulous cosmic justice, but to a real human society in which the ideal of justice can take form.

> For the species of rational beings is objectively in the idea of reason, destined
> for a social goal, namely the promotion of
> the highest as a social good.[2]

In the Religion the highest good acquires a social dimension. This is "because the highest moral good cannot be achieved merely by the exertions of the single individual toward his own moral perfection, but rather requires a union of such individuals into a whole toward the same goal -- into a system of well-disposed (wohlgesinnter) men, in which and through whose unity alone the highest moral good can come to pass -- the idea of such a whole, as a universal republic based on laws of virtue..."[3] The allusion of this passage is that the supreme

---

[1] Ibid. Schriften, VI, 97.

[2] RWL, p. 89. Ibid.

[3] Ibid. Schriften, VI, 97-8.

power transforming the world into the highest good has to be understood in a different sense from the strict idea of the will of God (the divine "omnipotence") described in the second Critique. The account offered in the second Critique establishes a dialectic between only principal agents -- the individual and his God. But in the Religion the dialectic involved in the concept of the highest good falls in a new light; it becomes a dialectic between man and society. Thus God's power to usher in the moral universe is transferred (though Kant makes clear that such a transfer is not by any means total) to man as a consciously unified collective. The task of promoting the highest good is no longer just a "matter of faith" -- a kind of pious trust that God will work everything out for the best -- but becomes a corporate labor.[1] By sloughing the pretense of moral self-sufficiency, man becomes truly "more than man;" he becomes more than man because, to a certain extent, he has undertaken the work of God.

The moral universe (the kingdom of ends) thus vanishes as an eternal order of reality outside history and sustained by some mysterious dispensation of the divine will. The moral universe becomes an historical product of man's sacrifice and dedication. To be sure, Kant does not specify exactly how far man is equipped to bring about the kingdom of ends through his own collective efforts. But we still note an important shift from an emphasis on the transcendent action of God -- an action which Kant holds up to as an article of moral faith -- to the

---

[1] Ernst Troeltsch in his untranslated study of Kant's philosophy of religion tries to bring out this neglected side of Kant's thought. Troeltsch implies that the one-sided emphasis on the "symbolization of religion and faith" without sufficient attention to the different slant of the philosophy of history is due to the "theological Kantians," who were concerned solely with questions of personal piety and individual religious experience. But, says Troeltsch, "Kant's philosophy of history deliberately presupposes the genus as its object and not the individual." Ernst Troeltsch, The Historical in Kant's Philosophy of Religion, trans. Clark Williamson (Unpublished typescript, Harvard University, 1966), p. 30. German edition, Das Historisch in Kants Religionsphilosophie (Berlin: Reuther Verlag, 1904), 46.

immanent activity of man. The quietude and passivity of faith give way to purposive social action. In a word, the private stance of self-perfection passes over into the demand for participation in an ongoing historical process. How Kant interprets this process we shall now investigate.

B. The Concept of Historical Progress

1. Nature, Teleology, and Morality

Emil Fackenheim has adroitly noted that "many expositors treat Kant's philosophy of history, but few treat it seriously."[1] This neglect may be due in part to the sketchy and topical form which his philosophy of history assumes. But there is perhaps a more compelling reason for the scholars' oversight. To begin with, the writings on history, in particular the essay entitled "Idea for a Universal History from a Cosmopolitan Point of View," present a picture of man and nature which seems to jar with the popular interpretation of Kant. Thus Kant's commentators are apt to make light of these writings as a king of aberration in the philosopher's reasoning. It is our contention, however, that, far from being some vexsome fly in the ointment of consistent Kant scholarship, this tabloid philosophy of history marks a major point of departure for projecting one possible course of development for Kant's thinking as a whole. That this line of development does not become explicit in the major writings of the critical corpus suggests perhaps that Kant is only experimenting with new approaches to the problems which he deals with. These new approaches might have been enlarged and defined in a systematic work if Kant had lived longer.

At any event, the new standpoint of the writings on history scotches the barely tenable thesis that the critical philosophy has an architectural unity. The "critical" perspective itself, engendered during the 1770's, represents a remarkable change from Kant's earlier thinking. It would be foolish to make the peremptory claim that Kant's ideas had no potential for further

---

[1] Emil Fackenheim, "Kant's Concept of History," Kant-Studien 48 (1956-57): 381.

development and refinement than the form in which history has left them. What is considered normative in Kant's thought is not necessarily his final say.

The new chord that Kant strikes in his treatment of history is the thesis that autonomy and rationality (in short, man's inherent "perfection") do not consist in timeless characteristics of men everywhere, but are the end products of historical evolution. Moreover, Kant implies that history itself (the nexus of human actions and interactions in which moral responsibility makes its appearance) has its origin and goal, not in the heaven of "noumena," but in the natural order. The point of view is, as Alfred Köster has observed, that "the history of man is a portion of the history of nature."[1] In our analysis of the third Critique we saw how the notion of purposiveness in nature provides, for Kant, a conceptual link between the transcendental world of morality and the immanent order of natural law. In "Idea for a Universal History" Kant tries to show that nature indeed can be said to have a central purpose: the purpose of bringing man to the fullness of his powers of reason and morality. The process of working out this purpose becomes human history. Moral agency, Kant argues in the third Critique, comprises the only actual instance of purposiveness in the world on which all other teleological notions are modelled. Man is the organism who transcends himself by projecting moral ends which he then tries to fulfill. All other purposiveness in nature must be compared with this kind of purposiveness and hence seen as analogous to it. But, Kant seems to indicate, if purposiveness is attributable to one part of nature (i.e., to man), is it right to deny purposiveness to nature as a whole?[2] Every human purpose, in a sense, is bound up with the greater purpose of nature. One's individual

---

[1] Adolf Köster, Der Junge Kant im Kampf und die Geschichte (Berlin: L. Simion, 1914), 49.

[2] Fackenheim, op. cit., p. 392. "Is it reasonable to assume a purposiveness in all parts of nature and to deny it to the whole?" OH ("idea"), p. 20. Schriften, VIII, 25.

moral acts do not arise and pass away in an eternity of transcentental consciousness, but have significance as part of the immanent and temporal purpose of the natural world. Nature's purpose (if, Kant suggests, we are to entertain the regulative idea of nature having a purpose) must be by and large a moral purpose. Its purpose is manifested in a process of human action beginning within nature as a nisus toward a higher life form and leading toward the development of that form as a creature with moral faculties. The teleological viewpoint of the "Idea" is thus a moral teleology. all personal acts have significance only with respect to the immanent end of the process we call history -- the end which is the establishment and spread of virtue.

The consideration of "history permits us," Kant says, "to hope that if we attend to the play of freedom of the human will in the large, we may be able to discern a regular movement in it, and that what seems complex and chaotic in the single individual may be seen from the standpoint of the human race as a whole to be a steady and progressive (fortgehende) though slow evolution of its original endowment (Anlagen)."[1] History is the inevitable process wherein "all natural capacities (Naturamlagen) of a creature are destined to evolve completely to their natural end."[2] Did not man's action belong instrumentally to this process, we would "no longer have a lawful but an aimless (zwecklos) course of nature, and blind chance (trostlose Ungefähr) takes the place of the guiding of reason."[3]

But "blind chance" happily does not rule human affairs. The latent perfection of the human species must reach fruition irrespective of men's familiar inclination to resist its growth. Detection of this pattern of evolution which brings purpose and coherence into the seemingly capricious chaos of human actions is the job of the philosopher of history.

---

[1] OH ("Idea"), p. 11. Schriften, VIII, 17.

[2] OH ("Idea"), p. 12. ("First Thesis"). Schriften, VIII, 18.

[3] OH ("Idea"), p. 13. Ibid.

> Since the philosopher cannot presuppose any
> [conscious] individual purpose among men in
> their great drama, there is no other expedient
> for him except to try to see if he can dis-
> cover a natural purpose in this idiotic course
> of things human. In keeping with this purpose,
> it might be possible to have a history with a
> <u>definite</u> <u>natural</u> <u>plan</u> for creatures who have no
> plan of their own.[1]

Kant says that nature <u>forces</u> man to become what he is destined to be, to realize his own generic perfection. The question arises, then, whether Kant has sacrificed his central contention that genuine moral actions must be self-legislated and not forced upon the agent from without. The idea that there exists a "plan of nature" superseding even the best-laid plans of the individual seems to clash with Kant's most basic tenets. It would appear as though Kant had traded the principle of autonomy for a heteronomous teleology of nature -- a teleology that takes precedence over the "personal teleology" of every moral agent. Earlier we had drawn the conclusion that there is only one genuine teleology that Kant allows: the system of moral purposes which men individually set before themselves and endeavor to carry out.

Most likely we would belie Kant's intention if we interpreted the sharp teleological language in the "Idea" as some kind of reversion to the dogmatic metaphysical position that there are objective purposes in nature. We should remember that in the third <u>Critique</u> Kant defends the use of teleological constructions for giving accounts of phenomena which general scientific laws and concepts are unable to explain completely. Such constructions are valid, Kant stresses, only so far as they show how the order of nature can be conjoined in thought with the order of morality. The idea of a "plan of nature" to which man's moral activity conforms, therefore, does not <u>explain</u> the origins of human autonomy and rationality in a theoretical or scientific fashion, so much as it serves as a heuristic concept for allowing us to think of morality as developing over

---

[1] <u>OH</u> ("Idea"), p. 12. <u>Ibid</u>.

time and in nature. Without such a heuristic concept, the
idea of moral progress would have little cogency. Morality
would be locked into a timeless supernatural realm with no
relationship to the world of nature. But if morality is to
be understood as progressive, it must be subject somehow to
the conditions of time. And the conditions of time belong to
the domain of nature. The idea of progress indicates that in
the span of history man is originally an insentient being of
nature and only at a later moment of development does he emerge
as a morally responsible creature. The call of reason to the
advancement of virtue and the promotion of the highest good
constitutes an imperative to continuing progress.

Thus the teleological view of nature which Kant sets
forth provides a unitary conception of how reason emerges and
develops out of the primordial animal state. Reason arises
out of nature, according to this view, and in turn subjects
nature to its norms. That is the dialectic of progress.
Nature gives birth to homo sapiens who directs his powers of
ratiocination back upon his natural environment and his own
natural instincts.[1] The dialectical movement is carried along
by two powerful forces shaping all human life: the mechanical
play of man's "natural" or sensible drives and the spontaneous
and creative promptings of his reason. History is the resolution of this clash of forces. History, moreover, is born
of a contrariety within the natural process itself. Nature
negates itself with the advent of man. Nature creates the
appropriate conditions for a creature to emerge who no longer
depends solely on the mechanisms of nature, but lives also by
his own autonomous abilities. The inherent tendency of nature
to negate itself in the appearance of the human species sums
up what Kant perhaps has in mind when he says that "nature
has willed" for man to "produce everything that goes beyond
the mechanical ordering (Anordnung) of his animal existence,

---

[1] "Thus nature produced Kepler, who subjected, in an unexpected way, the eccentric paths of the planets to definite laws: and she produced Newton, who explained these laws by a universal natural cause." Ibid.

and that he should partake of no other happiness or perfection than that which he himself, independently of instinct, has created by his own reason."[1]

At face value the notion of nature "willing" that man should will for himself seems a contradiction in terms. Yet the contradiction vanishes if we understand Kant's talk as though nature herself were an intelligent agent to mean that the potential for autonomy exists in nature prior to the growth of human reason. The "will" of nature is simply the latent will of man. The idea of nature's "will" consists of a regulative construct for judging how man's moral will can stand as the evolutionary end point of the natural processes. The same problem was faced by the philosophes of the eighteenth century: how could consciousness or mind arise out of unconscious matter? The eighteenth century thinkers often disposed of this dilemma by adopting the stance of materialism, by reducing human reason to, or regarding it as an epiphenomenon of matter. Kant, however, takes the "critical" approach. His first move is to divide reason and insentient nature into two separate spheres; but this ploy fails to allow for the fact of evolution. Thus he must recur to the principles of teleology, albeit a teleology for which "purposes" have to exact theoretical value. They are tools for conceptualization and nothing more.

In a second essay entitled "Conjectural (Mutmässlicher) Beginning of Human History" (1786), Kant turns to the problem of man's origins to illustrate the same theme. The very idea of a "beginning" (Anfang) to history, even more than the notion of a "plan of nature," offers no theoretical insights, according to Kant, into the real pattern of the development of mankind. Kant contends his account of the origin of the human race is plain "conjectures" which "cannot make too high a claim on one's assent." A fortiori they are "at best only... a permissible exercise of the imagination guided by reason,

---

[1] OH ("Idea"), p. 13. (Third Thesis). Italics mine. Schriften, VIII, 19.

undertaken for the sake of relaxation and mental health."[1]
Kant's "conjectures" are based on his rendition of the opening
chapters of Genesis. Fictive though the Genesis story may be,
it nevertheless, for Kant, contains a kernel of profound
truth. The leit-motif of the story, Kant tells us, is the
liberation of man's reason from its bondage to animality. The
myth of Adam's pristine innocence, couples with his loss of
that innocence in partaking of the tree of knowledge of good
and evil, graphically expresses the aboriginal rupture of
rationality in man from mere instinct.

> So long as inexperienced man obeyed the call
> of nature all was well with him. But soon
> reason began to stir. A sense different from
> that to which instinct was tied -- the sense,
> say, of sight -- presented other food than
> that normally consumed as similar to it; and
> reason, instituting a comparison, sought to
> enlarge its knowledge of foodstuffs beyond
> the bounds of instinctual knowledge.[2]

With his loss of dependence purely on instinct, man at the
same time brought into view new ends or purposes that were
not mere gratuities of nature, but ones presented by a faculty
all man's own and which were not the ends of any other species.
These ends were those fixed by reason.

> From this account of original human history
> we may conclude: man's departure from that
> paradise which his reason represents as the
> first abode of his species was nothing but
> the transition from an uncultured, merely
> animal condition to the state of humanity,
> from bondage to instinct to rational control
> (Leitung der Vernunft) -- in a word, from
> the tutelage (Vormundschaft) of nature to
> the state of freedom. Whether man has won
> or lost in this change is no longer an open
> question, if one considers the destiny of
> his species. This consists in nothing less
> than the progress toward perfection, be the
> first attempts toward that aim, or even the
> first long series of attempts, ever so faulty.[3]

---

[1] OH ("Conjectural"), p. 53. Schriften, VIII, 109.

[2] OH ("Conjectural"), p. 55. Schriften, VIII, 111.

[3] OH ("Conjectural"), p. 59-70. Schriften, VIII, 115.

A seemingly immoral act throws man into the state of freedom whereupon the exercise of rational moral choice is for the first time possible. The primordial act of evil marks the beginning of the growth of good in the world. The apparent paradox that evil itself has a higher purpose, insofar as its commission actually frees man to do the good, adds a meaning to the process of human evolution which is not possible so long as one considers nature as a realm alien to morality. The teleological metamorphosis of evil into good is a promise that counsels "contentment with Providence and with the course of human affairs (Dinge) considered as a whole."[1] A non-teleological view of nature tends to pit reason in a Manichean battle with the natural order. But Kant has opted for a more organic conception wherein morality struggles with and inevitably overcomes nature. Without some eye to a teleological unity of the natural world and rational autonomy, we could not make sense out of Kant's claim that nature itself *intends* the ultimate victory of morality in the course of the world. "For this course is not a decline from good to evil, but rather a gradual development from the worse to the better; and nature itself has given the vocation (ist berufen) to everyone to contribute as much to this progress (Fortschritte) as may be within his power."[2] The question we must put to Kant concerns the actual extent to which man's progress may fall "within his power."

The theme of the inexorability of progress suggests that man, for Kant, lives under the sway of a power greater than himself, a power that ruthlessly controls his history. Ordinarily we would tag the notion of such a power as God. And Kant himself tends to favor that notion in his account of God as the power which brings human life to perfection in the highest good. But the curious thing about the writings on history is that Kant employs virtually the same theological

---

[1] OH ("Conjectural"), p. 68. Schriften, VIII, 123.
[2] Ibid.

199

images of a supreme will and intention, with the exception that the God of history he now calls "nature." Nature, for Kant, becomes providential. It is incumbent upon us, therefore, to analyze briefly the significance of Kant's use of theological metaphors to describe the immanent evolutionary process.

2. The Providential View of Nature

The teleological language to which Kant resorts in his discussion of nature and history conjures up the old-fashioned theological doctrine of Providence. Indeed, Kant himself employs the term "Providence" (Vorsehung) to designate the nature of the process of human development.[1] Kant's talk about nature "willing" that man should take command of his own destiny, of having a "plan," (etc.) all in all demonstrates how Kant predicates of the world itself a divine purpose and will guiding history. The distinctive difference is that this guidance no longer comes from "above." Kant assigns the traditional attributes of a transcendent Deity to the immanent movements of the cosmos.

In light of Kant's obdurate demand for autonomous human action, we must shrink from inferring from these writings that

---

[1] E.g., "Such a justification of Nature -- or better, of Providence -- is no unimportant reason for choosing a standpoint toward world history." OH ("Idea"), p. 25. Schriften, VIII, 30. "It is true that Providence has assigned a toilsome road on earth..." OH ("Conjectural"),p. 66. Schriften, VIII, 121. Also, "contentment with Providence, and with the course of human affairs..." See above, p. 204, n. 1. "As a necessity working according to laws we do not know, we call it destiny (Schicksal). But, considering its design (Zweckmässigkeit), we call it "providence," inasmuch as we discern in it the profound wisdom of a higher cause which predetermines the course of nature and directs it to the objective final end of the human race." OH ("Perpetual Peace"), p. 107. Schriften, VIII, 360-1. "In the mechanism of nature, to which man belongs as a sensuous being, a form is exhibited which is basic to its existence...This perdetermination we call 'divine providence' generally..." OH ("Perpetual Peace"), p. 106n. Schriften, VIII, 361n. "As maintains nature in its course by universal laws of design, it is called 'ruling providence' (providentia gubernatrix); as directing nature to ends not foreseen by man and only conjectured from the actual result, it is called 'guiding providence' (providentia directrix)." Ibid.

Kant has, after all, settled on the idea of sovereign will which overrules all personal willing in the insuperable juggernaut of history. It has "concerned Nature," Kant writes, that man "should work himself upward so as to make himself, through his own actions, worthy of life and of well-being."[1] In a word, man himself becomes the sole historical agent. Man's moral purpose-making defines what should be the final purpose of the world. Nature does not actually "work out" a pre-existent purpose for the world of which man's purposes are subordinate instruments. Man can never be a mere means to a higher purpose than that dictated in practical reason. Kant's assertion that nature has a "purpose" serves only as a heuristic idea for showing how human purpose-making can be combined in a single conceptual scheme with the idea of nature as a total process. Man's reason and his purposive activity, like his animal endowments, are products of nature. The bare idea of man as a <u>causa noumenon</u> fails to indicate how human reason can be comprehended as a moment in the evolution of nature. The notion that nature as a pre-existent moral purpose locates the genesis of man's purpose-making in a state prior to consciousness and rationality. This, at least, is the best interpretation we can bring to bear on what may seem at first blush a curious resort on Kant's part to a metaphysics of nature. We must keep in mind that here, as elsewhere, Kant is interested primarily in devising philosophical constructs that unify diverse strands of experience, even if they do not explain the data of experience in a theoretically satisfying manner.

Kant's statements, like the one that "nature inexorably wills that the right should finally triumph,"[2] correspond in a manner of speaking to his notion, discussed earlier, that there exists a higher power (for instance, the notion of a divine will that realizes the highest good) working to create a universe which man on his own cannot effect. But in the case we are now considering, this higher power is portrayed,

---

[1] <u>OH</u> ("Idea"), p. 14. <u>Schriften</u>, VIII, 20.

[2] <u>Ibid</u>.

not merely as the agent who completes the remaining stages of
progress to which man is powerless to attain by himself (as
in the instance of the divine will which establishes the perfect highest good), but as the <u>initiator</u> <u>and</u> <u>sustainer</u> of
progress as a whole.

The significance of this enlargement of the idea of a higher
agency, on the face of it, poses some puzzling contradictions
to Kant's basic position. The role of God here is played by
nature which, in most of Kant's ethical theory, stands directly
over against (as the realm of phenomena) the sphere of moral
activity -- divine as well as human. In Kant's discussion of
the highest good, God is the agent who subjects nature to his
will, corresponding with the law of holiness. In the <u>Opus
Postumum</u> God and the natural world are opposing orders of
reality between which stands man, the "middle term." Moreover,
the view of history as the indefeasible plan of nature has all
the earmarks of a grand theodicy (an attempt at placing a
"moral" valuation on a scheme of seemingly immoral acts); but
the very presumption of theodicy we found earlier repudiated
in Kant.

Resolution of these apparent contradictions will not come
with even the most sedulous internal analysis of the concepts
Kant introduces in the essays on history. Any possible resolution, therefore, must hinge on our properly interpreting
the direction in which Kant's thought seems to be veering away
from the dualistic <u>Weltanschauung</u> so evident in the first two
Critiques and related treatises.[1] The essays on history intimate that idea of a transcendent "will of God" working itself

---

[1] It should be noted here that the organicism which seems
to be definitely emerging in the writings on history does not
entail a speculative claim concerning the inner secrets of the
universe in its entirety -- claims which the critical philosophy repudiates. "Providence" does not refer to a well-defined
pattern of events that can be cognized like Newtonian law.
"We do not observe or infer this providence in the cunning con-
trivances of nature, but...we can and must supply it from our
own minds in order to conceive of its possibility...The idea
of the relationship and harmony between these actions and the
end which reason directly assigns to us is transcendent from

out in history must be translated into the immanent processes of history itself. Heretofore we tried to show how the prima facie conception of independent divine action melts into illusion.[1] The import of the essays on history is to underscore that the dynamics of moral progress resides in the cultivation of the human will itself. This will has its origin and destiny not in God, but in the process of natural evolution for which the omega point is human autonomy. Nature "destines," Kant states in the "Idea," man to become the arbiter of his own destiny through moral activity. But this is just another way of saying that the "will" of nature is the nascent will of man. Man is the culmination of a creative process that begins from below and proceeds inexorably without any guidance from above. Man himself gradually takes over control of the process through increasing self-mastery and rule of the world in which he lives. There is seldom any mention of God in the writings on history.

But man's historical will is not at any past or present

---

a theoretical point of view... [Thus] use of the word 'nature' is more fitting to the limits of human reason and more modest than an expression indicating a providence unknown to us...the use of the word 'providence' here intimates the possession of wings like those of Icarus, conducting us toward the secret of its unfathomable (unergründlichen) purpose." OH ("Perpetual Peace"), pp. 106-8. Schriften, VIII, 362.

[1] Kant denies the idea of Providence as an independent divine activity. The concept of Providence as "intervention or concurrence (concursus) in producing an effect in the world of sense must be given up...We fall into...self-contradiction, for example, when we say that next to God, it was the physician who cured the ill, as if God had been his helper..." OH ("Perpetual Peace"), p. 107n. Schriften, VIII, 361-2n. "In a morally-practical point of view, however, which is directed exclusively to the supersensuous, the concept of the divine concursus is quite suitable and even necessary. We find this, for instance, in the belief that God will compensate for our own lack of justice, provided our intention was justice, provided our intention was genuine; that He will do so by means that are inconceivable to us, and that therefore we should not relent in our endeavor after the good. But it is self-evident that no one should try to explain a good action (as an event in the world) as a result of this concursus, for this would be a vain theoretical knowledge of the supersensuous and therefore absurd (ungereimt)." OH ("Perpetual Peace"), 107-8n. Schriften, VIII, 362n.

stage of history completely akin to God's will, for experience teaches us that man has never achieved full command of his natural endowments. How, then, can Kant dispense with the notion of God? Is the postulate of a supreme will still not necessary in order to make up for this historical lag? In the account of history Kant allows the lag to be compensated by a factor other than God: the cumulative progress of the race from one generation to another. The inevitable increase in virtue over the course of generations provides the necessary "guarantee" of a moral world that otherwise would be supplied by the will of God. Kant describes this guarantee as follows:

> It remains strange that the earlier generations appear to carry through their toilsome labor only for the sake of the later, to prepare for them a foundation on which the later generations could erect the higher edifice which was Nature's goal, and yet that only the latest of the generations should have the good fortune to inhabit the building on which a long line of their ancestors had (unintentionally) labored without being permitted to partake of the fortune they had prepared. However puzzling this may be, it is necessary if one assumes that a species of animals should have reason, and, as a class of rational beings each of whom dies while the species is immortal, should develop their capacities to perfection.[1]

The implication of the passage is telling. In the second Critique Kant offers the postulate of personal immortality as a warrant for progress in moral perfection. Yet we now find Kant saying that moral progress need not be pursued in the mysterious hereafter, but in the deathless progress of the race. Moral progress is achieved in history rather than beyond earthly existence. The imperfections of the individual are thus sublated into the perfectibility of the genus as a whole to which he belongs.[2]

---

[1] OH ("Idea"), p. 14. Schriften, VIII, 20. "One generation builds on the experience of the preceding one which has made progress in morality." Klaus Weyand, Kants Geschichtsphilosophie (Köln: Kölner Universitäts-Verlag, Kant-Studien Ergänzungsheft, 1964), 75.

[2] This view has been adopted by a number of commentators on

But if the race enjoys the perfectibility the individual lacks, are we not justified in concluding that the race thereby assumes the office of God? "In man (as the only rational creature on earth) those natural capacities which are directed to the use of his reason are to be fully developed only in the race, not in the individual." The race has the capacity to achieve what the lone individual in his frailty and finitude cannot. But this capacity Kant, in other contexts, ascribes to God. Syntactically it is easy to substitute the word "race" for "God." Kant's philosophy of religion is taken up into the philosophy of history. The element of "theodicy" in Kant's reckoning of human history is translated into an anthropodicy of the progress of the species.

Kant's anthropodicy of progress, moreover, injects a new meaning into the concept of the perfect highest good. The second Critique, we recall, showed how the idea of a highest good -- a world governed by perfect justice and containing the consonance of happiness with virtue -- becomes necessary for moral reason. Because such a world is a priori necessary,

---

Kant's philosophy of history. "Just as Kant had required in the philosophy of religion the postulate of immortality in order to guarantee the most complete approximation of virtue, so at the level of the philosophy of history he takes up the problem of the immortality of the race, in order to make possible the fullest development of all human tendencies and its closest approximation to the goal of human history." Ibid., pp. 184-5. The postulate of God's existence is supplanted by the "hidden plan of nature." Cf. also Kant "shifts the emphasis from the perfectibility of the individual to the perfectibility of the human species..." John Passmore, The Perfectibility of Man (New York: Charles Scribner's Sons, 1970), p. 217. Of course, we must remember that Kant himself is addressing a slightly different problem in this essay than in the second Critique. The argument of the second Critique is concerned to show how man qua individual can hope for moral progress toward perfection. Since men die before the progress is complete, they must look for continuance of their quest in the after-life. The idea of moral progress in history for the race as a whole solves the more abstract problem of how virtue in general will eventually come to dominate human affairs. But such an idea does not directly address itself to the existential question of how any given individual might perfect himself. The individual who scans the prospect of future generic development can hope for an easier road to virtue for posterity, but not necessarily for himself.

Kant further argues, we must postulate the existence of a
supreme agent with the capacity to realize perfect justice
in the universe. Kant's account of history, however, suggests
one alternative to belief in God as the guarantor of perfect
justice. No longer must we view justice in the world solely
as the consequence of a divine act, but also as the result of
man's historical struggle to secure an order of interpersonal
relations that allows for an equitable distribution of rewards. Such an order lies in the conception of a just society.
Indeed, the very notion of "justice" itself has an original
socio-political meaning. The theological meaning is a secondary derivation. Kant's interpretation of history persuades
us that the idea of cosmic justice is merely a mythical
equivalent for the attainment of a perfect social order. The
divine will which guarantees this justice can be translated
into the human effort to establish such an order.[1] Kant's
view of history, therefore, represents a secularization of
the theological concept of Providence. The highest good becomes the founding of world justice.[2]

---

[1] Again, we should note here that the notion of God's justice proferred in the second Critique is designed to meet the problem of justice in the universe corresponding to one's personal moral efforts. Ultimately, justice for the individual will be secured in the universal society, but until the advent of that society man must rely on belief in the beneficence of a power that transcends merely human dispensations. The idea of divine justice represents a mythical solution to the problem; the idea of a just society involves a real solution, albeit a solution that must be deferred to future epoch. In Marxist parlance, we may say that the solution of the second critique is necessary, like all religious solutions, as a proximate reconciliation of a contradiction that exists in present social relations. But once those social relations are transformed, the contradiction will disappear and the idea of God will prove otiose. Naturally, we must offer this analysis as primarily an interpretation of a certain direction in Kant's thought. Kant never makes any explicit attempt to tie the solution to the issue of justice in the essays on history to the solution of the second Critique.

[2] Cf. Kant's rendering of the highest good as "social," above, p. 194, n. 1.

3. The Socialization of the Race

The second thesis of Kant's essay on the "Idea for a Universal History" runs as follows: "In man (as the only rational creature on earth) those natural capacities which are directed to the use of his reason are to be fully developed only in the race (Gattung), not in the individual."[1] Kant goes on, however, to delimit the concept of generic perfectibility more concretely. "If it is asked," Kant says, "whether the human race at large is progressing perpetually toward the better, the important thing is not the natural history of man (whether new races may arise in the future), but rather his moral history (Sittengeschichte)..." More precisely, however, we must understand "his history not as a species according to the generic notion (singulorum), but as the totality (Ganzen) of men united socially on earth and apportioned into peoples (Völkerschaften)..."[2] As we have already seen, moral progress depends, for Kant, on the gradual formation of a universal social order committed to the ideals of morality and justice. The progress of the race consists in its steady socialization. Yet the process of socialization does not proceed at an equable pace, but is punctuated with setbacks and violent conflicts. Kant does not adopt a simple meliorist's view of history. Meliorism is the doctrine that the world, slowly and uneventfully, is becoming better, and that man, through prudent planning and foresight, is the supervisor of change. Kant, of course, foreglimpses the day when man can take charge of progress, yet he is prophetically aware of man's destructive energies and his retrograde tendencies which curtail his own steady advancement. Man exhibits almost as great an antipathy to the construction of social harmony as an affinity for it. Kant read enough of Thomas Hobbes to be convinced of the anti-social impulses in the human animal.

---

[1] OH ("Idea"), p. 13. Schriften, VIII, 18.

[2] OH ("Question"), p. 137. SF: Schriften, VII, 79.

Kant, therefore, comes up with another of his putative paradoxes: the development of social order among men eventuates from <u>disorder</u>. Kant outlines this stance in the "Fourth Thesis" of the "Idea." "The means employed by Nature to bring about the development of all the capacities of men is their antagonism in society, so far as this is, in the end, the cause of lawful order among men."[1] Kant characterizes this "antagonism" as the "unsocial sociability" (<u>ungesellig Geselligkeit</u>) of men, i.e., their propensity to enter into society, bound together by a mutual opposition which constantly threatens to break up the society."[2] Every man harbors within himself "the unsocial characteristic of wishing to have everything go according to his own wish." For that reason "he expects opposition on all sides because, in knowing himself, he knows that he, on his own part, is inclined to oppose others." But this opposition "awakens all his powers," stimulates the urge for competition and the desire "to achieve a rank among his fellows whom he cannot tolerate but from whom he cannot withdraw."[3] In a far more sanguine tone than Kant's lament in the <u>Religion</u> for the tenacity of radical evil in human affairs,[4] Kant signs paens to the brutality and violence that has marred man's history.

> Thanks be to Nature, then, for the incompatibility, for heartless competitive vanity (<u>missgünftig wetteifernde Eitelkeit</u>), for the insatiable desire to possess and to rule! Without them, all the excellent natural capacities of humanity would forever sleep, undeveloped. Man wishes concord; but Nature knows better what is good for the race; she wills discord. He wishes to live comfortably and pleasantly; Nature wills that he should be plunged from sloth and passive contentment into labor and trouble, in order that he may find means of extricating himself from them.

---

[1] <u>OH</u> ("Idea"), p. 15. <u>Schriften</u>, VIII, 20.

[2] <u>Ibid</u>.

[3] <u>Ibid</u>. <u>Schriften</u>, VIII, 21.

[4] Cf. above, p. 129.

> The natural urges to this, the sources of
> unsociableness and mutual opposition (durch-
> gängigen Widerstandes) from which so many
> evils arise, drive men to new exertions of
> their forces and thus to the manifold dev-
> elopment of their capacities. They thereby
> perhaps show the ordering of a wise Creator
> and not the hand of an evil spirit, who
> bungled in his great work or spoiled it
> out of envy.[1]

Remarkably, we find in passages such as this one a prefiguration of Hegel's idea of the "cunning of reason" -- the view that there is a rational pattern amid the irrational welter of man's passions and expressions of self-interest, that history uses human conflict to achieve a final goal of which the actual agents in the drama of events are not immediately conscious or committed to realizing.[2] Kant, of course, does not share Hegel's assumption that the intricate tapestry of history can be "comprehended" in respect to the real processes involved. The "justification of Nature," of which Kant speaks,[3] is no speculative _tour de force_. The "idea" of history which Kant presents has no constitutive value, but is akin to the "regulative ideas" proposed in the _Critique of Pure Reason_. The function of "this Idea" is to "serve as a guiding thread (Leitfaden) for presenting as a system, at least in broad outlines, what would otherwise be a planless conglomeration (planloses Aggregat) of human

---

[1] OH ("Idea"), p. 16. Schriften, VIII, 21-2.

[2] Cf. Hegel's account of "world-historical men" whose passions and appetites advance the development of the "universal" or "Idea" of history. "This may be called the cunning of reason (List der Vernunft) -- that it sets the passions to work for itself..." C.W.F. Hegel, The Philosophy of History, trans. J. Sibree (New York: Dover Publications, 1956), p. 33. Compare this with Kant's statement that "nature guarantees perpetual peace by the mechanism of the human passions." OH ("Perpetual Peace"), p. 114. Schriften, VIII, 368. The comparison of Kant with Hegel is also made by Goldmann, op. cit. and Karl Jaspers, Philosophy and the World, trans. E. B. Ashton (Chicago: Henry Regnery Company, 1963), p. 109.

[3] OH ("Idea"), p. 25. Schriften, VIII, 30.

actions."¹ The concept of a purpose to historical events, which seemingly have no express purpose, is a rational construct useful for the observer of human affairs in bringing unity and coherence out of a riot of mere impressions. But this idea does not merely assist in the development of a theory of history, just as the regulative ideas of the first Critique serve as appliances for scientific inquiry. The idea of history has a practical role to play; it provides a foundation for hope that one's moral actions are not whimsical gestures to fate, but pregnant moments in an ongoing process toward the realization of the highest good.² Although Kant nowhere explicitly defines the function of the idea in such a way, such a function is perhaps what he has in mind when he argues that he does not "want to displace the work of practicing empirical historians with the Idea of world history."³ For the idea of history "is to some extent based upon an a priori principle."⁴ The idea of history falls in the same category with all other practical ideas or "beliefs." Beliefs are instrumental in furnishing a total frame of meaning for moral action. Belief in the purposefulness of the historical process is necessary to man if he is to "grasp," as Kant puts its, "the burden of history we shall leave to [our descendents] after a few centuries."⁵ The recurring question, however, is whether belief in the purposefulness of history has more practical value than simple belief in God. We shall weigh that question in our concluding remarks.

---

¹OH ("Idea"), p. 24. Schriften, VIII, 29.

²Kant looks at "history as the temporal development of human community toward the realization of the highest good through which we can fulfill in our concrete present life a moral vocation and attain the highest good." Goldman, op. cit., 215.

³OH ("Idea"), p. 25. Schriften, VIII, 30.

⁴Ibid.

⁵Ibid.

For Kant, the purposefulness of history is expressed, not simply in the uninterrupted advance of virtue (the idea of moral progress apart from a concrete, historical context of action is a tenuous abstraction), but in the development of a society in which morality can flourish. The social context of moral progress is specified in the fifth thesis: "The greatest problem for the human race, to the solution of which Nature drives man, is the achievement of a universal civic society (<u>allgemein bürgerlichen Gesselschaft</u>) which administers law among men."[1] A society "which administers law" is vital to the attainment of moral perfection; for law guarantees security and domestic tranquillity in which man's tender moral aptitudes can be cultivated and individuals do not exhaust themselves in the struggle for self-preservation.[2] Law guarantees a state in which there can be the "most exact definition of freedom and fixing of its limits so that it may be consistent with the freedom of others."[3] Freedom merely to do as one pleases -- the lonely and anxiety-ridden freedom of man for himself in the state of nature -- allows a person no opportunity to improve his state of life beyond concern with his day-to-day welfare. But in a "civic union" (<u>bürgerliche Vereinigung</u>) the passions and aggressions of men are bridled sufficiently to permit occupation with developing the higher forms of moral culture. Kant draws a simile with the way trees grow in a forest:

> each tree needs the others, since each in seeking to take the air and sunlight from others must strive upward, and thereby each realizes a beautiful, straight nature, while those that live in isolated freedom put out braches at random and grow stunted, crooked, and twisted.[4]

---

[1] <u>OH</u> ("Idea"), p. 16. <u>Schriften</u>, VIII, 22.

[2] "The friction among men, the inevitable antagonism which is a part of even the largest societies and political bodies, is used by Nature as a means to establish a condition of quiet and security." <u>OH</u> ("Idea"), p. 18. <u>Schriften</u>, VIII, 24.

[3] <u>OH</u> ("Idea"), p. 16. <u>Schriften</u>, VIII, 22.

[4] <u>OH</u> ("Idea"), p. 17. <u>Ibid</u>.

211

The "civic union" that establishes the conditions for the growth of morality, however, must have world-wide scope. Without this union wars and other kinds of internecine violence continually threaten every member of the human race. The development of order within a particular society is not in itself adequate to foster moral progress. Just because men subscribe to the norms and statutes of a particular society does not mean they will respect the integrity of men in other communities. War is all too often the result of one nation-state striving to impose its own norms and institutions on other peoples, to enforce its own parochial ethos in contempt of other values and moral traditions. If the power to foist particularized notions of right and wrong on one's neighbors were checked, a major source of war would dry up.

War, therefore, can be eliminated by the creation of a universal society in which the "law of the land" is essentially a universal law. In the "Idea" Kant adopts the point of view that man must ultimately be subjected to the universal moral law, first of all, through the positive force of a constitution of world-wide government. "Man is an animal," Kant contends, "which, if it lives among others of its kind, requires a master," a master who "will break his will and force him to obey a will that is universally valid, under which each can be free. But whence does he get this master? Only from the human race."[1] The race becomes the master of man in political form: as a "league of nations" (Völkerbund),[2] a "lawful civic state" (gesetzmässigen bürgerlichen Verfassung),[3] or an "international government" (grossen Staatskorner).[4] Under the tutelage of this "master" man is impressed into a state of morality which would be impossible for him acting alone. History, thus, leads to the establishment of a "universal cosmopolitan con-

---

[1] Ibid. Schriften, VIII, 23.

[2] OH ("Idea"), p. 19. Schriften, VIII, 24.

[3] OH ("Idea"), p. 18. Ibid.

[4] OH ("Idea"), p. 23. Schriften, VIII, 28.

dition (<u>allgemeiner</u> <u>weltbürgerlicher</u> <u>Zustand</u>), which Nature has as her ultimate purpose," and which "will come into being as the womb wherein all the original capacities of the human race can develop."[1] A "state of peace is established in which laws have force"[2] -- the "perpetual peace" (<u>ewiger</u> <u>Friede</u>) preserved by an international order. Secured through a perfect constitution, the state of perpetual peace provides the proper environment for man's moral life. External constraints are necessary to the cultivation of inner freedom, the freedom of autonomy. A good constitution fosters a "good will." "A good constitution is not to be expected from morality, but conversely, a good moral condition of a people is to be expected only under a good constitution."[3]

Generally speaking, Kant has offered one of the first inklings of the modern sociological perspective: the moral behavior is not <u>sui generis</u>, but a product of socialization. In fine, it is the view that moral behavior must be conditioned or inculcated by forces or pressures from within one's social <u>milieu</u>. Thus the moral values to which a man in conscience subscribes represent the internalization of outside norms. Morality becomes, in short, a social creation.[4]

But does not Kant's view that morality depends on the constraints of society seem to fly in the face of the principle of autonomy? If man is shaped by outside influences, rather

---

[1] <u>Ibid</u>.

[2] <u>OH</u> ("Perpetual Peace"), p. 112. <u>Schriften</u>, VIII, 366.

[3] <u>OH</u> ("Perpetual Peace"), p. 112-3. <u>Ibid</u>.

[4] Cf. Carl Friedrich, <u>Inevitable Peace</u> (Cambridge: Harvard University Press, 1948), p. 62f. Friedrich maintains that the idea of positive social laws as the necessary determinant of morality is an "assumption" that is "deeply rooted in Kant's whole system of philosophy." Cf. also Theodore Ruyssen, "Philosophie de l'Histoire selon Kant," <u>La Philosophie Politique de Kant</u>, Annales de Philosophie Politique (Paris: Presses Universitaires de France, 1962), 33-51.

than primarily making what he is himself through the laws of
his own reason, is this not an unmistakable volteface for
Kant's ethical system? Kant is not really saying that society
coerces man into obeying the moral law in violation of his
own will and in a way not certified by the recommendations of
his own reason. If the law of practical reason is to become
a principle of willing, it must be adopted as one's own law.
But that is not to say the positive form of the moral law
cannot first be proposed ab extra to man's reasoning faculties
through the process of education. In his essay on pedagogy
Kant defines education as primarily "discipline" (Zucht),
"teaching" (Unterweisung), and "culture" (Bildung)."[1] Education is the formation (bilden) through rigorous training
of moral character; it is the process of instilling the highest values of a society in the consciences of its members.
So far as a world society is concerned, the task of education
is to imprint upon men's minds the necessity of respect for
the universal law of reason. The decision to adopt the law as
a maxim is one's own decision.

Yet education alone cannot cement reverence itself for
the law. It can only make a public case for the necessity of
a universal moral standard; it has no power to make reason
give its final assent to the moral law and appropriate it as
a rule of one's own will. The power of inducing assent must
come from within the agent; it cannot be enforced from without.
The power of assent springs from a well-developed faculty of
reason. Thus what is needed, in addition to education, is a
steady growth of man's powers of autonomous reason in guiding
the moral life. This process Kant calls "enlightenment"
(Aufklärung). Enlightenment is "man's release from his self-incurred [minority] (Unmündigkeit)."[2] "Minority," Kant con-

---

[1] E, p. 1. Schriften, IX, 441.

[2] OH ("Enlightenment"), p. 3. Schriften, VIII, 35. I have
translated the term Unmündigkeit as "minority," instead of as
"tutelage," as occurs in the Beck translation. The former translation seems to give a more precise rendering of Kant's meaning. Enlightenment consists in man's release from his own
immaturity, his adolescence in the conduct of his moral affairs.

tinues, "is man's inability to make use of his understanding without direction from another."[1] In his immaturity man depends on the authority of an Other -- whether it be his family, his nation, or his God -- to instruct him how he should conduct himself in the world.[2] The moral law, like other laws, becomes nothing more than a positive law, not an inner law of his own conscience. Through enlightenment man's dependence on outside authorities and constraints is cast aside.

Kant emphasizes that enlightenment is a virtue only the individual can nourish within himself. Yet the conditions for the individual's undertaking his own enlightenment are laid down by society. The solitary agent cannot achieve genuine enlightenment. "For any single individual to work himself out of the life under tutelage which has become almost his nature is very difficult."[3] Yet "that the public should enlighten itself is more possible."[4] Public enlightenment will come when a social order has been constructed that grants man the equanimity and liberty to enhance their rational faculties "if only freedom is granted, enlightenment is sure to follow."

The socialization of man into the state of morality, therefore, does not directly go against the rule of autonomy. Society only makes moral progress possible; it does not create the good dispositions or intentions logically prior to moral acts. Cultivation of the good will must be an autonomous act of the moral agent. In this respect, the world-wide civic

---

[1] "It is easy not to be of age. If I have a book which understands for me, a pastor who has a conscience for me, a physician who decides my diet, and so forth, I need not troubl myself. I need not think, if I can only pay -- others will readily undertake the irksome work for me." Ibid.

[2] Ibid.

[3] OH ("Enlightenment"), p. 4. Schriften, VIII, 36.

[4] Ibid.

[5] Ibid.

union which Kant urges only represents the outward form of
the moral life of mankind. Its constitution provides the
positive canons of justice and the mechanisms of social control, but does not create automatically the personal attitude
of moral commitment and solidarity necessary for the unity of
the human race. True moral solidarity issues from the inner
commitment of many wills to the universal law of reason, which
is basically the public law of the peoples of the world written
into men's hearts.

Inside the husk of human solidarity (the world political
order) Kant envisages, therefore, the growth of a community of
virtue whose members, not only obey the universal positive
laws, but gradually appropriate the objective norms of reasons
into the moral maxims. Perviously we discussed how the concept of the moral law entails a community of moral agents
acting out of respect for each other's persons. Such a community Kant calls a "kingdom of ends." The kingdom of ends is,
first of all, an a priori conception of the form human interaction would take, if all men adopted the rule of the end-initself as their maxims. But, like all a priori concepts of
practical reason, the kingdom of ends demands realization in
the natural order. The kingdom of ends must be translated
from the heaven of transcendental ideals to a visible, earthly
association of men. The realized kingdom of ends becomes the
highest good in its social aspect. Sometimes Kant gives it
the name of "ethical commonwealth," sometimes "kingdom of
God" (Reich Gottes).[1] In the Religion he calls the empirical
manifestation of the kingdom of ends by its traditional title --
the "church."[2] The church is that historically enduring

---

[1]"Christian ethics supplies the defect of the second indispensable component of the highest good by presenting a world hwerein reasonable beings single-mindedly devote themselves to the moral law; this is the Kingdom of God, in which nature and morality come into harmony..." CP_rR, p. 133. Schriften, V, 133.

[2]"The true (visible) church is that which exhibits the (moral) kingdom of God on earth so far as it can be brought to pass by men." RWL, p. 92. Schriften, VI, 101.

communion of men that strives to actualize the kingdom of ends within their own circle as well as in their dealings with other men. But such a church is not the same as the familiar institutional church with its rites, priests, creeds, and dogma -- the passel of religious trappings Kant calls "ecclesiastical faith." It is the church of enlightened autonomous agents, who have learned to shun superstition and follow their own reason. Kant views history as the process in which this enlightened moral communion slowly takes over the whole of public life. Indeed, the process has already begun and is irreversible.

> If now one asks, What period in the entire known history of the church up to now is the best? I have no scruple in answering, the present. And this, because, if the seed of the true religious faith, as it is now being sown in Christendom, through only by a few, is allowed more and more to grow unhindered, we may look for a continuous approximation to that church, eternally uniting all men, which constitutes the visible representation (the schema) of an invisible kingdom of God on earth.[1]

Kant's cause for historical optimism does not stem so much from a review of man's past as from his discernment of what is now taking place, how current events augur the future course of human action. "We have good reason to say," Kant writes, "that 'the kingdom of God is come into us,'" because such a kingdom has "gained somewhere a public foothold, even though the actual establishment of this state is still infinitely removed from us."[2] The ethical commonwealth, the kingdom of

---

[1] RWL, p 122. Schriften, VI, 131-2.

[2] It should be noted that Kant, in the Religion, does not draw any actual connection between the idea of the ethical commonwealth and the concept of "perpetual peace" through international order, which he develops in the essays on history. Our analysis here is an extrapolation from Kant's remarks in the essays that the formation of political harmony is the necessary pre-condition for morality. In the Religion Kant emphasizes, however, that morality must develop within a community of virtue. The "two-stage" theory of progress noted below is an attempt to adjust the Religion with the essays.

virtue -- these represent the maturation of man's moral relations with one another. Establishment of an order of international justice through a federation of nation states lays the groundwork for the growth of moral solidarity in the race.[1] Through "the mechanism of human passions" nature converts man into a social and political animal out of which can evolve his higher rational talents.

The moral process, then, supersedes the original social impulse in man's development. The progress of the race passes through two distinct stages: (1) the pacification of man's original bellicosity in the state of nature; (2) the moralization of man in community. The internationsl civic union serves as the chrysallis in which the butterfly that is the kingdom of ends can emerge. The component of "justice" in the highest good is secured immanently and historically through the creation of stable judicial institutions; the component of virtue is attained in the life of the church.

Yet the moralization of man in the church, as opposed to his mere socialization in civic union, turns out to be a more arduous and monumental task than the establishment of justice. Whereas justice requires only an artificial mechanism for meting out rewards and punishments, morality demands the cultivation of good maxims, of the right intentions in men. In other words, justice is an external problem, morality an internal one. No political body can enforce virtue after the fashion of some world-wide Genevan Consistory.[2] Kant makes the distinction between a "juridico-civil (political state" and the "ethico-civil state" or the ethical commonwealth. A juridico-civil state "is the relation of men to each other in which they all alike stand socially under public

---

[1]Cf. OH ("Perpetual Peace"), p. 114. Schriften, VIII, 368,

[2]"...woe to the legislator who wishes to establish through force a polity directed to ethical ends! For in doing so he would not merely achieve the very opposite of an ethical polity but also undermine his political state and make it insecure." RWL, p. 87. Schriften, VI, 96.

juridical laws (which are, as a class, laws of co-ercion)."
An ethico-civil state, on the other hand, "is that in which
they are united under non-coercive laws, i.e., laws of virtue
alone."[1] Laws of virtue, because they are ordinances of the
"heart" and hence non-coercive in the judicial sense, cannot
be enforced with the same ease and effectiveness as the laws
of a political commonwealth. Dissemblance can mask bad intentions. Thus the ethical commonwealth must have a law-maker
and governor, "'one who knows the heart,' in order to see the
innermost parts (Innerste) of the disposition of each individual
and, as is necessary in every commonwealth, to bring it about
that each receives whatever his actions are worth."[2] Yet,
Kant adds, "this is the concept of God as moral ruler of the
world."[3] For that reason, it is necessary to conceive of the
ethical commonwealth "as a people under divine commands, i.e.,
as a people of God, and indeed under laws of virtue."[4]

God becomes the conscience of the ethical community. He
ensures that the invisible law of moral intention becomes
binding on all its members. The project of establishing a
universal civil society, therefore, is an open historical
challenge for man. But the founding of a moral community which
brings man to his final perfection as a rational agent requires, Kant indicates, the intervention of a super-human power.

This analysis again outlines a different kind of argument
than the one in the second Critique for belief in a God who
realizes the highest good. The concept of God ultimately will

---

[1] Ibid. Schriften, VI, 95. In the "ethical commonwealth all the laws as expressly designed to promote the morality of action (which is something inner, and hence cannot be subject to public human laws) whereas, in contrast, these public laws and thus would go to constitute a judicial commonwealth -- are directed only toward the legality of actions, which meets the eye, and not toward (inner) morality, which alone is in question here." RWL, p. 90. Schriften, VI, 98-9.

[2] RWL, p. 91. Schriften, VI, 99.

[3] Ibid.

[4] RWL, p. 92. Schriften, VI, 100.

no longer be needed to guarantee justice in an unjust universe.
The creation of justice -- the outward allocation of tangible
rewards to moral merit -- comes about through the socio-
political processes. With the arrival of social justice, God
will become superfluous in securing the second or "perfect"
condition of the highest good. On the other hand, in the
Religion God is deemed necessary to guarantee the first or
"supreme" condition of the highest good -- the preservation
of good intentions. God is the founder of the community of
righteous men. In the essays on history, we find the notion
that immanent historical processes, God notwithstanding, impel
the development and perfection of man's moral conduct (albeit
through society); but in the Religion Kant insists that "to
found a moral people of God is...a task whose consummation can
be looked for not from men but only from God Himself."[1] The
idea of a divine moral agent, Kant seems to be saying in this
passage, becomes necessary, providing we wish to view history
as progressing, not only toward the erection of social institutions that favor moral growth, but also toward purifica-
tion of man's inner life -- his reason and moral decision-
making.

On the other hand, in the Religion Kant goes on to amend
his statement that only God can secure the ethical commonwealth.
Though God may be the guarantor of the ethical commonwealth,
man is its _executor_. Though man may believe in the reality
of a higher power who realizes the kingdom of ends in history,
he

> ...is not entitled on this account to be idle
> in this business and to let Providence rule,
> as though each could apply himself exclusively
> to his own private moral affairs and relinquish
> to a higher wisdom all the affairs of the human
> race (as regards its moral destiny). Rather,
> man must proceed as though everything depended
> on him; only on this condition dare he hope
> that higher wisdom will grant the completion
> (Vollendung) of his well-intentioned (wohl-
> gemeinten) endeavors.[2]

---

[1] RWL, p. 92. Schriften, VI, 100.

[2] Ibid. Schriften, VI, 100-1. Italics mine.

Man must act "as though everything depended on him." The idea of a Providence which accomplishes for man what he alone is obliged to do strikes Kant as deleterious to morality. In this sense, the idea of Providence, for Kant, is as otiose as the notion of grace. Kant demands that man must act alone mindless of any prospect that he will attain his objective. Any suggestion that man, instead, can depend on the work of an agent more powerful than himself -- an agent waiting in the wings of history to pick up where man has left off -- must be abandoned. Otherwise, the formula for action becomes a heteronomous one. Only when man has struggled for complete self-mastery is he entitled to "hope" for the "completion" of his efforts.

But what exactly is contained in this hope? The principle of autonomy rules out the idea of a God who meddles in man's moral career. The injunction to act "as though" one were entirely alone on the stage of history makes the idea of human self-sufficiency a kind of practical postulate with as much heuristic value as the postulate of God. Do the two postulates conflict? Not necessarily. They would conflict only at the perfection of human development. Should man eliminate radical evil from his nature and gain control of the natural world, the idea would no longer have any practical efficacy. The "postulate" of self-sufficiency presents man with a vision of what he should strive to become. The postulate of God, so to speak, "fills in the gap" between this vision of perfection and man's present inability to accomplish that perfection. Kant does not express unflinching confidence that the gap can ever be closed. The implication of his argument is that some idea of God will always be necessary. But the gap can be increasingly <u>narrowed</u> through moral progress. As time goes on, the God-postulate will gradually lose its overshadowing role in the conduct of human affairs. Kant would remain true to the inner logic of his own philosophical views if he had recognized that the God-postulate can ultimately be dispensed with. The God-postulate, we have argued, in keeping

with Kant's own cardinal tenets, must come to light as a kind
of "interim" postulate that continues in force as long as man
is on his pilgrimage to holiness. But the postulate is only
necessary so long as this condition persists.

The content of man's hope, therefore, lies in an anticipation of his own success in the struggle for moral perfection.
He may hope for the workings of a "higher wisdom," but any
idea of a higher wisdom with a plan for the universe that is
not man's own plan is both theoretically and practically empty.
This came to light in our analysis of Kant's rejection of
theodicy. The idea of a higher wisdom, therefore, is a kind
of coded expression for the ambiguity of the perceived future.
The actual course of future events is opaque to our vision;
we can only project it imaginatively or symbolically. Any
certain knowledge of the future (our "wisdom") is veiled by
the limits of sense-experience. The "higher wisdom" or real
pattern of future happenings is unknowable. The question
that concerns Kant, then, is <u>not</u> what we can know of the
future. In much of his writings, Kant symbolizes the hope of
the future in terms of God's sovereign will. But we must
reformulate this hope in terms of man's own action in history,
in terms of the divine potential of the race. Whether divine
perfection in the sense of a cessation of the process of
development is a real possibility remains a moot point. In
his essay on "The End of All Things" (<u>Das</u> <u>Ende</u> <u>aller</u> <u>Dinge</u>)
Kant claims that perfection in time is an absurd notion; for
true perfection would signal the end of time, the end of
progress -- yet man is a being who cannot escape time. Thus
there can be no true <u>eschaton</u> to history. On the other hand,
progress itself can become the object of hope. Man can look
toward the cumulative development of the race as the practical
symbol which guarantees his present moral activity and impels
him into the future. Though man may never, in fact, become
God, he can yet become "godlike." Man becomes godlike through
the gradual moral perfection of the race. The God of theism
passes over into a sort of God of process. History becomes
the deification of man and the hominization of God.

CONCLUSION

It has been our design in this lengthy probe of the Kantian texts to unfurl the logic of Kant's account of what it means to be a moral agent. In addition, we have extensively considered Kant's idea of God as such an agent. Our conclusions are as follows:

(1) Kant tests the worth of all moral action against the immanent criteria of man's practical reason. Moral action inter alia must be (a) self-legislated or "autonomous"; (b) the product of a will motivated by objective principles or universalizable rules of conduct. These criteria are discernible a priori by every rational being. Even God's "action" must conform to these criteria. Thus, in exploring the meaning of the term "God" in Kant's thought, we do not commence with his "theology" and proceed to his ethics. Conversely, we begin with the principles of his moral philosophy and reason how the concept of God is necessary in light of such basic principles. Hence, we have dissected Kant's notion of a moral agent in general before treating his idea of divine agency. The implication to be drawn from this procedure is that Kant makes man, insofar as the latter is a being endowed with reason and capable of immediately recognizing moral truths, is the measure of God. The moral law that confounds every human conscience becomes the Archimedean point for reflection on "divine things."

(2) Since man is the measure of God, the idea of God reflects something essential about man. In Kant's philosophy the idea of God represents the perfection of man as a moral agent. Kant does not draw this conclusion outright himself, but the logic of his presentation of the concept of God leads us to it. Reason obliges man to achieve a life of perfect virtue, to become "holy." God, therefore, is the model of a

"holy" being whose will is, "in fact," commensurate with the pure will which man feels he <u>ought</u> to have. Reason persuades man to strive with all his powers to promote the highest good in the world, to bring the law of nature into concord with the moral law. God, therefore, represents the being who effects this concord. In a word, God stands for the fruition of man's highest moral <u>intentions</u>. He signifies what man thinks he ought to be, what man himself wants and labors to become, even though the latter comes to realize his congenital incapacity to do exactly what reason prescribes.

(3) Man's finite ability to control nature, together with the persistence of radical evil in his moral maxims, forestalls him from reaching the perfection his reason demands. The result is that man is an habitual "split-personality." His personality is composed of an intentional or God-aspiring self (projected as a powerful "Other") which struggles for realization in the world and which vies with his empirical, fallible self that chronically resists the moral law. In the idea of God man stands "outside of himself" in the heaven of ideals. In the idea of God man, to use Hegel's language, <u>alienates</u> himself in a profound way. He objectifies his ideal self as a powerful Other. This alienation can only be overcome so far as man attains the perfection represented in the idea of God; but such perfection cannot be reached in a man's short span of years. It is possible, however, for man to hope that perfection will be reached -- that alienation will be overcome -- within the sweeping passage of human history.

(4) Kant's notion of history as inevitable progress offers a new solution to the problems of the moral life which is not found in the rest of his practical philosophy. <u>Qua</u> solitary individual, man remains forever alienated from his conception of what he ought to be. He stands powerless before the insuperable forces of nature <u>outside</u> him and before the impulses to evil <u>within</u> himself. Thus reason shows he need believe in a God who will complete his moral intentions which are blocked by his own disabilities. Such, at least, is the

kind of argument we find in the second Critique and in the
Religion. Yet, as a member of the human race, as a participant
in its limitless progress, man can hope for perfection in a
way that is not possible should he consider himself in isolation from his congeners. For history promises the unending
and cumulative growth of human morality. The development of
the race through history is an immanent process of nature.
Out of nature arises the phenomenon of human society which,
in turn, provides the milieu for further growth of morality.
The concept of inexorable progress, therefore, comes to serve
as a more telling and perhaps more "realistic" symbol for
man's hope than the notion of God's will. The "will of
nature" takes over as a secularized version of the "will of
God." Divine action in history is supplanted by human action.
Kant's recurrent preference for the language of theism, however, tends to cloud this transition from the symbols of
transcendence to the symbols of immance. To the question,
"What may I hope?" Kant is inclined to answer "Hope that God
will bring about the moral universe." But Kant's view of
history suggests a more apt answer, "Hope that human progress
itself will eventuate in the moral world which reason sets
as its purpose."

* * * * * * * * * * * * * * * * *

There is a distinct trend within Kant's thought that
points beyond theism. Already we have analyzed how Kant
denies (sometimes explicitly, sometimes implicitly) the meaningfulness of an idea of a God who exists independently of
man's moral consciousness. God, on the contrary, is merely
an idea construct that serves a "need" of reason. This stance
we may dub Kant's "critical theism." Critical theism maintains that even though God cannot be said to have any independent existence apart from man, the conception of such an
independent being has a certain value, inasmuch as it serves
to regulate and direct our moral lives. Yet, from the standpoint of autonomy, the idea of an independent being or agent
who enacts for man what he is obliged to do for himself seems

strikingly inconsistent. Kant's theism, therefore, appears
au fond a redundant mythology that obscures the real drift of
his moral philosophy: the thesis that man's self-perfection
must ensue from his own efforts.

The new "critical" perspective, in contrast with "critical
theism," which we find emerging from the philosophy of history,
is the inevitable upshot of the dissolution of Kant's theism.
We shall call this new perspective that of historical <u>immanence</u>.
History, not God, comes to serve as the regulative idea for
ordering human morality. The idea of Almighty God no longer
provides consolation for the complexities and contradictions
of human experience; rather, we must look to history for such
consolation, to the ongoing life of the species. Man's source
of hope for the possibility of his own self-transcendence,
therefore, resides not in some super-human will, but in the
collective will of the universal moral community coming to
perfection over the distance of generations. To take this
tack, of course, urges us to relinquish the need for finding
solutions to the strictly existential questions of personal
immortality and immediate rewards for our efforts at virtue.
We are proposing a secular answer to the traditional
religious quest. The response to this quest offered in the
essays on history perhaps point away from the purely religious
point of view. Thus we see how Kant has done the spadework
for the critique of theology and the rise of a dialectics of
history in the thought of Hegel and Marx. Kant becomes an
important watershed for these streams of philosophical history.

From the theological standpoint, the impact of the critical
philosophy is to supply some important clues concerning how
man, while divested of belief in a power qualitatively different
from himself, may come to claim ultimate responsibility
for ordering and reshaping the world. The process of reshaping
involves both moral reform of personal lives and the
construction of a new system of human association (the universal
community) embodying rational ethical principles. The
development of the kingdom of ends, as a purely rational para-

digm for human relations, supersedes the revelational concept of the 'Word' as the goal and pattern of history. For man, if we stretch the inner logic of Kant's thought to its outer limit, is now bidden to grasp the reins of history, to struggle for his own kingdom with every ounce of commitment. The result is that the erstwhile God of history is now transformed into the developing powers of that pre-eminent historical being -- man. The historical challenge, for Kant, is to ensure the full development of these powers.

"There are," Kant notes,

> many germs lying undeveloped in man. It is for us to make these germs grow, by developing his natural gifts in their due proportion, and to see that he fulfills his destiny.[1]

Kant's counsel to man goes one step beyond Socrates. Not only does he recommend, "know thyself," but also, "cultivate thyself." In cultivating himself man fulfills a destiny that is all his own. Kant's counsel, therefore, is to snatch human destiny away from the gods and remand it to its rightful owner.

---

[1] E, p. 9. *Schriften*, IX, 445.

BIBLIOGRAPHY

Acton, Harry B. Kant's Moral Philosophy. New York: St. Martin's Press, 1970.

Adickes, Erich. Kants Opus Postumum, Dargestellt und Beurteilt. Kant-Studien, Ergänzungsheft 50 (1920).

Allison, Henry E. Lessing and the Enlightenment. Ann Arbor: University of Michigan Press, 1966.

Antonopoulos, Georg. Der Mensch als Burger zweier Welten. Bonn: Bouvier Verlag, 1958.

Aquinas, Saint Thomas. Summa Theologica. Translated by Blackfriars. New York: McGraw-Hill, 1963.

Axinn, Sidney. "Kant, Authority, and the French Revolution." Journal of the History of Ideas 32 (July-September 1971): 423-32.

Ballard, Edward G. "The Kantian Solution to the Problem of Man." Tulane Studies in Philosophy 3 (1954): 7-40.

Barth, Karl. "An Introductory Essay." Translated by James Luther Adams. In Ludwig Feurebach, The Essence of Christianity. Translated by George Eliot. New York: Harper & Row, Torchbook Edition, 1957. The German text is contained as a chapter in Die Theologie und die Kirche. Zollekon-Zürich: Evangelischer Verlag, 1928, Vol. 2, pp. 212-29.

Beck, Lewis W. A Commentary on Kant's Critique of Practical Reason. Chicago: The University of Chicago Press, 1960.

_____. Early German Philosophy. Cambridge: Harvard University Press, 1969.

_____. "Kant and the Right of Revolution." Journal of the History of Ideas 32 (July-September 1971): 411-22

Bloch, Ernst. Das Prinzip Hoffnung. Bd. 2 of Gesamtausgabe. Frankfurt-am-Main: Suhrkamp Verlag, 1955.

Bohatec, Joseph. Die Religionsphilosophie Kants in der 'Religion innherhalb der Grenzen der blossen Vernunft' mit besonderer Berücksichtigung ihrer theologischdomatischen Quellen. Hamburg: Hoffman und Campe, 1938.

Bolzano, Bernard. _Paradoxes of the Infinite_. Translated by Fr. Prihonsky. New Haven: Yale University Press, 1950.

Bossart, W. H. "Kant's Doctrine of the Reciprocity of Freedom and Reason." _International Philosophical Quarterly_ 8 (September 1968): 334-55.

Brown, D. G. _Action_. Toronto: University of Toronto Press, 1968.

Brown, S. M., Jr. "Does Ought Imply Can?" _Ethics_ 60 (1950): 275-84.

Bruch, Jean Louis. _La Philosophie Religieuse de Kant_. Paris: Aubier, 1968.

Burleigh, T. Wilkins. "Teleology in Kant's Philosophy of History." _History and Theory_ 5 (1966): 172-85.

Bury, J. B. _The Idea of Progress_. London: Macmillan and Company, 1920.

Care, Norman, and Landesman, Charles, eds. _Readings in the Theory of Action_. Bloomington: Indiana University Press, 1968.

Cassirer, Ernst. _Rousseau, Kant, and Goethe_. Translated by James Gutmann, P. O. Kristeller, and John Randall, Jr. Princeton: Princeton University Press, 1945.

Chojnacki, P. _Die Ethik Kants und die Ethik des Sozialismus_. Freiburg/Schweiz: Studia Friburgensia, 1924.

Collingwood, R. G. _The Idea of History_. New York: Oxford University Press, 1956.

_____. _The Idea of Nature_. New York: Oxford University Press, 1960.

_____. _Metaphysics_. Oxford: Oxford University Press, 1940.

Collins, James D. _The Emergence of Philosophy of Religion_. New Haven: Yale University Press, 1967.

Dakin, A. Hazard. "Kant and Religion." In _The Heritage of Kant_, edited by G. T. Whitney and D. F. Bowers. Princeton: Princeton University Press, 1939.

Dempf, Alois. _Das Unendliche in der mittelalterlichen Metaphysik und in der Kantischen Dialektik_. Münster in Westfalen: Aschendorffschen Verlagsbuchhandlung, 1926.

Duncan, Alastair R. C. _Practical Reason and Morality_. Edinburgh: Nelson and Company, 1957.

Ebbinghaus, Julius. *Kants Lehre vom ewigen Frieden und die Kriegsschuldfrage*. Tübingen: J.C.B. Mohr, 1929.

Eisler, Rudolf, ed. *Kant-Lexikon*. Berlin: E. S. Mittler und Sohn, 1930.

Emmett, Dorothy. *The Nature of Metaphysical Thinking*. London: Macmillan and Company, 1946.

England, F. E. *Kant's Conception of God*. London: Allen & Unwin, 1929.

Ewing, Alfred C. *Kant's Treatment of Causality*. London: Kegan Paul, 1924.

Fackenheim, Emil L. "Kant's Concept of History." *Kant-Studien* 48 (1956-7): 370-92.

Farrer, Austin. *Finite and Infinite*. Glasgow: The University of Glasgow Press, 1943.

Ferre, Frederick. *Language, Logic, and God*. New York: Harper & Row, Torchbook Edition, 1961.

Feuerbach, Ludwig. *Principles of the Philosophy of the Future*. Translated by Manfred Vogel. New York: Bobbs-Merrill, Library of Liberal Arts, 1966.

Friedrich, Carl J. *Inevitable Peace*. Cambridge: Harvard University Press, 1948.

Frost, Walter. "Kants Teleologie." *Kant-Studien* 11 (1906): 297-347.

Goldman, Lucien. *Mensch, Gemeinschaft, und Welt in der Philosophie Immanuel Kants*. Zürich: Europa Verlag, 1945.

Gotschalk, D. W. "The Central Doctrine of the Kantian Ethics." in *The Heritage of Kant*, edited by G. T. Whitney and D. F. Bowers. Princeton: Princeton University Press, 1939.

Hampshire, Stuart. *Thought and Action*. New York: The Viking Press, 1959.

Harris, H. S. "The Young Hegel and the Postulates of Practical Reason." In *Hegel and the Philosophy of Religion: The Wofford Symposium*, edited by Darrel Christensen. The Hague: Martinus Nijhoff, 1970.

Hegel, G. W. F. *The Philosophy of History*. Translated by J. Sibree, New York: Dover Publications, 1956.

Hendel, Charles. *The Philosophy of Kant and Our Modern World*. New York: The Liberal Arts Press, 1957.

Hoekstra, Tjeerd. *Immanente Kritik zur Kantischen Religionsphilosophie*. Kampen: J. H. Kok, 1906.

Hospers, John. *Human Conduct*. New York: Harcourt, Brace & World, 1961.

Hume, David. *Dialogues Concerning Natural Religion*, edited by Norman Kemp Smith. New York: Thomas Nelson and Sons, 1947.

_____. *An Inquiry Concerning Human Understanding*. New York: Bobbs-Merrill, Library of Liberal Arts, 1955.

Jansen, Bernard. *La Philosophie Religieuse de Kant*. Translated by Pierre Chaillet. Paris: Librairie Philosophique J. Vrin, 1934.

Jaspers, Karl. *Philosophy and the World*. Translated by E. B. Ashton. Chicago: Henry Regnery Company, 1963.

James, William. *Essays on Faith and Morals*. New York: The World Publishing Company, Meridian Books, 1962.

Joël, Karl. *Kant als Vollender des Humanismus*. Tübingen: J. C. B. Mohr, 1924.

Jones, W. T. *Morality and Freedom in Kant*. London: Oxford University Press, 1940.

_____. "Purpose, Nature, and the Moral Law." In *The Heritage of Kant*, edited by G. T. Whitney and D. F. Bowers. Princeton: Princeton University Press, 1939.

Katzer, Ernst. *Luther und Kant*. Giessen: A. Töpelmann, 1910.

Kelly, George A. "Rousseau, Kant, and History." *Journal of the History of Ideas* 29 (July-September 1968): 347-64.

Kemp. J. *Reason, Action and Morality*. New York: The Humanities Press, 1964.

Klinke, Willibald. *Kant for Everyman*. Translated by Michael Bullock. New York: Collier Books, 1962.

Knox, Sir Malcolm. *Action*. London: George Allen & Unwin, 1968.

Körner, S. *Kant*. Baltimore: Penguin Books, 1955.

Köster, Adolf. *Der junge Kant im Kampf um die Geschichte*. Berlin: L. Simion, 1914.

Kremer, Josef. "Das Problem der Theodicee in der Philosophie und Literatur des 18. Jahrhunderts mit besonderer Rücksicht auf Kant und Schiller." *Kant-Studien* 13 (1909).

Kroner, Richard. *Kant's Weltanschauung*. Translated by John E. Smity. Chicago: University of Chicago Press, 1956.

_____. *Von Kant bis Hegel*. Tubingen: Mohr Verlag, 1961.

Lenfers, Dietmar. *Kants Weg von der Teleologie zur Theologie: Interpretationen zur Kants Kritik der Urteilscraft*. Unpublished inaugural dissertation, University of Köln, 1965.

Lessing, Gotthold. *Theological Writings*. Translated by Henry Chadwick. Stanford: Stanford University Press, 1965.

Lovejoy, Arthur O. *The Great Chain of Being*. New York: Harper & Row, Torchbook Edition, 1960.

Liddell, Brendan. *Kant on the Foundation of Morality*. Bloomington: Indiana University Press, 1970.

Lindsay, A. D. *Kant*. London: Ernest Benn, 1934.

Lotz, Johannes B. *Kant und die Scholastik Heute*. München: Verlag Berchmanskolleg, 1955.

Löwith, Karl. *Gott, Mensch und Welt in der Metaphysik von Descartes bis zur Neitzsche*. Göttingen: Vandenhöck und Ruprecht, 1967.

Luther, Martin. *Werke*. Vol. 40. Weimar: Hermann Böhlhaus, 1914.

MacMurray, John. *The Self as Agent*. London: Faber and Faber, 1954.

Mead, George Herbert. *Selected Writings*, edited by Andrew Reck. New York: Bobbs-Merrill, Library of Liberal Arts, 1964.

Mischel, Theodore, ed. *Human Action: Conceptual and Empirical Issues*. New York: The Academic Press, 1969.

_____. "Kant and the Possibility of a Science of Psychology." *The Monist* 51 (1967): 6-20.

Murphy, Jeffrie. *Kant: The Philosophy of Right*. New York: St. Martin's Press, 1970.

Nell, Onora S. *Universalizability*. Unpublished doctoral dissertation, Harvard University, 1969.

Newman, John H. *An Essay on the Grammar of Assent*. New York: The Catholic Publication Society, 1870.

Passmore, John. *The Perfectibility of Man*. New York: Charles Scribner's Sons, 1970.

Paton, H. J. *The Categorical Imperative*. London: Hutchinson and Company, 1965.

Paulsen, Friedrich. *Immanuel Kant: His Life and Doctrine*. Translated by J. E. Creighton and Albert Lefebre. New York: Charles Scribner's Sons, 1902.

Peters, Eugene. *Descriptions of God in the Later Writings of Kant*. Unpublished doctoral dissertation, Harvard University, 1968.

Porter, Noah. *Kant's Ethics*. Chicago: S. C. Griggs and Company, 1886.

Price, H. H. *Belief*. London: George Allen & Unwin, 1969.

Quinton, Anthony. "Knowledge and Belief." In *The Encyclopedia of Philosophy* X. Vol. 2, pp. 345-52.

Ramsey, Ian. *Religious Language*. New York: The Macmillan Company, 1957.

Ross, Sir David. *Kant's Ethical Theory*. Oxford: The Clarendon Press, 1954.

Rousseau, Jean-Jacques. *The Social Contract and Other Discourses*. New York: Everyman's Library, 1950.

Ruyssen, Theodore. "Philosophie de l'Histoire selon Kant." In *La Philosophie Politique de Kant*. Annales de Philosophie Politique. Paris: Presses Universitaires de France, 1962.

Sander, Josef. *Die Begründung der Notwehr in der Philosophie von Kant und Hegel*. Bleichenrode an Harz: C. Nieft, 1939.

Scheler, Max. *Der Formalismus in der Ethik und die Materie Wertethik*. Bd. 2 of Gessammelte Werke. Bern: A. Francke, 1954.

Schilpp, Paul A. *Kant's Pre-Critical Ethics*. Evanston: Northwestern University Press, 1960.

Schmalenbach, Herman. *Die Kantische Philosophie und die Religion*. Göttingen: Vandenhöck und Ruprecht, 1926.

Schrader, George A. "Kant's Presumed Repudiation of the Moral Arguments in the *Opus Postumum*: An Examination of Adickes' Interpretation." *Philosophy* 31 (1951): 228-41.

Schroeder, H. H. "Some Common Misinterpretations of the Kantian Ethics." Philosophical Review 49 (1940): 424-46.

Sidgwick, Henry. The Methods of Ethics. London: Macmillan and Company, 1901.

Silber, John. "The Ethical Significance of Kant's Religion." Introductory essay to Kant's Religion within the Limits of Reason Alone. Translated by Theodore Greene and Hoyt Hudson. New York: Harper & Row, Torchbook Edition, 1960.

Skinner, B. F. Science and Human Behavior. New York: The Macmillan Company, 1953.

Smith, Norman Kemp. A Commentary to Kant's Critique of Pure Reason. London: Macmillan and Company, 1918.

Teale, A. E. Kantian Ethics. London: Oxford University Press, 1951.

Torrey, Henry, ed. The Philosophy of Descartes. New York: Henry Holt and Company, 1892.

Troeltsch, Ernst. Das Historische in Kants Religionsphilosophie. Berlin: Reuther Verlag, 1904. The Historical in Kant's Philosophy of Religion. Translated by Clark Williamson. Unpublished typescript, Harvard University, 1966.

de Vleeschauwer, H. J. "Entwurf einer Kant-Bibliographie." Kant-Studien 57 (1966): 457-83.

Walsh, William H. Kant's Moral Theology. London: Oxford University Press, 1963.

_____. Philosophy of History: An Introduction. New York: Harper & Row, Torchbook Edition, 1960.

Wand, Bernard. "Religious Concepts and Moral Theory: Luther and Kant." Journal of the History of Philosophy 9 (July 1971): 329-48.

Warnock, G. J. "Kant." In A Critical History of Western Philosophy, edited by D. J. O'Connor. New York: The Free Press of Glencoe, 1964.

Webb, Clement. Kant's Philosophy of Religion. Oxford: Clarendon Press, 1926.

Weyand, Klaus. Kants Geschichtsphilosophie. Kant-Studien, Ergänzungsheft (1964).

White, Alan R., ed. The Philosophy of Action. London: Oxford University Press, 1968.

Whittemore, Robert. "The Metaphysics of the Seven Formulations of the Moral Argument." *Tulane Studies in Philosophy* 3 (1954): 133-61.

Wittgenstein, Ludwig. *Tractatus Logico-Philosophicus*. London: Routledge & Kegan Paul, 1961.

Wolff, Robert Paul. *Kant: A Collection of Critical Essays*. Garden City: Doubleday and Company, Anchor Books, 1967.

Wood, Allen W. *Kant's Moral Religion*. Ithaca: Cornell University Press, 1970.

DATE DUE

MAY 24 2004			
MAY 23 2007			